THE VISUAL GUILLOTINE

THE VISUAL
THE CINEMATIC CUT AND
GUILLOTINE
POLITICS IN LATIN AMERICA

THOMAS MATUSIAK

MINNESOTA

University of Minnesota Press | Minneapolis | London

The University of Minnesota Press gratefully acknowledges the generous assistance provided for the publication of this book by the University of Miami.

Portions of chapters 3 and 4 are adapted from “Crímenes cinematográficos: Decapitación y montaje,” *Cuadernos de Literatura* 23, no. 46 (2019): 47–72. Portions of chapter 5 are adapted from “Latin American Post-Cinema and the Afterlives of Film Theory,” *Revista de Estudios Hispánicos* (forthcoming); and from “Losing Our Heads: Madness and Cinema in Carl Theodor Dreyer and Javier Téllez,” *Romance Quarterly* 69, no. 4 (2022): 198–213; reprinted by permission of the publisher Taylor & Francis Ltd, http://www.tandfonline.com. The conclusion is adapted from “Invitation to a Beheading: The Visual Guillotine and the Politics of the Audiovisual Apparatus,” *LASA Forum* 56, no. 1 (2025), https://forum.lasaweb.org/; reprinted by permission of the Latin American Studies Association.

Published by the University of Minnesota Press
111 Third Avenue South, Suite 290
Minneapolis, MN 55401-2520
http://www.upress.umn.edu

ISBN 978-1-5179-1552-0 (hc)
ISBN 978-1-5179-1553-7 (pb)

LC record available at https://lccn.loc.gov/2026022159.
LC ebook record available at https://lccn.loc.gov/2026022160.

Printed on acid-free paper

CONTENTS

INTRODUCTION
SHARPENING THE GUILLOTINE

As we enter the cinema, the spatial arrangement of the movie theater organizes the audience into a neat row of bodies. Gazing forward toward the screen, our fellow spectators appear visually and metaphorically beheaded. The light of the projection illuminates the silhouettes of these heads as they float above their seats. Immobilized, we lose our heads and enter a collective state of cinematic hypnosis. Our consciousness of time, space, and our bodies fades as we are immersed in the spectacle and gaze at the close-up of a celebrated actor. The edge of the frame cuts the field of vision and beheads this figure for our viewing pleasure. In a ritual that has taken place earlier, the blade of the splicer—the device that cuts and stitches fragments of film together—rises and falls on the editing table. Holding a sequence of frames that contain a face in close-up, the cutter mutilates the body of the film. The editors repeat this quintessentially filmic gesture thousands of times throughout the production. This body in pieces constitutes the raw material of a film. Enchanted by these ephemeral heads that vanish in the darkness, the fetishistic spectator will later hunt down the actor's star image, which circulates through the wider apparatus of film publicity. Searching a fan magazine with scissors in hand, this modern headhunter decapitates the actor's figure and adds another totem to her collection. An actor decapitated by the auteur; a fragment of film dismembered during editing; a headshot dissected by the spectator. These scenes underscore the symbolic violence implicit in the logic of fragmentation that organizes the aesthetic, material, and discursive practices associated with the moving image.

The Visual Guillotine: The Cinematic Cut and Politics in Latin America proposes a theory of cinema that centers the relation between body, apparatus, and image. Through a corpus that spans the 1930s to the present, I trace the politics of the cinematic cut back to the guillotine. This apparatus anticipates modern media by mechanizing a primordial violence that creates a spectacle of the serial production of the body in pieces. Through its characteristic tools of montage and the close-up, cinema is a machine that continuously produces severed heads. If the scaffold cuts one body after another, so too does the splicer that mutilates the roll of film, or the camera's frame. In the heads projected on the screen—beheaded by the close-up—we witness a return to the ritual of decapitation in a rationalized, modern form. Likewise, the eruption of energy provoked by the shock of montage approximates revolutionary pathos. In this book, I ask why cinema is structured around cutting and how this violence gives form to audiovisual politics. The logic of the cut structures the moving image across formal and material practices, from editing to framing, and I reflect on how the inscription of symbolic violence within audiovisual form stages political concepts and positions the spectator as a political subject.

As a mass medium, cinema was one of the most politically transformative cultural forms of modernity. From Mexico to Cuba and beyond, the revolutions and radical movements that marked Latin America's twentieth century were accompanied by and institutionalized through cinema. The modern nation-state, positioning itself as the agent of Latin American modernity, wielded cinema as a tool of hegemony. By representing the national popular—"the people," *el pueblo*—they reinforced collective identity and secured the consent of the governed. By the 1960s, counterhegemonic filmmakers throughout the region, who collectively articulated the New Latin American Cinema (NLAC), disrupted the stylized images of the people that served the interests of the state. Joining the aesthetic and political avant-gardes, filmmakers experimented with audiovisual form to enact a revolutionary *pueblo*. Nevertheless, by the 1980s this regional project met its end with the rise of repressive dictatorships, neoliberal economic policies, and accelerated globalization. National film industries collapsed, and filmmakers found themselves pressured to privilege commercial viability over political commitments. Many producers and filmmakers turned to transnational financing and international markets after the loss of state subsidies. The 1980s and 1990s thus mark a threshold separating the popular, autonomous, and identitarian cinema of national film industries and the NLAC from the depoliticized and global filmmaking that has taken hold in the twenty-first century.[1] Yet while Latin American film history tends to emphasize this rupture, my account of the visual guillotine traces continuities in the politicization of audiovisual form.

In theorizing the cinematic cut, this book seeks to expand the conceptualization of audiovisual politics beyond questions of representation and identity that underlie conventional accounts of Latin American cinema. I define the visual guillotine as the expression of the political through the form of the cinematic cut. As an instrument of revolution, the guillotine has come to symbolize the emergence of political modernity. With the decapitation of the king, power passed to the people, who surrounded the scaffold as a mass of spectators. Put differently, the cut that mechanically reproduced severed heads gave form to popular sovereignty. *The Visual Guillotine* explores how this inscription of politics in the cut survives in the audiovisual apparatus. Across five chapters, I study how Latin American filmmakers stage political concepts through the cinematic cut. From the national cinemas of the 1930s and the NLAC of the 1960s and 1970s, to the expanded and postcinematic forms that mark contemporary audiovisual production, I trace the mutations of audiovisual politics. Though I maintain the conventional periodization described above, my concept of the visual guillotine identifies a politics of form that is proper to the audiovisual apparatus.[2] By identifying the figuration of politics with the cinematic cut, rather than a mimetic and identitarian image that precedes form, I trace continuities across the ruptures that separate the conventionally defined stages of Latin American film history. The cinematic cut structured the hegemonic politics of national cinemas as well as the revolutionary intensities of the NLAC. These filmmakers aligned the politics of the cut with popular sovereignty, wielding the visual guillotine to reproduce an image of the people or to release revolutionary intensities. New conceptualizations of politics emerged in the 1990s, as neoliberalism provoked the crisis of the nation-state and the *pueblo*. The cinematic cut also mutated during this decade, with electronic and digital media displacing analog film. Yet the visual guillotine persists despite these transformations to both politics and cinema. The confluence of the severed head and audiovisual form returns in the images of explicit violence that have accompanied the unending cycle of global conflict in the twenty-first century. After the exhaustion of the concepts that defined political modernity—popular sovereignty, the nation-state, hegemony—the confluence of the severed head and the cut gives form to necropolitical configurations of power in the present. Under what Sayak Valencia has termed "gore capitalism," the cinematic cut is weaponized by those who seek to paralyze the public sphere through horrorism in the unrestricted pursuit of capital.

Surveying Latin American cinema from the 1930s to the present, I trace continuities in the politics of the cut across the thresholds enacted by periodization. I echo Laura Podalsky's conclusion that, without discarding conventional models of Latin American film history, we must overcome their shortcomings and signal continuities despite transformations to political and infrastructural conditions.[3] Thus, while cinema and politics mutate in the 1990s, the politics of form that defines the visual guillotine persists. Rather than a predetermined politics that is already represented in the image, preceding form, the visual guillotine offers the *potential* of politics. Depending on how the authors of the moving image wield it, the politics of the cut may be revolutionary or reactionary. As a result, in addition to my theoretical argument I develop a practice of critical reading—what I refer to in chapter 3 as countermontage—that responds to this contemporary appropriation of the visual guillotine and invites the reader to reflect on the expansion of the cut and its politics in our postcinematic era.

The Severed Head and Audiovisual Form

In theorizing cinematic politics through the image of the severed head, I draw on a tradition of aesthetic thought that locates the origins of figuration—and by extension the production of subjectivity through representation and identification—with the symbolic violence of beheading. In her book *The Severed Head,* Julia Kristeva traces the contemporary spectacle of the fragmented body to the ancient skull rites that marked the emergence of visual culture. For Kristeva, the dismemberment and display of the sacrificed body marks the first example of representation because it converts the severed head into a signifier within a new symbolic order. In other words, Kristeva identifies the origins of visual signification, of human communication through images and symbols, with decapitation.[4] While art and religion later replaced such violent rituals, beheading resurfaces throughout cultural history.[5] Drawing on her background in psychoanalysis, Kristeva associates the sense of loss that gives rise to subjectivity with the cut that decapitates. The origins of subjectivity, she argues, can be found in these prehistoric rites. In gazing at the severed head, early humans expressed their desire for identification with the other.[6] The violence of decapitation is later sublimated through the image, giving rise to art, photography, and cinema. While Kristeva's archaeological account of the relation between decapitation and visuality stops short of the mechanically reproduced image, she signals the survival of the severed head in cinema: "The cinema will not be outdone. It will take over for the history of painting and thus, inevitably, of decapitation. Especially, of decapitation."[7] Why does Kristeva insist on the relation between cinema and the severed head? The answer to this question cannot be limited to the fact that fragmentation is essential to cinematic form. After all, any moving image longer than a single shot requires a cut. Rather than recording an inventory of splices and critiquing how filmmakers have wielded them for political ends, I trace a theory of the cinematic cut that would link the moving image to other cultural and political forms by relating this symbolic violence to the production of subjectivity. If we revisit the relation between the political subject, the body, and representation through the concept of the cut, then we can begin to understand not just *how* cinematic form manipulates symbolic violence, but *why*.

The art historian Linda Nochlin further explicates the relation between the severed head and representation since the end of the eighteenth century, arguing that the social, psychological, and metaphysical shocks of modernity found their visual expression in the metaphor of the body in pieces.[8] Nochlin grounds this argument in her observations regarding the framing of the body in painting. Beginning with the wealth of imagery inspired by the spectacle of the guillotine, artists represented modernity's rupture with tradition, and the nostalgic desire for a lost wholeness, by cutting the human form with the frame of the image. The fragmented body produced by cropping the image became a metaphor for the perceptual violence of modernity. This preoccupation with the fragment only intensified with the development of modernism across the arts. The avant-gardes embraced rupture over unity, and two of the most distinctive modern aesthetic techniques—collage and montage—both depended on the cut. The formal language of moving images reaffirms the significance of the fragment in modern visuality. Nevertheless, Nochlin's account omits cinema.

The first filmmakers were already experimenting with the force of the cinematic cut by the end of the nineteenth century. As they began to explore the formal possibilities of cinema, Thomas Edison and Georges Méliès entertained audiences by harnessing the cinematic cut to create a spectacle of bodily fragmentation. For example, in *Un homme de tête* (*The Four Troublesome Heads,* 1898), Méliès playfully beheads himself for the camera. This effect is generated through the substitution splice, the earliest example of editing. As Méliès holds his hands to his head, about to decapitate himself, the film cuts to a shot of the filmmaker with a black sack over his head. This matches the black background and makes him appear headless. As a result, the decapitation on-screen coincides with the cinematic cut. Méliès likely borrowed this tactic from Edison, who in *The Execution of Mary, Queen of Scots* (1895) took advantage of the substitution splice to simulate a beheading. As the executioner's blade rises, the filmmaker cuts and substitutes the actor playing the queen with a mannequin, which is swiftly decapitated. Examining Edison's film as one of the earliest representations of death in cinema, Scott Combs ties *The Execution of Mary, Queen of Scots* to the legacy of the guillotine in visual culture, in which spectacular violence is displaced onto the cinematic cut.[9] Within my account of the cinematic cut, Edison was the first theorist of the visual guillotine. The French filmmaker Ferdinand Zecca repeats this strategy in *Histoire d'un crime* (1901) when he explicitly associates the cinematic cut with the guillotine. The film's narrative follows a criminal who is arrested for murder, tried, and executed by guillotine. Once the criminal is inserted into the apparatus, Zecca cuts and replaces this body with a mannequin; he then splices in the footage of the mannequin's decapitation to simulate the beheading. Again, the structural violence of film form substitutes the cut that decapitates this figure.

In the decades following these early experiments, as the classical style of narrative cinema became the medium's dominant mode, filmmakers and film theorists continued to highlight the visual and symbolic violence implicit in cinematic form and materiality. By the 1920s both montage and the close-up had become indispensable to cinematic narration. However, when first introduced these devices shocked audiences who had not yet become accustomed to cinema's fragmented structure. For example, Combs suggests that the substitution splice that permitted Edison to simulate decapitation went undetected by early audiences. As a result, these edits would have startled early spectators.[10] In an anecdote I will return to in chapter 1, the film theorist Béla Balázs recounts the experiences of a peasant girl from Siberia who, upon visiting Moscow, sees a film for the first time. The girl's reaction verges on trauma as she describes a ghastly scene of bodies mutilated through the combined effects of the close-up and montage.[11] Apocryphal or not, Balázs's anecdote acknowledges that the visual dismemberment of the actor initially disturbed audiences. In disrupting the stream of images through montage and fragmenting the actor's body through the close-up, early filmmakers distinguished this new medium from theater. Yet the first close-ups provoked disgust among audiences, who were accustomed to observing the entire body perform on the stage. Reviews of films featuring close-ups considered these images grotesque and chastised filmmakers for "depicting the repulsive naturalism of gigantic heads."[12] D. W. Griffith, who is credited with institutionalizing the close-up in narrative form, was infamously scorned by his producers for reducing the actor to a monstrous image of a severed head.[13] Given such reactions to the spectacle of cinematic fragmentation, early film theory relied on metaphors of violence to elucidate the formal properties of this developing medium. Surveying both film theory and modernist cinema, Karla Oeler observes that meditations on montage and framing frequently invoked murder. In her words, "montage famously serves as a vehicle for conveying violence (e.g., the shower sequence in *Psycho*). What often escapes consideration, however, is that the reverse is also true: deadly violence, throughout the history of film-theoretical writing, has . . . often served as a metaphor *for* montage."[14] Oeler invokes a broader definition of montage, which includes both editing and framing. Film theorists such as Sergei Eisenstein extended montage to shot composition. The excess of Eisenstein's obsession with the cut could not be contained within the editing room; the principles of montage also applied to the violent fragmentation of the actor's body. Heads and individual limbs could be severed by the frame and rearranged in a new symbolic order. Like a doll, the actor's body was segmented and easily disarticulated. Thus while Oeler concludes that murder shadowed the theory and practice of montage throughout film history, the cinematic cut alludes to a specific form of violence. As in the example from Hitchcock that Oeler cites, these devices rely on the cut. If cinema is analogous to murder, then it is to the expressive crimes of dismemberment and decapitation.

My theory of the cinematic cut traces the formal, material, and symbolic violence of film form back to the guillotine. This device resuscitates the primordial violence of decapitation at the end of the eighteenth century, yet its influence stretches beyond the French Revolution and capital punishment. The guillotine transforms the relation between political violence and the image in its afterlife, conditioning the relation between media and modernity. By mechanizing violence and creating a spectacle of the serial production of the severed head, the guillotine anticipates modern media. In the words of Patrick Wald Lasowski, "The guillotine has not disappeared. It haunts the century of progress and continues in modern times. It conditions the relationship between modernity and the image."[15] Lasowski argues that the instantaneity of the mechanized cut, as well as its immobilization of the body, ties photographic portraiture to the guillotine.[16] Cinema inherits and radicalizes this legacy. The French film theorist Raymond Bellour traces a genealogy of cinematic affect back to the guillotine. Bellour concerns himself with how the spectacle entranced the crowd at different moments in modernity. The guillotine is an early example of an apparatus of spectacle; since this machine automates the production of an image for the visual pleasure of the crowd—specifically the image of a severed head—Bellour compares the guillotine's operator with the projectionist, and the window of the guillotine, where the condemned rested his head prior to execution, to the screen.[17] With the rest of his body concealed by the apparatus, the victim's head appeared suspended above the crowd, as if foreshadowing the close-up. My metaphor of the visual guillotine ties cinema's central position in modern political aesthetics to this relation between cutting film and cutting bodies.

Filmmakers and editors similarly trace the cinematic cut back to the guillotine. In his now-classic account of film editing, Walter Murch reminds us that watching a film entails observing an unremitting sequence of cuts. Murch radicalizes the notion of the cut to include any moment an image is displaced. Consequently, he argues, "The truth of the matter is that film is actually being 'cut' twenty-four frames a second."[18] In the act of analog projection, the film, divided into individual frames, is fed through the projector. The motor pulls each frame up to the lens. The shutter of the lens opens, and the frame is held still for one-twenty-fourth of a second so that light emitted from a bulb in the back of the machine may shine through the film.[19] This light, carrying the image, travels through the lens and is projected onto a surface. The shutter then closes, the motor advances to the subsequent frame, and the process is repeated twenty-four times a second. Each frame contains a separate still image, and thus each time the shutter closes constitutes a cut in Murch's definition because it provides the illusion of movement through displacement. The progression from one frame to the next is thus its own form of montage. In this case, the shutter's frame within the machine, ceaselessly opening and closing, cuts the projected cinematic image, just as a guillotine, constantly rising and falling, cuts the bodies of its victims. And yet the apparatus conceals this element of its operation; it is the sheer number of cuts and the rapid pace of the projector's operation that in fact provides the illusion of uninterrupted motion. Murch emphasizes the effect of this visual dislocation on the spectator, describing it as producing "a mental jarring—a jump—that is comparatively disturbing."[20] Murch thus ties cinematic affect not only to the form or content of the moving image but to its materiality as well.

As an editor and sound designer with a long career in Hollywood, Murch can attest to cinema's hidden cruelties. He explicitly associates montage and beheading when comparing the cinematic body to the victim of the guillotine. In his view, the cutting room resembles a torture chamber:

> Why do cuts work? We *know* that they do. And yet it is still surprising when you think about it because of the violence of what is actually taking place. . . . I recall once coming back to the editing room after a few weeks in the mixing theater (where all movements are smooth and incremental) and being appalled at the brutality of the process of cutting. The "patient" is pinned to the slab and: Whack! Either/Or! This not That! In or Out! We chop up the poor film in a miniature guillotine and then stick the dismembered pieces together like Dr. Frankenstein's monster.[21]

Murch's invocation of the guillotine here is not exceptional. This bloody spectacle anticipated cinematic violence and has served as a metaphor of montage since approximately the 1920s, when film editing became mechanized with the invention of the Moviola and film splicer. Previously, an editor would cut the film strip using only a pair of scissors or a sharp razor, and then glue these fragments together. Such rudimentary editing was less efficient, as the editor, faced with hundreds of feet of film, could not easily amplify frames in order to determine the most effective cut. Even when aided by a magnifying glass, the incision was much less precise.

Soon the editing process was modernized in the hopes of executing splices with greater speed and efficiency. Introduced in the early 1920s, the Moviola featured a small screen that enlarged an individual frame from a film strip. Editors could proceed through raw footage frame by frame, backwards and forwards, to locate the most effective cut.[22] The editor would mark the splice and then execute the cut using a splicer. Many models exist; to give one example, a tape splicer contains a blade on the edge of the device that rises and falls. This is the guillotine that cuts the cinematic body. Sprocket holes on the edge of the splicer's bed immobilize the film and allow for a clean cut. Once two splices are ready to be joined, the editor aligns them and applies a piece of clear tape from the base of the device over the film. To complete the process, a handle is pulled down over this wound, cutting the tape and pressing it over the cut to join the two fragments. The taping is then repeated over the other side of the film for greater stability. Thanks to the Moviola, editors, now working within growing industries, were able to make decisions on splices faster and work with greater quantities of film. As Murch's account demonstrates, the logic underlying such advancements in film editing mirrors the technological justification for the guillotine. As an instrument of capital punishment, the scaffold replaced the executioner's sword in the name of technological and political progress, scale, and precision.

In a series of photographs he took as a study of his editing table, Mexican experimental filmmaker Teo Hernández (1939–92) makes the violence of montage explicit. Hernández focuses on a Super 8mm Moviola, which he places on a red surface. In front of the device is a film splicer, and to the side is a Super 8mm camera. In the first image, the

Moviola's screen is in use and the room is dark. The photograph is illuminated in chiaroscuro, and as a result the apparatus itself is obscured. Wrapped in darkness, the technology of mediation fades from thought while the image on its screen draws the eye. Unlike the black box of the movie theater, however, the materiality of the apparatus is not rendered entirely invisible. Its outline is apparent, but it remains in the shadows. Here, Hernández highlights a violent side of cinema the spectator typically doesn't see. This is cinema's violent primal scene, and a macabre air envelops the liminal space of the editing room. The frame from an unknown film is visible on the Moviola's screen, and the severed head of an actor in close-up floats in the darkness. The man's expression mimics the synthetic head he holds up next to him, suggesting that, like this doll, the actor's body also exists to be manipulated, cut up, and rearranged by the filmmaker. In staging the Moviola with this image, Hernández relates the fragmentation of the actor's body through the framing of the image with the dissection of the body of the film through montage. Consequently, Hernández does not limit his photographic study to the specificity of either film editing or the close-up but instead reflects on the broader logic of the cinematic cut.

In a subsequent photograph, the Moviola is out of use and its screen is blank. The table is lit from above and illuminates the apparatus: its materiality is the focus of the image. The film has been threaded through the splicer, and the blade of the guillotine is raised menacingly. The striking red color of the editing table evokes the image of blood. In a third photograph, Hernández abandons the Moviola and splicer to stage a sacrificial altar in his editing room. In the center is a disarticulated doll with its head cocked, posed behind glass and with a key resting at its feet. The doll's construction highlights its fragmented body; its form is segmented into detachable limbs. As a result, the doll recalls the materiality of the film, which is also an assemblage of minimal units. Furthermore, the juxtaposition of the man's head with the head of a doll in the frame displayed on the Moviola in the previous image, as well as the unnatural expression that both these two figures share, reinforces the association between the disarticulated doll and the synthetic body of the actor. As I have already mentioned, early film theorists extended the principles of montage to shot composition and reduced the actor's body to an assemblage of limbs that could be severed by the frame and rearranged according to montage principles. Hernández's focus on the doll's segmented body recalls such theories of the violence of the cinematic cut. To the right of the doll is the black-and-white photograph of a crucifix, which invokes the theme of sacrifice. Hernández thus appears to construct a sacrificial altar in his editing room, where we might imagine the filmmaker offering the mutilated scraps of film he discards in this ritual space. In associating the violence of the cinematic cut with ritual, Hernández returns to the genealogy traced by Kristeva. The prehistoric rites of beheading that gave rise to representation survive in the structural violence of the apparatus: its construction of a moving image through symbolic dismemberment and decapitation. In this bloodless and otherwise unexceptional scene, the filmmaker is not concerned with staging violence through cinema but with exhibiting the violence *of* cinema. The violence of audiovisual form thus continues a genealogy initiated with the very origins of representation.

Cinema and Politics in Latin America's Cruel Modernity

The guillotine politicized the relation between decapitation and the image that characterized the origins of subjectivity. As a tool of revolution, this public spectacle inaugurated a modern political aesthetics. The guillotine positioned its audience as a collective of political subjects through the decapitation of the sovereign body and display of the severed head. With the beheading of the king, sovereignty passed to the masses that surrounded the scaffold. Both the emergence of the people as a community of spectators and the representation of the guillotine's politics through the image of the severed head are integral to the aesthetics of modern sovereignty. The guillotine must not only put the sovereign to death; it must also display the severed head for the crowd to see. In witnessing the beheading of the sovereign body, power is transferred to the people.[23] By means of this decapitation, the mechanically reproduced cut gives form to an image of sovereignty. Abstracted from the body, stripped of the essence of humanism associated with the face, the severed head becomes a political sign. The guillotine thus adds a third category to the association explored by Kristeva, relating the severed head to the origins of figuration, subjectivity, and politics.

Cinema succeeded the guillotine as an apparatus of political aesthetics, becoming a revolutionary technology within decades of its invention.

Since Walter Benjamin's reflections on the aestheticization of politics and the politicization of aesthetics in the age of the technologically reproduced image, theorists have more closely associated cinema with the political than any other medium. Yet what does it mean for cinema to be political? For Benjamin, the audiovisual apparatus reduced the distance between reality and the image, making social and material relations more immediate and encouraging the audience to change this reality. Cinema, in other words, was a revolutionary medium. In reassessing the entanglement of cinema, politics, and philosophy, Nico Baumbach contrasts Benjamin's argument that cinema is an engine of revolution—a vehicle for popular representation and political praxis—with the conceptualization of politics by film theorists in the 1970's and 1980s.[24] Collectively grouped under the label of apparatus theory, or screen theory, thinkers such as Jean-Luc Comolli, Jean Narboni, Jean-Lois Baudry, and Laura Mulvey narrowed their definition of politics to the category of ideology. Apparatus theory displaced Lacanian psychoanalysis and Althusserian Marxism to the field of cinema, arguing that structures of power predetermined the development of aesthetic form, cinematic technology, and the material configuration of exhibition. Concealed from the spectator, the materiality and aesthetics of the apparatus—the framing of the shot, the cutting that takes place in the editing room, the spatial arrangement of the movie theater—position the spectator as a political subject. Furthermore, the illusionism of narrative film reinforced existing power structures by encouraging the oppressed classes to identify with a false image of themselves, thereby stifling the possibility of dissent. This leads Baumbach to conclude, "Cinema's essence in this understanding is not political so much as antipolitical."[25] Cinematic politics resided in ideology critique that exposed and interrupted this antipolitics by disrupting the pleasures of narrative illusionism through a psychoanalytic and semiotic theory of the apparatus, as well as avant-garde aesthetics. As a result, the film theory of the 1970s and 1980s could not surpass its negativity to assert its own politics.

Given that the definition of cinematic politics has been contested throughout the history of film theory, we cannot take this category for granted. Without abandoning the core concepts of apparatus theory, such as the role of cinematic suture in determining politicized subject positions, my account of the visual guillotine exceeds the conceptualization of politics as ideology and critique. Instead, my approach emerges from the tradition of Latin American cultural studies, which grounds its critique of political aesthetics in the concepts of sovereignty and the *pueblo*. I begin with a brief overview of how this field has understood politics before narrowing my attention to cinema's position in these debates.

The nation was the primary agent of Latin American modernity, and Latin American cultural studies has long understood the cultural production of the late nineteenth and twentieth centuries in relation to the social and political processes that sustained the nation-state. This tradition assumes a Schmittian definition of politics, which distills the autonomy of the political to the distinction between friend and enemy, a grouping that is determined by the sovereign. The sovereign state relies on the category of the popular—the people, *el pueblo*—to legitimate its power. Throughout modernity, the state grounded its authority in the will of the people and realized its hegemony through cinema, literature, and other cultural forms. Through a politics of representation, the state established a pact with the people that legitimated its sovereignty. In Latin America, culture was essential to the movement from revolution, in which the people emerged as a political category that overthrew the (neo)colonial regime, to the nation-state. Subsequently, the state relied on cultural forms—from the novel to narrative cinema and beyond—to define the limits of national identity. Put differently, culture was subordinated to hegemony, serving the representational regime of sovereignty. The formation and legitimacy of the nation-state depended on the integration of the national popular as political subject, which it achieved through hegemonic representations of the people. Latin American cultural studies thus understands the cultural expression of modernity as politically determined in relation to sovereignty and the process of hegemony that legitimated the nation-state through the representation of the people.

By 1990, Latin America found itself reeling from economic turmoil, recent dictatorships and civil conflicts, the failure of the revolutionary project, and the rise of postnational cultures. The advance of neoliberalism cast doubt on the authority of the nation-state, whose sovereignty was threatened by rapid globalization and the subordination of the sphere of the political to the economic. The modern nation-state had entered a deep crisis, leading scholars of Latin American cultural studies to question the continued legitimacy of the conceptual foundations of political modernity. With the eclipse of the nation, Gareth Williams argues, Latin America found itself on the other side of the popular. Unmoored by transnationalization, the *pueblo* lost its political agency and the state no longer legitimated its power through hegemony.[26] Jon Beasley-Murray echoes this conclusion, affirming that hegemony has exhausted its conceptual potential and that politics operates outside representation. In adapting the concept of hegemony, Latin American cultural studies had hitherto assumed the consent of the people to be the basis of state sovereignty. Skeptical of "the people," Beasley-Murray conceptualizes the masses in terms of the multitude, understood as a collective that anticipates the constitution of the people as the political subject. As a presubjective mass, the multitude cannot be represented and cannot provide or withdraw consent to be governed.[27] Thus, both Williams and Beasley-Murray diagnose the crisis of the nation-state as a crisis of popular representation, a conclusion that has profound consequences for accounts of cinematic politics, which have long been organized around the concepts of hegemony and the popular.

The Latin American nation-state that grounded its authority in the representation of the *pueblo* rested on a foundation of sovereign violence. Schmitt famously defines the sovereign as the one who holds the right to introduce the state of exception, leading Jean Franco to define Latin America's cruel modernity as a succession of struggles over the sovereign right to exert this extralegal violence. The sovereign enforces the borders of national identity and violently excludes social groups, such as Indigenous and Afro-descendant communities, that are deemed an obstacle to modernization and progress.[28] Throughout the region, the nation-state repeatedly suspended the law in the pursuit of modernity. The spectacular violence that has marked Latin America's political history—from the conquest to the independence movements, the series of massacres that defined the twentieth century, and the criminal politics of the present—is thus not an exception within the spirit of progress identified with modernity and the liberal nation-state, but a structural fixture of its development.[29] Sergio Villalobos-Ruminott excavates the ideological underpinnings of teleological accounts of Latin American history that culminate in the nation-state as an agent of modernity and development.[30] Villalobos-Ruminott critiques this narrative of progress that neoliberal elites have celebrated in the twenty-first century when marking the bicentenary of Latin American independence movements. Against this celebration of the nation-state, Villalobos-Ruminott traces the mutation of sovereignty since the conquest. In the nineteenth century, imperial sovereignty underwent a metamorphosis, reconfiguring itself in terms of state sovereignty. In the interregnum that marks the contemporary crisis of the nation-state, sovereignty has transformed itself once again, according to the codes of neoliberal capital and its unfettered flow across national borders. This postnational sovereignty coincides with contemporary biopolitical and necropolitical forms of power. Tracing continuities throughout Latin American history, as opposed to the ruptures and successive stages of teleological models that risk overdetermining the role of the state, Villalobos-Ruminott identifies a return to the pact between the globalism of imperial sovereignty and the violent origins of capitalism in the colony.[31] From the Spanish empire to the neoliberal present, we can trace a genealogy of sovereign violence whose maximum expression is the image of the severed head. Achille Mbembe identifies the plantation as an emblematic example of the sovereign's right to suspend the law and exert unchecked violence.[32] In Mbembe's words, "the colonies are the location par excellence where the controls and guarantees of judicial order can be suspended—the zone where the violence of the state of exception is deemed to operate in the service of 'civilization.'"[33] The violence of the plantation anticipates the necropolitical logic of the guillotine, which gives birth to popular sovereignty. Mbembe's theory of necropolitics has been indispensable for contemporary Latin American cultural studies, as the field traces a genealogical account of how cultural forms create political subjects through violence and its representation. The region has produced some of the most cutting-edge scholarship on violence and contemporary politics—much of it untranslated—thereby reversing the perverse logic of intellectual extractivism according to which Latin America offers up its dead for the theories and analysis of scholars in the Global North. The thought of these contemporary Latin American theorists, including Rita Segato, Rossana Reguillo, and Sayak Valencia, offers a point of departure for my reflection on the survival of the visual guillotine today.

Mexico has become a prominent example of the mutation of sovereignty and crisis of the nation-state that has drawn the attention of

Latin American cultural studies in the twenty-first century. The impunity that characterizes both the narco-conflict and wave of femicides since the 1990s, both examples of the confluence of the unhinged pursuit of capital and brutal violence under neoliberalism, exhibits the dissolution of the social contract and exhaustion of the people in the shift from popular to necropolitical sovereignty. Segato, Reguillo, and Valencia have argued that the severed heads and mutilated bodies that haunt the claims to neoliberal progress are not barbaric exceptions but instead the product of the systematic shift toward necropolitical sovereignty and gore capitalism. While the modern state sought to manage its population by exerting disciplinary power over the body, Segato and Reguillo argue that death has become a form of governmentality today and identify the roots of this genealogy in the colonial past. Reguillo observes the rise of a paralegal order in Mexico in which criminal organizations challenge the state's monopoly on violence and territorial control. With the erosion of the social contract in a society that privileges the well-being of financial capital over its citizenry, the rule of law gives way and the border between politics and criminality blurs.[34] In other words, the resurgence of decapitation that is commonly reduced to the barbarism of narco-violence is instead a contemporary form of necropolitics, or of managing marginalized communities through death. Drawing on theories of performance, Reguillo defines the contemporary decapitations that have undermined the public sphere in Mexico as expressive acts that consolidate new forms of necropolitical sovereignty through the display of the severed head. Engaging Reguillo's argument, I look specifically at how this violent reconfiguration of politics has manifested in audiovisual practices that have emerged from the conflict. If in modernity cinema fulfilled a hegemonic function, legitimating the power of the state by representing the people, I identify a pact between the audiovisual and the necropolitical that appropriates the politics of the cut.

Latin American film studies has long privileged the question of cinema's hegemonic function, defining cinematic politics in terms of representation. Consequently, national cinemas and narrative film have been the field's primary objects of study. Beginning in the 1990s and early aughts, when the field began to coalesce institutionally, scholars of Latin American cinema grounded their methodology in national film history, a trend that continues today.[35] This scholarship has taken a politics of representation as its axiomatic foundation.

While historical scholarship continues to emphasize the politics of representation within national cinemas, scholars studying contemporary cinema have underscored the decline of the national framework and turn to transnationalism provoked by the crisis of the nation-state under the neoliberal model. So strong was the association of Latin American cinema with the *pueblo* that the rise of postnational cultures in the 1990s led Néstor García Canclini to question the existence of Latin American cinema by the end of the millennium.[36] While Latin American cinema still thrives, García Canclini could not conceive of filmmaking practices outside of the politics of popular representation. Writing in 1997, García Canclini was reacting to the collapse of national film industries and rise of cinematic transnationalism. Beginning in the 1980s, Latin American cinema entered a prolonged period of crisis and restructuring, with the filmgoing public cut in half throughout this decade.[37] In Mexico, the privatization of the film sector led to the widespread closure of state-subsidized movie theaters, while the signing of NAFTA flooded the Mexican market with Hollywood imports. Ignacio Sánchez Prado concludes that these trends "rendered meaningless the political potential of Mexican film."[38] The gutting of the Instituto Mexicano de Cinematografía (Mexican Film Institute), Argentina's Instituto Nacional de Cine y Artes Audiovisuales (National Institute of Cinema and Audiovisual Arts), and Brazil's state-owned Embrafilme drove the neoliberal reform of Latin America's largest film industries.[39] Consequently, filmmakers turned to private financing, transnational funding schemes such as Ibermedia, and arthouse incubators such as the Rotterdam International Film Festival's Hubert Bals Fund. The link that had tied cinema to the representation of the people and the hegemony of the nation-state had been severed. This transformation has produced a cinema that critics such as García Canclini largely perceive as depoliticized and increasingly concerned with either commercial success or the cultural capital of European film festivals. Yet despite these conclusions, the transformation of funding, exhibition, and spectatorship in recent decades does not preclude cinematic politics. Rather, as Gonzalo Aguilar has observed, critics have regarded this cinema as depoliticized because they continue to insist on a politics of representation that is out of step with the political realities of the present.[40]

The challenge for scholars of contemporary Latin American cultural studies has been to reconceptualize audiovisual politics beyond the sphere of popular representation. More recently, Aguilar has revisited the theoretical and historiographical models that privileged the category of the people. A crucial example is Glauber Rocha's explicit rejection of the category of the *pueblo* in 1971. Speaking at a conference at Columbia University, Rocha rebels against the postulates of Third Cinema as outlined by Fernando Solanas and Octavio Getino when he derides "the people" as a "myth of the bourgeoisie" that perpetuates colonial reason.[41] In place of a politics of representation, which aligns with Rocha's previous call for an aesthetics of hunger, the filmmaker advocates for an aesthetics of dreams characterized by a politics of affect. Such a cinema would espouse a revolutionary unreason that would channel "the irrational forces of the poor masses."[42] Embracing the radical potential of the multitude, which operates through the release of intensities as opposed to the representation of the people that territorializes this presubjective mass, Rocha calls for a posthegemonic politics of cinema. Thus, Aguilar underscores an audiovisual politics in the NLAC that runs counter to the movement's long-standing association with a politics of representation, anticipating the exhaustion of the people in the cinema of the 1990s.[43] Rudy Pradenas traces this historical revision back even further in Latin American film history. Pradenas critiques the historiographic and theoretical foundations of Latin American film studies, arguing that they privilege a conceptualization of cinematic politics that achieved its zenith in the NLAC. This identitarian cinema privileges narrative over form, overshadowing other modes of cinema and politics that do not share its commitments to popular representation.[44] Through the anti-identitarian concept of anonymity, Pradenas revisits accounts of early cinema in Latin America and frames the region's tradition of cinematic politics beyond the scope of representation. The work of Aguilar and Pradenas thus represents a shift in Latin American film studies that marks a new conceptualization of politics beyond representation, centering instead questions of form, affect, and materiality.

Despite the exhaustion of the *pueblo,* which coincides with the eclipse of analog film and rise of electronic and digital media, moving images continue to stage the political through the form of the cut. Most recently, the relation between the severed head and the image has resurfaced in the decapitation video. This grizzly new genre has come to represent the extremity of screen violence in our postcinematic age, and the recordings of beheadings that have emerged from the conflicts in the Middle East have already drawn the attention of filmmakers and film theorists.[45] However, the relation that these snuff films establish between the moving image and the severed head is particularly prevalent today. In Mexico, criminal organizations weaponized the growing popularity of streaming technologies and began uploading decapitation videos to the internet in 2006. Anthropologists, critics, and theorists have interpreted the severed head as the maximum expression of the country's widespread violence, as power has consolidated around organized crime and the public display of the body in pieces. I refer to these images as *cinematic crimes* in order to emphasize their production value and form. Their authors, consciously or not, identify the relation between the cinematic cut and the severed head that is implicit in audiovisual politics.

As a political and visual apparatus, the guillotine continued the association between sovereignty, the severed head, and spectacle. Cinema inherits the guillotine through this mechanization of the cut. Like the guillotine, cinema was an apparatus of spectacle that staged popular sovereignty through the cut. The concomitance of the cut and sovereign violence continues in our necropolitical present. In the chapters that follow, I examine how filmmakers themselves theorize the inscription of political violence in the cut. By exploring the long-established relation between cutting film and cutting bodies, filmmakers relate the structural violence of the audiovisual to the political. This corpus asserts that cinema is an inherently political medium when it triangulates modern sovereignty, violence, and visuality. A potential for a cinematic politics that exceeds representation resides within the cut, though it may be wielded for a variety of ends. What I call the visual guillotine organizes the relation between body, image, and technology in cinema around the symbolic violence of cutting. The works I examine throughout this book interrupt and exaggerate the violence of the cinematic cut, making the logic of the visual guillotine explicit. This corpus draws the audience's attention to the symbolic violence that organizes cinema, often shocking the audience through extreme uses of montage or the close-up. By exaggerating cinema's obsession with cutting, their authors theorize the visual guillotine. Moving from the level of representation to questions of form and materiality, I examine how they express political concepts and situate spectators as political subjects.

Cutting the Corpus

The guillotine, like cinema, was both a political apparatus and an image-making device. It continued the relation between the severed head and the image that Kristeva traces to the very origins of visual culture. As a result, a cultural and political history of violence is fossilized in audiovisual form. The filmmakers I study theorize cinema's political force by relating the formal violence of the cut to decapitation. In the first chapter, my account of the visual guillotine unfolds by tracing a political history of the close-up in Latin American cinema from the studio era of the 1930s and 1940s to the militant aesthetics that swept the NLAC in the late 1960s and 1970s. My observations depart from the excess of theoretical reflection that the close-up has provoked given the cultural weight assigned to its most common object: the amplified face. The close-up has been the site of humanist aesthetics throughout film history, and theories of this device have vacillated between a commitment to the audience's identification with a human essence outwardly projected through the face, on the one hand, and a morbid fascination with the close-up's power to deface and dehumanize the actor, on the other. For example, Jacques Aumont has observed that while classical cinema privileged the close-up to encourage the audience's identification with the depths of human experience expressed through the face, this form underwent a transformation in postwar cinema, when modernist filmmakers reckoning with the cruelties of the twentieth century channeled the experience of destruction toward the face. Amid this crisis of humanism, the close-up ceased to be a medium for identification and instead became an instrument of disfiguration and defacement.[46] Nonetheless, in the European context these practices remained largely within the realm of the aesthetic avant-garde. While relating modernist abstraction to the disasters of the twentieth century, Aumont overlooks the politics of this gesture.

In tracing a political genealogy of the close-up in Latin American cinema, I observe a similar shift from humanist identification to modernist defacement. Working within the conventions of the classical style, filmmakers contributed to projects of cultural nationalism by emphasizing the human qualities of the face in aesthetically refined close-ups. Treating the face as a window into the soul of the nation, state-sponsored studios encouraged the spectator to identify with this face and form part of the national community. However, decades later militant filmmakers radically opposed these hegemonic images. Aligned with revolutionary movements, they embraced radical aesthetics and politics by foregrounding the formal violence of this device to represent political violence by defacing the body politic. These filmmakers continued to treat the close-up as a tool of political allegory but charged this form with negativity. Here I identify a parallel with Aumont's account of cinematic defacement. In seeking to bolster the revolutionary cause, Latin America's militant cinema united the aesthetic and political avant-gardes. Radical politics required radical forms, and in these examples the modernist aesthetic of defacement identified by Aumont serves to represent the dehumanizing violence directed at the people. Militant cinema encouraged the spectator to identify with these destroyed faces that represented the violence directed at the *pueblo* so that the audience would join the revolutionary cause in defense of its dignity. Defaced, these visibly severed heads lost their human qualities and became political signs.

Throughout film history, reflections on the politics of cinematic form have privileged montage for its potential to radicalize audiences. To paraphrase Oeler, throughout film history montage is shadowed by the guillotine.[47] In the second chapter I continue my reflection on the intersection of the two avant-gardes in the NLAC by examining how Fernando Birri and Glauber Rocha reaffirm the relation between montage and revolutionary violence when they relate the cinematic cut to beheading. Inspired by Eisenstein's unfinished project on the Mexican Revolution, the late films of Birri and Rocha relate the cinematic cut to revolutionary affect. By overwhelming the spectator through an excess of cuts, or unsettling the spectator through a titillating absence of montage, Birri's *Org* (1978) and Rocha's *Cabezas cortadas* (*Severed Heads,* 1970) induce states in the audience that mimic the affective intensity of revolution. Steeped in the filmmakers' wistful meditations on the radical movements of the 1960s, these films communicate revolutionary affect through formal experimentation. While contemporary film studies has largely turned away from the formal concerns of classic film theory toward questions of cinematic affect, I follow recent efforts by theorists such as Eugenie Brinkema to reflect on the relationship between affect and form. However, whereas Brinkema steers clear of cinematic politics, this chapter associates the form of the cinematic cut with a revolutionary affect that stems from the guillotine.

The radical politics of the NLAC provoked violent repression from authoritarian governments throughout Latin America, leading filmmakers such as Birri and Rocha to exile themselves in Europe. Two of the most prominent figures within the NLAC, their style mutated after authoritarian governments repressed militant movements throughout the region. *Org* and *Cabezas cortadas* have received limited critical attention, in part because of their stylistic divergence from Birri's and Rocha's earlier work. These disparities have long provoked debate on the periodization of the NLAC. I draw on recent revisions of this movement, especially the work of Laura Podalsky, to explain why this reflection on montage and political affect emerges only amid the decline of the movement in the region. I observe that, while explicitly political, the montage of the late NLAC abandons the revolutionary didacticism that film historians have long identified with the NLAC. Exemplified by the experimental films of Santiago Álvarez and by Solanas and Getino's militant essay film *La hora de los hornos* (*The Hour of the Furnaces,* 1968), these works overwhelmingly drew on documentary and the type of intellectual montage theorized by Soviet filmmakers—especially Dziga Vertov and Eisenstein. However, this first phase of NLAC waned at the end of the 1960s. Disenchanted with this failure of cinematic militancy, filmmakers began to abandon their commitment to intellectual montage and experimented more freely with the affective force of the cinematic cut. Rather than employ montage to reason with the spectator that militancy was a logical response to neocolonialist exploitation, this later montage used the cut to overwhelm the audience and re-create the ecstasy of revolution. This is cinema as guillotine: abandoning revolutionary reason, the violence of the cut induces a sublime state.

The third chapter theorizes the displacement of violence onto the cinematic cut in the present. The mutation of politics and aesthetics at the end of the twentieth century has reoriented this visual guillotine. The neoliberal policies and accelerated globalization that followed the Cold War reshaped both the state and cultural production. One of the primary concerns of contemporary Latin American cultural studies has been theorizing the new cultural forms that have emerged from this crisis of the liberal nation-state and its pact with popular sovereignty. I join this debate by examining how the relation between the cinematic cut and politics mutates in the audiovisual production associated with what is popularly referred to as the Mexican narco-conflict. Yet rather than study the representation of narco-violence on-screen, I am specifically concerned with how the erosion of cinema's commitment to the popular, which defined the medium's political commitments throughout modernity, revived a politics of form. Following the eclipse of the NLAC, the 1980s and 1990s saw the transformation of cinematic politics in Latin America. Throughout the region, the introduction of neoliberal policies and accelerated globalization in the final decades of the twentieth century cast doubt on the *pueblo* as collective political actor. For example, in Argentina, where filmmakers aligned with revolutionary movements had sought to represent and construct the people, the 1990s saw cinema abandon this political category. Though this was not a coordinated or programmatic move, the *pueblo* splintered into a plurality of political identities that were not traditionally represented in this category.[48] Mexican cinema underwent a similar transformation in this decade, when the state abandoned its long-standing support of the national film industry. From the Golden Age of the 1930s and 1940s to the Nueva Ola (New Wave) of the late 1960s and 1970s, Mexican filmmakers served the cultural hegemony of *mexicanidad* (Mexicanness). With the neoliberal reforms of the 1980s and the enactment of NAFTA in 1994, Mexican cinema gradually abandoned the popular and began to represent the concerns of the new middle class that emerged in the wake of neoliberalism.[49] My reflections on the politics of the cinematic cut in chapter 3 are situated in this context, with the emergence of new forms of audiovisual politics.

As I have already mentioned, in contemporary Mexico criminal organizations record beheadings and disseminate these images online. These decapitation videos have become a prominent terror tactic under new forms of sovereignty that depend on the manipulation and display of the severed head. These recordings weaponize the cinematic cut through their use of montage and close-ups to horrify the public. Jean-Louis Comolli, famous for his ideological critique of the cinematic apparatus in the 1960s and 1970s, has recently pointed to the decapitation videos produced in Iraq and Syria as the locus of audiovisual politics today. I open a dialogue with Comolli based on similar images from the Mexican context. To this end, I examine these videos in formal, aesthetic, and political terms. I argue that they must be understood in relation to the cinematic apparatus; these moving images politicize film form—the cinematic cut—as it survives in video. The materials analyzed in this chapter come from a series of such videos. I highlight the transformation of both politics and moving-image practices since the 1990s to track how the politics of the visual guillotine shifts from the radicalism of the NLAC to contemporary necropolitics. Amid these broader transformations, the cinematic cut, once wielded for its revolutionary potential, becomes weaponized by the opposite end of the political spectrum.

I consider the politics of engaging these images as both documents of the ongoing conflict and contemporary aesthetic objects. To avoid falling into the political trap set by their authors—that is, a mode of viewing that spectacularizes violence and thus erases the victim—I intervene in these images through a process of countermontage. Drawing on Laura Mulvey's theorization of stillness and death in digital media, I use the freeze-frame to capture images of the victims in these videos and reorder them through the practice of montage. Thinkers including Aby Warburg, Walter Benjamin, and Georges Didi-Huberman have emphasized how the juxtaposition of images can create flashes of insight that contradict the message these same images convey. Herein lies the political potential of montage. My reflection on the aesthetics and politics of the decapitation video proceeds by extracting stills from these videos and juxtaposing them with images of cinematic violence taken from film history. I thus imagine possibilities for disarming the decapitation video by turning the logic of the visual guillotine against itself.

Filmmakers and artists have been quick to react to the decapitation videos that have emerged from the narco-conflict. The shift in the political register of this visual guillotine interpellates filmmakers. Whereas the force of montage and the close-up has helped radical filmmakers represent revolutionary violence for emancipatory ends, criminal organizations weaponize the cinematic cut. Put differently, the decapitation video turns the politics of cinematic form on its head and forces filmmakers to revive reflections on the relation between the audiovisual apparatus, the body, and violence. In the fourth chapter I examine narrative, documentary, and experimental films that capture the cinematic logic of these gruesome videos. Filmmakers including Carlos Reygadas, Amat Escalante, and Everardo González, as well as the audiovisual collective Los Ingrávidos, expose the visual logic of this violence. Their films critically reflect on the role of the audiovisual apparatus within this conflict. Across cinematic modes, these filmmakers stage the relation between the moving image and the severed head in order to understand the decapitation video's appropriation of the cinematic cut in a reactionary register. By returning to the relation between cutting images and cutting bodies, this corpus reframes the decapitation video not as a performance of barbarism but as a cinematic crime that enacts a political agenda. Since the culture industry serves the security strategy of the Mexican state by representing narco-violence as barbaric, the critical examination of the politics of audiovisual form in these self-reflexive films is politically urgent. Furthermore, the materials analyzed in this chapter examine the mutation of the visual guillotine in the technology shift from cinema to digital media, reconsidering the remains of radical cinema in the present. Finally, in addition to their critique of form and technology, these materials meditate on the place of the spectator amid the weaponization of the visual guillotine. The decapitation video exploits the affect inscribed in the cut, which modernist filmmakers such as Birri and Rocha associated with the intensities of revolution. In these materials, the cinematic cut loses its connection to its radical history. Rather than inspire revolutionary praxis, the visual guillotine paralyzes the public sphere in horror.

In the final chapter, I conclude my account of the politics of the cinematic cut by examining the spectator's role in the visual guillotine. The focus is on the spectator's interpellation and participation in these processes of cutting. I open a dialogue between my concept of the visual guillotine and classic models of cinematic suture that emerged from the apparatus theory of the 1970s. Adapting Lacanian psychoanalysis, suture theory sought to account for the formation of cinematic subjects through the audience's immersion in the spectacle and identification with the protagonist. Film theorists such as Kaja Silverman and Stephen Heath posited that the cinematic cut structured this process; for example, through a facial close-up and a cut to a countershot, a filmmaker could encourage the audience to identify with the spectator's gaze.

In the psychoanalytic framework of suture theory, this cut represented the psychic lack that the spectator sought to resolve through this process of identification. Consequently, the premise of suture theory—the formation of the subject through the cinematic cut—bears striking similarity to Kristeva's reflections on the image of the severed head. Thus, I conclude my account of the visual guillotine by zooming out from my concerns with sovereignty to engage other conceptualizations of cinematic politics. In the first half of this chapter, I examine self-reflexive short films by Alejandro Jodorowsky and Mariana Rondón that reinforce this relation between the severed head and subjectivity by visualizing subject formation through a symbolic beheading. These films meditate on the process of cinematic identification, which in classical cinema relies on the cinematic cut, by staging the scene of identification through the symbolic decapitation of the spectator. Jodorowsky and Rondón reimagine suture as the transposition of two severed heads: one represented on-screen, which is the object of the spectator's desire, and another in the audience, suspended above their seat and transfixed by the moving image. The fetishistic spectator produced by the form of classical cinema desires to possess the head projected in the darkness.

The second half of this chapter takes up the politicization of suture within critiques of fetishization by feminist film theorists and filmmakers. Combining psychoanalysis, ideology critique, and formal analysis, theorists such as Laura Mulvey and Linda Williams famously aligned fetishistic spectatorship with the formal and material structure of the cinematic apparatus. Sutured into the narrative, the spectator identifies with the male gaze of the film that seeks to resolve the threat of sexual difference through a perverse dominance over the female body. I revive these concerns in my reflection on suture and the severed head. If Jodorowsky and Rondón imagine the scene of identification as a transposition of heads, then the sadism of the fetishistic spectator may be recast as a desire to decapitate the female form. Freud associates the cultural weight of the decapitation of the Gorgon with a desire to resolve castration anxiety. The sight of the Medusa paralyzed the male gaze because it represented female lack, and this sexual difference is resolved through decapitation.[50] Mulvey invokes Freud's reflection on the decapitation of the Medusa in her reflections on fetishization and the commodification of the female form through the close-up. I depart from Mulvey's psychoanalytic reflections on decapitation and fetishization in my analysis of the severed head in films by María Luisa Bemberg and Lucrecia Martel. In comparing the critique of fetishization through the decapitation of the female form in Bemberg's *El mundo de la mujer* (*Woman's World,* 1972) and Martel's *La mujer sin cabeza* (*The Headless Woman,* 2008), I hope to demonstrate the continued relevance of classic film theory. The material structure of the audiovisual apparatus that shaped feminist film theory has mutated with the shift to electronic and digital media. However, Martel has continued to reflect on fetishization in her digital shorts, which experiment with new forms of cutting and dominating the body, such as pixelation. Similarly, cinema's expansion beyond the traditional venue of the movie theater—its reimagination of exhibition through dialogues between film and contemporary art that have led to the relatively recent popularity of film installation—have prompted new reflections on spectatorship. I conclude my reflection on spectatorship and the severed head by examining the critique of fetishization and gender in the expanded cinema of Venezuelan artist Javier Téllez. Together with Martel's digital shorts, this work reimagines the legacy of the cinematic cut in our postcinematic age.

Governing the logic of the visual guillotine is the cinematic cut, which transcends any single formal or discursive practice. The violent logic of the cut, which determined cinematic politics and survives in digital video, places the severed head at the heart of cinematic politics. Like the guillotine, the editor's blade rises and falls, the shutter of the projector opens and closes, and the frame of the camera beheads the actor. This logic has always structured the cinematic apparatus; we have only needed a corpus that would call it to our attention. My own role as a corpus is to listen to these works and arrange them so that this theory of the visual guillotine emerges from their juxtaposition. Latin American cinema is essential to this account; it is the combination of theory and praxis in the materials I organize here—through which this apparatus is exhibited—that allows me to elaborate this account of the politics of the cinematic cut. These filmmakers propose that violence relies on image-making and, in turn, that moving images require violence. In arranging their contributions as if in a collage, *The Visual Guillotine* traces the contours of a Latin American film theory.

1

DEFACEMENT

THE POLITICS OF THE CLOSE-UP IN THE VISUAL GUILLOTINE

Before Soviet filmmakers of the 1920s defined montage as the essence of film, early film theorists identified cinema's medium specificity with the close-up. The breadth and intensity of reflection on this device leads Mary Ann Doane to conclude that the close-up "has been accompanied by an excessive discourse or, at the very least, a discourse about excess."[1] Throughout film history, interpretations of the close-up have never been stable.[2] Film theorists have vacillated between a morbid fascination with the close-up's power to mutilate the actor and its ability to connect with the depths of human expression through its most common object: the amplified face. The contradictions of the close-up—including this tension between the humanizing image and the threat of dehumanizing violence—have made it difficult to define. Yet one trait has remained constant: the close-up has been conceived in relation to the face and its defacement. This image of the human relies on the decapitation of the body by the camera's frame. The threat of defacement always looms behind the close-up, even when it proclaims its humanism. I attribute the intensity, volume, and range of thought that the close-up has inspired among film theorists—as well as its political significance—to the visual and symbolic violence of this formal device. The excessive discourse surrounding the close-up, sometimes praising its humanistic force, sometimes recoiling at such perverse mutilation, channels the structural violence and affect of the visual guillotine.

The specter of the severed head looms over the close-up. In her hybrid autobiography, Mexican author Margo Glantz captures this when recalling how Norma Shearer's performance in *Marie Antoinette* (1938) deeply affected her as a young woman. The close-ups of Shearer provoked such a strong reaction in the author that she was ejected from the theater for her emotional outburst even before Antoinette's execution.[3] Glantz's reaction mirrors those of the diegetic spectators who crowd the scaffold at the culmination of the film. As Shearer's Antoinette is being led to the guillotine, the close-up of her head anticipating her decapitation, a young woman bursts from the crowd with her hands outstretched, wailing and reaching for the queen before a guard apprehends her and escorts her away from the spectacle. The scene represents an uncanny doubling of Glantz's reaction to these close-ups that closes the figurative distance between the guillotine and the scene of projection. These anxieties reaffirm Doane's conclusion that "the most heavily used close-up, that of the face, fragments the body, decapitating it."[4] Given the sensibilities of classical Hollywood, Shearer's beheading is only implied through the symbolic violence of the camera's frame. As the queen awaits her fate, her head is superimposed in double exposure. Next, a close-up of the guillotine adds a third layer to the image as its blade slowly ascends. Blocking out this face, its sharp edges coincide with the limits of the frame. Glantz's anecdote highlights the symbolic violence of the close-up by tracing its formal operation to the guillotine. The guillotine encodes itself in the close-up. The edges of the frame sever the head from its body and display this spectacular image for the crowd. Glantz is not alone in forging this association. Throughout the first half of the twentieth century, film and media theorists have referred to the edges of the frame in terms of scalpels, razors, and other menacing blades.[5] Such metaphors express a theme that underlies the concern with fragmentation in modern aesthetics: to frame an image is to cut the field of vision. The violence of this process is heightened when the pro-filmic figure is a body.

The guillotine was both a political tool and a spectacle that mechanically reproduced severed heads. Audiences surrounded the scaffold in hopes of catching a glimpse of these images. In addition to physicians, who attended public beheadings out of scientific interest, artists lined the stage in order to represent the act of beheading. However, those contributing to the guillotine's vast visual archive faced a seemingly insurmountable challenge. The guillotine produced death instantaneously: in the blink of an eye, the blade fell and severed the head from its body. The act of beheading was unwatchable, both because of its graphic violence and extreme rapidity. The cut itself could not be represented given its temporality. The physical act of beheading eluded figuration, so artists seeking to re-create the hypnotic power of this spectacle centered their gaze on the single image that the guillotine mechanically reproduced: the severed head.[6] Since this machine had automated the spectacle of decapitation, film theorist Raymond Bellour has compared the guillotine's operator with the projectionist. Liberated of the task of producing an image of the severed head by manually beheading the victim, the executioner is reconfigured as a technician. Furthermore, Bellour compares the window of the guillotine, where the condemned rested his head prior to execution, to the screen. With the rest of his body concealed by the apparatus, the victim's head appeared suspended above the crowd, as if foreshadowing the close-up.[7] Just as the guillotine displayed an image of the body in pieces, so too does the cinematic apparatus project a severed head onto the surface. This visual decapitation only increased the titillating anticipation of the final cut among the crowd. In Bellour's argument, the association between guillotine and cinema demonstrates the continuity of affect that is inscribed within the cut. The spectacle of fragmentation shocks the audience. As we see in Glantz's anecdote, the close-up of the star communicates a pathos capable of overwhelming the spectator.

In this chapter, I begin my account of the visual guillotine with the close-up. Even in recent years, long after this device has lost its aura amid technological convergence and intermedial aesthetics, film theorists continue to revisit the close-up. Yet despite the richness of reflection that has emerged in the wake of cinematic modernism, in the work of Doane, Noa Steimatsky, and Jacques Aumont, theories of the close-up continue to overlook the politics of this device. While each of these accounts has shaped my argument, my concept of the visual guillotine addresses the lack of discussion surrounding the politics of the close-up. Doane gestures in this direction with her indispensable reflection on race and the claims to the universality of the close-up in classical film theory. This critique makes possible my examination of the racial politics of the facial close-up in the Mexican studio system, but it falls short of a broader theoretical engagement of politics. In what follows, I trace a political history of the close-up in Latin American cinema, from the studio era of the 1930s and 1940s to the counterhegemonic and militant aesthetics of the New Latin American Cinema (NLAC) in the late 1960s and 1970s, and open a conversation between film form and the iconography of populism in the region. Specifically, I examine how the fragmentation of the body underlying the facial close-up—its visual dismemberment by the frame—represents the concept of popular sovereignty that may be traced back to the guillotine.[8]

In this account, the politics of the close-up derives from the tension between the humanist image of the face and its defacement. This historical context is marked by cinema's place within a broader iconography of populism, in which the face forms the nucleus of political representation. This face, especially when juxtaposed with a wider shot of the crowd or inserted into a sequence of close-ups, expresses the pathos of the people. Through the facial close-up, filmmakers visualized the struggles of the people as a collective political subject and sought to inscribe the spectator in the national and regional community through the face-to-face encounter. Gazing at the facial close-up, the spectator identifies as a member of this collective.

I distinguish three moments in the development of this politics of the close-up. In the first, the state-supported studio systems elaborated what I term the hegemonic close-up to maintain social, political, and economic hierarchies by fabricating a face for the nation. The decline of the studio era and rise of independent productions at the end of the 1950s initiates a second phase. Filmmakers rebelled against these hegemonic politics in the early years of the NLAC. At this time, what I call the utopian close-up replaced the glamorous face of the movie star with the image of pathos present in the face of the nonprofessional actor. Embracing both social documentary and neorealist narrative, counterhegemonic filmmakers traveled to underdeveloped regions to capture the true face of the people and elaborate an authentic populist image. The utopian close-up sought to represent the people, but it also aspired to be an event: through the spectator's identification with this image, a new collective emerged and demanded representation. While the hegemonic and utopian close-ups differed in their political register, either fabricating a hegemonic image of the *pueblo* to consolidate power or representing the politically disenfranchised from below, both employ a humanist logic to construct community through the audience's identification with the face. The final phase of this history abandons the representative politics of the face and instead wields the symbolic violence of the close-up to represent neocolonial assault on the *pueblo*.

When the NLAC was met with political repression, the humanism that previously enabled the facial politics of the close-up began to give way. In observing how radical filmmakers developed an aesthetics of cinematic defacement, I depart from Aumont's reflection on the status of the face in modernist cinema. Whereas silent cinema embraced the facial close-up as an expression of a universal human essence, filmmakers reckoning with the horrors of war and the Holocaust used this form to disfigure the pro-filmic body. While these strategies develop in postwar European cinema, I displace Aumont's theory of cinematic defacement to the context of neocolonial violence and anticolonial militancy in Latin America. In the face of repression by authoritarian governments, the militant filmmakers of the 1960s and 1970s similarly reckoned with a crisis of humanism and foregrounded the violence of the close-up to give form to political violence. At the intersection of the political and cinematic avant-gardes, defacement came to represent the exploitation of the *pueblo*. The genealogy of the close-up in this chapter thus traces the politics of the cinematic cut by highlighting this violence and centering this tension between the face and its defacement.

The Violence of the Close-up and the Shocks of Modernity

Before the close-up became integrated into the narrative system of classical cinema, its violence shocked early audiences. Béla Balázs provides a likely apocryphal anecdote from the early years of film reception in Russia that nevertheless registers the disruptive qualities of the close-up. To illustrate the novelty of the cinematic cut and the violence with which it was received in a visual culture that was unaccustomed to the fragmented experience of modernity, Balázs tells the story of a Siberian peasant girl who experiences the cinema for the first time while on a trip to Moscow. Describing her experience after the projection, the girl could not contain her shock. Balázs recalls her repulsion, writing, "Oh, it was horrible! I can't believe they allow such dreadful things to be shown here in

Moscow! . . . Human beings were torn to pieces and the heads thrown one way and the bodies the other and the hands somewhere else again."[9] Balázs draws on this anecdote to illustrate how contemporary spectators had come to accept the fragmentary structure of film narration, despite the underlying violence of its form. Furthermore, the example suggests that these shocks were acutely felt in contexts of underdevelopment that reckoned with an uneven modernity. However, early audiences in the global center also demonstrated a morbid fascination with this visual violence. Proto-close-ups in the cinema of attractions entertained audiences by enlarging and disfiguring faces. Though the shock of the close-up gradually wore off, filmmakers who experimented with this device early on encountered resistance. The disorientation the close-up provoked through its manipulation of scale was perceived as a form of violence. For early audiences, the close-up violated the principles of bodily unity in theatrical performance and created a perverse spectacle of dismemberment.

At once perturbing and titillating, the close-up channeled broader concerns surrounding the legibility of the body and the face in modernity. The severed heads projected on-screen continued a tradition introduced in nineteenth-century painting, which gradually abandoned the principle of bodily integrity by cropping the body in the frame of the artwork.[10] The arrival of photography accelerated modernity's tendency toward a fragmented visuality and implicated the image of the body in pieces in new modes of social control. The emergence of the crowd as a political force, as well as the rise of urban anonymity and crime, led to the disciplining of the body through physiognomy and criminology. Anxieties surrounding the opacity of the face were at the center of these debates. To render the face transparent and discipline the modern subject through its image, the biometric system designed by Alphonse Bertillon relied on facial measurements and photographic portraiture. Bertillon insisted on the physiognomic transparency of the face, which outwardly projected deviancy, to identify criminal types and predict repeat offenses. This instrumentalization of the face by disciplinary power resonated in Latin America, given its turbulent and uneven experience of modernity. The legibility of the racialized face was of particular concern, and Bertillonage was adapted within ethnographic expeditions.[11] In Mexico, the pseudoscientific claims advanced by physiognomic discourses gained traction under the regime of Porfirio Díaz, who adapted them in the service of wider modernization projects. Mexico became a pioneer of criminological photography by the turn of the century, amassing troves of biometric photographs in its efforts to document criminal types.[12] The ideology of this social project was clear, and the physiognomic photograph became another avenue for legitimizing the racial hierarchies of Mexican society. In this archive of expressionless faces, the majority bearing Indigenous features, the bodies before the camera are stripped of subjectivity and dehumanized by disciplinary power. Having their likeness reduced to biometric data, they are defaced. This assault on the humanism of the face in modernity marks the beginning of a facial politics in Latin America, in which cinema intervenes through the close-up.

Anxieties surrounding the face in modernity led to a humanist resurgence that sought to reclaim this image through the scale and magnification permitted by the close-up. Film theorists responded to the assimilation of the close-up within the system of classical narration, which had emerged by the 1920s, by praising cinema's power to amplify the details of the human face. Inaugurating a humanist tradition of the close-up, Balázs goes as far as equating this device with the concept of faciality. By extracting an object from the accelerated pace of modern life and amplifying it in the cinema, the close-up allows the filmmaker to isolate what Balázs calls "the face of things."[13] In other words, even when it does not amplify a human face, the close-up anthropomorphizes the object in its frame. Balázs's contemporaries satirized his excessive humanism, and critics have since noted the contradictions within his theory. Despite its excessive insistence on the face, the threat of defacement lurks behind this humanist account as the border between face and object becomes blurred. Indeed, Aumont observes that this insistence on the face in silent cinema is already the first phase of its ruination.[14] Aumont's critique extends to Balázs's contemporary Jean Epstein, who develops his theory of *photogenie* in relation to the close-up and the perception of the face's micromovements. In an infamous passage, Epstein describes the beauty of a close-up that captures a face breaking into a smile in almost mystical terms. Nonetheless, this ekphrasis betrays a perverse fascination with the violence of the close-up. As the muscles tense and the edges of the lips begin to curl upward, "Everything is movement, imbalance, crisis. Crack. The mouth gives way, like a ripe fruit splitting open.

As if slit by a scalpel, a keyboard-like smile cuts laterally into the corner of the lips."[15] Though Epstein declares the sublime beauty of the facial close-up, this image and the experience it evokes are not immune from the violence of the apparatus. While the close-up permitted both a humanist encounter with the face and a transcendental experience tied to the essence of cinema, it was a double-edged blade that threatened to deface. As Balázs and Epstein demonstrate, the excessive discourse surrounding the close-up is driven by a tension between its potential for humanist expression and the threat of a dehumanizing violence that severs the head in the frame. Such are the contradictions of the close-up, which Deleuze underscores when he asserts, "the facial close-up is both the face and its effacement."[16] A politics of the close-up emerges from this dialectic, and Latin American cinema develops its own tradition of the close-up in the contexts of these debates.

The Hegemonic Close-up and the Face of the Nation

A politics of the close-up begins with humanist theories of this device, whose insistence on the mimetic face enables political representation in cinema. Embedded in the classical style of narration that dominated film production approximately from the 1920s onward, the close-up staged a face-to-face encounter with the audience. The instrumentalization of the close-up by classical film form, such as the convention of the shot/countershot, encouraged the spectator to decode the microgestures of the actor's face and identify with an outwardly projected essence. With the emergence of classical narration in the silent era, film theorists praised the close-up's ability to transform the face into a vehicle of human expression. Writing in almost mystical terms, Balázs and Epstein identified this device with cinema's specificity as an artistic medium because it captured the ineffable character of inner experience. The close-up became the degree zero of representation: it exhibited the mysteries of the human soul by amplifying the mimetic face to a scale never seen before. Through this device, cinema allowed spectators to suspend language and return to a primordial, prelinguistic mode of communication that had been lost. Through the power of the close-up, cinema recovered the face—and consequently the soul—in modernity. Balázs held that the close-up abstracted an image of the human from the diegesis. Transcending linguistic and cultural barriers, the close-up permitted a universal communication.[17] This image allowed spectators to identify with the human form represented in the face, which would advance the construction of a global community. Yet while Balázs insists on the potential of the facial close-up for a humanist cinema, this theory activates other forms of violence by defining the universal face represented by the close-up as a European face with white features. In his words, "The cinematograph is a machine that in its own way will create a living, concrete internationalism: *the unique, shared psyche of the white man*. We can go further. By suggesting a uniform ideal of beauty as the universal goal of selected breeding, the film will help to produce a uniform type of the white race."[18] Consequently, the community made possible by the universal language of the facial close-up in fact served to reinforce the racial hierarchies of colonial modernity by erasing the threat of difference.[19] Balázs thus inaugurates a political tradition of the close-up. His observation that the close-up permits the formation of a collective through identification with an essence mediated by the face proves influential for my argument because it determines who belongs to the political community. My account of the close-up in Latin American cinema examines how such claims to universality supported systems of oppression.

In the 1930s and 1940s, state-sponsored film industries contributed to projects of cultural nationalism by articulating a politics of representation through the facial close-up. What I call the hegemonic close-up imposed a face on the people, forming a national community through the audience's identification with this image. Employed in the service of the state, these close-ups served to maintain social, political, and economic hierarchies. In his history of Latin American cinema, Paul Schroeder Rodríguez underscores the role of film studios in consolidating power within the politics of corporatism that marked these decades. As Schroeder Rodríguez explains, corporatism was a cultural discourse of modernity that incorporated other cultural and political forms.[20] Film studios, particularly in Lázaro Cárdenas's Mexico and Juan Perón's Argentina, were forced to mediate between corporatist states, the people, and capital. Within the discourse of corporatism, cinema became a powerful tool for exercising hegemony by encouraging the audience to identify with the image of a national culture that the state-backed studios crafted through narrative, landscape, music, gestures, costumes, and the faces of the star system. Political representation depended on a definition of the people, and the national community emerged from the masses' identification with these cinematic faces.

The close-up became a political form that organized this logic of representation, as studios imbued cinema with a populist spirit. In his iconography of populism, Georges Didi-Huberman argues that throughout modernity the people manifested through the figure of the face.[21] Cropped out of the crowd and often juxtaposed through montage, the close-up of the anonymous face visualizes popular sovereignty. Across media, the face gives form to the collective political subject. Yet the constitution of the people through the image of the face is not an innocent act, as this abstraction of the face carries with it the violence implicit in any act of framing. To remove the face from the crowd, to sever it from the body politic for the purpose of political representation, is to expose it to violence. This is no longer the face of an individual that projects an inner human essence, but a face converted into the site of political struggle. The cut that isolates this face in the frame gives form to the pathos that defines the people; its violence represents the oppression of the people and releases a political intensity that further unites this collective. Paraphrasing Deleuze, this populist iconography vacillates between the *face* and its *defacement*. Through the work of the visual guillotine—its conversion of this image into a political sign through the close-up—the face becomes a severed head: the figuration of popular sovereignty.

Mexico offers a compelling example of the politics of the close-up, as its government financed the development of one of the region's most prolific national cinemas from the 1930s to the 1950s. After the Mexican Revolution left the country fractured, the government erected a monolithic national culture. While studios imported the classical Hollywood style, they politicized many of its formal elements. The close-up fulfilled both a narrative and political function by imagining the face of the nation. An early example can be seen in Fernando de Fuentes's *¡Vámonos con Pancho Villa!* (*Let's Go with Pancho Villa!,* 1936). The film was funded by the government of Lázaro Cárdenas (1934–40), which sought to make good on the revolution's promise to serve the disenfranchised *pueblo*—the people—by realizing land and labor reforms. Cardenas's populist nation building extended to cultural policy, and what is now known as the Golden Age of Mexican cinema emerged thanks to subsidies for national film production during his presidency. Centering

Figure 1. Faces in the crowd. *¡Vámonos con Pancho Villa!,* dir. Fernando de Fuentes, 1936.

Figure 2. The face of the national popular, political subject of the Mexican Revolution. *¡Vámonos con Pancho Villa!,* dir. Fernando de Fuentes, 1936.

on the suffering of peasants in the cruel northern campaigns of the revolution, the narrative of *Vámonos* represents the plight of the rural classes that Cárdenas's policies sought to alleviate.

De Fuentes integrates the populism of *cardenismo* through his use of the close-up to represent the misery of the rural poor. Far from a hagiography of the revolutionary leader, de Fuentes presents a disenchanted account of the revolution. The film follows the tragedies that befall a group of idealistic young men, known as Los Leones de San Pablo, after they join Villa's forces. De Fuentes introduces Villa as Los Leones arrive at his camp. The roar of a crowd is heard as a group of peasants throngs around an open train car. At first, the film represents the crowd as a faceless mass. The spectator recognizes the peasants through close-ups of their upturned hats, which they hope to fill with the corn that the general is distributing. Positioned above the crowd, the camera then pans up further to Villa as he describes this food as the fruit of the revolution. During the proclamation of these revolutionary ideals, the camera cuts to the crowd as seen from Villa's perspective. After a wide shot of the group, de Fuentes cuts to a montage of close-ups that detail the faces in the crowd as they push forward to receive their share of corn (Figures 1–2). These close-ups, which interrupt the action by abstracting these faces from time and space, contrast with the tumultuous movement of the crowd. In this way, de Fuentes represents the spirit of the national popular amid the chaos of the revolution. The faces of these extras contrast with Domingo Soler's elaborated performance of Villa. Yet de Fuentes's populist form cannot escape the hegemonic representation of the people. The close-ups are clearly stylized through lighting and makeup. Rather than offering an authentic and spontaneous image of the popular classes, they impose a face on the nation. This is the image of the *pueblo* that Cárdenas would like to project, as one of the targets of his economic reforms was the poor peasantry of northern Mexico. The high angle of the close-up signals the hierarchy of power that determines this populist image. Sharing Villa's perspective, the camera is positioned above the crowd and looks down on the faces of the people. Thus, even though *Vámonos* offers a critical image of Villa—the brief and idealistic speech when distributing corn contrasts starkly with the representations of the general's cruelty later in the film—de Fuentes associates *cardenismo* with the populist ideals of the revolution.

The cinematic populism seen in *¡Vámonos con Pancho Villa!* characterized the Golden Age of Mexican cinema as it developed in the wake of Cárdenas's presidency. Yet despite its attempts to address the people, *Vámonos* was a commercial failure among audiences who were still reckoning with the memory of revolutionary violence. Concerns with history and the fate of the revolutionary *pueblo* gave way to melodramatic narratives that paid homage to tradition while abstracting history.[22] A national star system bolstered these efforts by providing a pantheon of glamorous faces with which audiences could identify. These stars assumed national types in a didactic cinema that taught the popular classes when to laugh or cry, and whom to exalt or villainize.[23] In other words, the development of its own star system permitted Mexican cinema to continue to realize a representational politics through the facial close-up. Yet while serving the hegemonic objective of political integration, Emilio "El Indio" Fernández's films substituted the populist aesthetic seen in *Vámonos* for the glamorous close-ups that the Mexican studios adapted from Hollywood. Transplanted to this context, the close-up of the star's face took on a political function.

As a beloved and politically influential star within the Mexican studio system, Dolores del Río's iconic face became a symbol of national identity. Born in Mexico, del Río first achieved fame in Hollywood. Although many Mexicans worked in the film industry, the majority could not advance beyond low-level jobs due to entrenched racism. Even actors who achieved a degree of success were often relegated to playing racist stereotypes, though occasionally white-passing Mexicans and Latinos broke out. When constructing her star image, del Río and her agent Edwin Carewe navigated Hollywood's racism by emphasizing her family's Spanish lineage and lack of racial mixture, as well as her European training and multilingualism.[24] A sign of her successful whitening, del Río's face would eventually be used to promote cosmetics and the latest fashion, formally encoding her body with the ideals of Western beauty. While Hollywood converted del Río into an icon of "universal" (white) attractiveness, this remained a crucial element of her star image even when the actress returned to Mexico in 1942. By this time, Mexican cinema had taken on an important role in the politics of *indigenismo* and *mestizaje* promoted by the postrevolutionary government. Filmmakers, artists, and intellectuals appropriated Indigenous themes to construct a monolithic national subject. Yet despite this romanticization of Indigenous culture, *indigenismo* maintained the racist structures of the Díaz era as it became entwined with the cult of the *mestizo,* or the Mexican of mixed Indigenous-European heritage. The *mestizo* became the model of a new national subject that combined symbolic elements of Indigenous heritage with European features. Consequently, *mestizaje* cannot be separated from a racial politics of whitening that shaped the Golden Age of Mexican cinema.[25] I turn to one of the most emblematic films of this period, Fernández's *María Candelaria* (1943), to situate the facial close-ups of Dolores del Río within the context of the racial politics of postrevolutionary Mexico.

María Candelaria's melodramatic narrative recounts the tragedy that befalls an exceptionally beautiful Indigenous woman, played by del Río, as recounted in a flashback by a successful artist who painted her portrait. Ostracized for being the daughter of a sex worker, María Candelaria is engaged to Lorenzo Rafael, a young Indigenous man from her community. The two raise a pig in hopes of funding their marriage, though Don Damián—the owner of the local general store—threatens to take the animal in order to cover a small debt. One day the artist spots María as she sells flowers in the market and asks to paint her portrait, though the jealous Lorenzo refuses to consent. When Lorenzo is imprisoned for stealing quinine tablets from Don Damián's store to treat María's malaria, she nonetheless agrees to sit for the artist in exchange for his support in freeing her betrothed. After painting her face, he asks her to pose nude and she refuses. The artist finishes the portrait with the body of another model, but rumor has spread and the Indigenous community stones María to death.

Though the film centers the theme of Indigenous beauty, Fernández casts del Río, who built her star image on a carefully constructed whiteness, in the titular role. When the artist introduces his account, he describes María as "an Indian of pure Mexican race." Pointing to the portrait, he compares her to "the beauty of the ancient princesses the *conquistadores* came to conquer." The film represents this Indigenous beauty through the aesthetic of glamour that emerged from Hollywood and conquered the world by projecting an image of Western beauty that became accepted as universal. Glamour thus took on an ideological function, colonizing the cinematic imaginary throughout the world through an artificial construction of the face.[26] Departing from the humanism of the silent era, glamour functioned by way of the facial close-up. However, rather than probe the depths of the soul through the face, as Balázs would have it, these glamorous close-ups imposed a mask through makeup and lighting.

This incorporation of the classical image of glamour in Mexican cinema cannot be removed from the problem of difference that shaped the nation. Seeking to participate in a universal discourse of modernity, Mexico was nevertheless forced to contend with the diversity of its population. Drawing on the same physiognomic discourse that shaped Balázs's theory of the facial close-up, political elites represented the face of the nation as possessing white features while identifying Indigenous faces with criminal and degenerate elements. This logic continued in its classical cinema, as Fernández and his cinematographer, Gabriel Figueroa, further whitened del Río when lighting her close-ups (Figure 3). In contrast,

Figure 3. A luminous Dolores del Río, who in a racial masquerade portrays the ideal of Indigenous beauty. *María Candelaria,* dir. Emilio Fernández, 1943.

Indigenous actors were darkened and generally not filmed in close-up.[27] Consequently, *María Candelaria* expresses the racial politics of Mexican cultural nationalism through film form. Del Río's face becomes a vehicle of hegemonic politics, subjected to what Carlos Monsiváis has called a "facial ideology" that served the Partido Revolucionario Institucional, Mexico's postrevolutionary political party that governed uninterrupted until the end of the century.[28] With the success of Fernández's cinema, the actress becomes the face of the nation.

The emergence of the classical Hollywood style and star system transformed the close-up while preserving the expression of transcendental beauty that Balázs and Epstein first celebrated. The face remained the privileged object of the close-up with the transition to sound, but the addition of the voice decentered its communicative function. No longer a window of the soul, the close-up fulfilled a crucial function in the process of signification. The face was subjected to a grammar of match cuts and countershots; no longer did it spontaneously express inner turmoil or passion.[29] Given the sheer quantity of close-ups that the system of classical narration required, the humanism with which Balázs defined the close-up becomes impossible as the spectator is saturated with faces. Additionally, these faces were constantly the subject of intervention by cameras, makeup, and the publicity apparatus of film studios. In the studio systems, the humanist aura of the face receded following its commodification. To account for such effacement in the dehumanizing engine of capital, the classical cinema supplemented a weakened humanism with the glamour aesthetic.[30] Fernández and Figueroa transplant this aesthetic to Mexico, adapting the economic objectives of the star system to serve national politics. This adds a political layer to the facial close-up of the star. As we see in the case of Mexico, national cinema identifies the face of the star with that of the nation. This is the facial ideology theorized by Monsiváis: del Río's face becomes politically contested within the project of cultural nationalism. The actor's head, severed by the frame and suspended in the darkness of the cinema, stages the racial politics of Mexican cultural nationalism. While these close-ups preserve the utopianism that Balázs originally assigned to the face, its politics serve the interests of the state. These close-ups convert the face of the star into a political sign. In this visual guillotine, the facial close-up, which severs a head in the frame, is presented as an index of popular sovereignty.

The Utopian Close-up as Event in the New Latin American Cinema

The hegemonic close-up, which adapted the forms of classical cinema to national politics, was not limited to Mexico. In a context that was similarly marked by the politics of corporatism, Argentina also relied on a national film industry and star system to consolidate power by representing the face of the people in close-up.[31] While the question of national identity remained at the forefront of Latin American cinema, it began to adopt new forms by the end of the 1950s. This period saw a heightened resistance to corporatism, which gave rise to revolutionary movements.[32] Such a reaction produced a shift in the politics of the close-up, as these emancipatory movements addressed the masses through the moving image. The transition from an industrial model to independent productions was further aided by the fact that the major studios in Mexico and Argentina entered a period of crisis as viewership dropped and worn aesthetic models no longer maintained the same appeal among audiences. Under the influence of neorealism, independent filmmakers developed new strategies of political representation that corrected the shortcomings of film studios. If the hegemonic close-up imposed a face on the people, the NLAC sought to emancipate spectators from this false image and replace it with an authentic populist aesthetic. While opposing the star system and abandoning its glamour, these filmmakers maintained a political utopianism: by representing the face in close-up they sought to give form to the people. Filming from below, they adopted documentary tactics to lend an immediacy and political urgency to the face. Such filmmakers rejected the stylized close-ups of the stars and instead registered the real faces of the rural and urban margins. The utopian humanism with which Balázs first approached the close-up is still present in these images. In these early years of the NLAC, they continued the humanist tradition of the close-up and employed this device in the service of emancipatory politics.

The reception of neorealism in Latin America posed a challenge to the hegemonic close-up. In Italy, postwar filmmakers, seeking to elaborate an authentic response to the devastation that surrounded them, replaced the superficial star image with the anonymous face in the crowd.[33] Simultaneously, classical cinema had begun to exhaust the expressive power of the face by converting it into an engine of capital. The publicity apparatus of the film industry had instrumentalized the face, which it heavily modified by means of cosmetics, lighting, and other devices, to appeal to a universal audience. The star's face had taken on commercial value and adorned lobby cards, posters, advertisements, calendars, and other ephemera. Its expressive ties to the human began to weaken. Neorealism inherited Balázs's obsession with the close-up's power to project human essence; nonetheless, by centering the face of the nonprofessional actor, the neorealist close-up was, in Aumont's estimation, "the first properly human face in cinema."[34] The neorealists attached a new value to the close-up, imagining "new modalities and potentialities of the cinematic face."[35] The face of the nonprofessional actor was to offer access to the human soul following the horrors of war and the clichéd imagery of the culture industry. These films sought to evade the commodification of the face and return to its mimetic power by appealing to the features of the everyman. Through these utopian close-ups, filmmakers sought to enact a political event: the creation of a national and regional community of the popular through the spectator's identification with the face. Like the images examined above, these close-ups rely on the power of the face to establish a political collective. However, by shifting the political register of the close-up, the NLAC crafted an emancipatory image.

Margot Benacerraf's *Araya* (1959) occupies a central role in this corpus as one of the earliest denunciations of the perils of underdevelopment. Distancing herself from classical documentary, Benacerraf aligns *Araya* with a modernist aesthetic. Despite elaborating her social commentary through the register of actualities, Benacerraf herself describes the film as "a great metaphor, a poem."[36] The film, produced independently in Venezuela, represents a twenty-four-hour period in the harsh lives of salt miners and fishermen along the remote Araya Peninsula. The film is less committed to ethnographic empiricism than to tracing the history of Araya's extractive economy through a lyrical meditation on landscape, gesture, and physiognomy. In vacillating between a macrohistorical narrative and microhistorical account of three families, the film departs from conventional uses of the close-up. *Araya* juxtaposes epic landscapes with details of the worker's body in its movement between the mythic scale of history and the specific, material circumstances of the workers.

Benacerraf liberates the close-up of its narrative and testimonial functions and intensifies its expressive force by deploying this form sparingly, in juxtaposition with sweeping panoramas of mountains and the sea. Intercut with these sublime views, the worker's face takes on monumental proportions. In highlighting the film's formal experimentation with the close-up, I follow Javier Campo in drawing attention to the camera's relation to the body in *Araya.* Throughout the film, Benacerraf fragments the workers to register their labor in poetic detail. Exquisitely choreographed, these close-ups of the salt miners' rhythmic movements reinforce the film's mythic dimension and communicate the filmmaker's interest in the repetition of these same gestures over centuries.[37] Benacerraf's spare yet calculated representation of the face complements the camera's fragmentation of the body and imbues *Araya* with a humanist spirit that reinforces the claims to universality that have marked the film's legacy (Figure 4).[38] Echoing Balázs's utopian theory of the close-up, the filmmaker constructs a transnational community through the audience's recognition of the faces of the toiling workers. While these facial close-ups issue an ethical claim to the audience, their function is not limited to the denunciation of exploitation through the representation of pathos. Through its framing of the face, the close-up gives form to this people and its traditions.

Figure 4. A young girl aids her family of salt miners in Araya. *Araya,* dir. Margo Benacerraf, 1959.

The film begins with panoramic shots of the topography of the Araya Peninsula. Set to a dynamic score, this arid landscape appears devoid of human life. Only when the camera climbs one of the monumental salt mounds does Benacerraf reveal a flurry of activity below. The film emphasizes the timelessness of the workers' gestures: the ancestors of the men and women we see have been repeating these actions for centuries. Much of the sequence is filmed in medium or long shots to capture the scale of this labor.[39] Benacerraf further emphasizes the human through scale when she contrasts the enormous, manually constructed pyramids of salt with a distant mountain range. She achieves this through depth of field, framing the salt in the foreground and mountains in the background to emphasize the humble salt miners' power to shape the landscape. The frame fills with bodies moving in unison to emphasize the collaboration this work requires. The crowd is humanized by intermittently inserting close-ups of the laborers. Contrasted with the monumental salt piles, the face has an imposing effect on the spectator. Through such juxtaposition, the worker's face reinforces the film's narrative of an ideal humanity outside of time. *Araya* also emphasizes the humanity of these subjects by moving from the general—the crowd of laboring bodies—to the individual face. Benacerraf reveals her guiding concern in the film's conclusion. After depicting the miners hard at work, the screen suddenly erupts with images of machinery. Modernization has arrived in Araya, and salt mining is mechanizing. The film's slow and lyrical meditation on traditional salt production is replaced with an aggressive montage of drills, trucks, and bulldozers. Meanwhile, the documentary voice-over questions what will become of the salt workers and their culture, which has lived in harmony with nature for centuries. In this context, Benacerraf's close-ups represent the human face of tradition that is at stake.

In addition to registering Araya's colonial history through the repertoire of labor, Benacerraf represents its past through the facial close-up. In the filmmaker's words, "The physiognomy of these people—the fishermen, the salt miners—testified to this same closed way of life."[40] While signaling that these workers will likely be swallowed up in the modernization of Araya, the film does not defend the artisanal production of salt that organizes these workers' lives and culture given its origins in Spanish colonialism. *Araya* leaves the audience to reflect on the workers' fates in the wake of modernization. However, Benacerraf's close-ups remind urban audiences that these faces—worn from exposure to salt and sun—have been marginalized from the nation. By exhibiting the transhistorical pathos of this people through the facial close-up, *Araya* gives form to a community. While critical of the colonial repertoire implicit in the artisanal tradition of salt production, *Araya* cannot be reduced to a cinema of denunciation. In the audience's recognition of the faces in close-up, the people emerge as a political category that demands recognition. In this way, the film's representation of pathos constructs community through the human image represented in the facial close-up. In this visual decapitation, the image of the severed head cut from the body and amplified on the screen, *Araya* gives form to politics. When the spectator witnesses this symbolic beheading, the borders between self and other erode, and community emerges.

As Benacerraf developed her politics of form in *Araya,* Fernando Birri employed similar strategies in Argentina. After studying at the Centro Sperimentale in Rome, Birri returned to his homeland eager to create a national popular cinema. Without simply transplanting Italian neorealism to Latin America, he preserved its spirit of "revolutionary humanism."[41] His first film, *Tire dié* (1958/1960), draws heavily on the close-up of the face to give form to political community. A manifesto-film of the Documentary School of Santa Fe, which Birri founded at the Universidad del Litoral in 1956, *Tire dié* documents life in the social margins. The film's title refers to the poor children who beg along the railway leading into Santa Fe. As trains slowly cross a river and approach Santa Fe, the children run along the rails of the bridge yelling "¡Tire dié!" ("Throw me a dime!") to the passengers. The face of the child, framed in close-up, lies at the heart of the film's social denunciation (Figure 5). Sutured with images of the children's squalid living conditions, the facial close-up organizes the film's testimonial narrative. In each of the interviews that compose this social survey, the documentary subjects face the camera directly and demand recognition from the audience. This face-to-face lays the groundwork for Birri's politics.

Birri's close-ups exceed a testimonial function. From the sphere of representation, *Tire dié* passes into political praxis. In the emotional climax of the film, Birri documents the children who risk their lives to beg along the train tracks. The sequence alternates between tracking shots

Figure 5. The close-up of an impoverished child interpellates the spectator. *Tire dié*, dir. Fernando Birri, 1958/1960.

of the children taken from the train and countershots of the passengers from the perspective of the tracks. Suturing facial close-ups with images of the collective, Birri stages a face-to-face encounter between the impoverished children and the middle-class passenger. *Tire dié* seeks to establish a critical national consciousness through this humanist apparatus. In Birri's montage of close-ups, the *pueblo* is constructed in the spatiotemporal distance that separates these faces. This tactic extends the populist iconography that shaped modern politics, which creates an image of the national popular through a dialectic that vacillates between the anonymous face and the crowd. An individual close-up, no matter how humanizing, cannot enact a community; the utopian close-up must pass from the personal to the collective. It frames an anonymous face from the crowd but must inscribe this image in an assemblage. In Didi-Huberman's words, "what must be exposed is the people, not the 'I.' But it is necessary to address singular bodies to expose the people in a construction—a series, a montage—capable of sustaining their faces."[42] Thus, Birri's enactment of the national popular occurs in the intervals between these images. Moving from the individual face to the crowd, the humanism of the utopian close-up opens the possibility of representation, identification, and community. Birri thus enacts the people through a politics of form. Political community is not represented; it emerges through the cinematic cut, with montage and the close-up functioning here as complementary elements of this visual guillotine. The display of these subjects, beheaded by the cut of the close-up, stages popular sovereignty. The spectator participates in this process when decoding this assemblage and identifying with these fragmented images. In other words, Birri's utopian close-up is both representation and event. By displaying the facial close-up of the marginalized subject and establishing a relation with the face of the spectator in the audience, *Tire dié* aspires to create political community.

The representation of the national popular through the facial close-up is not without its dangers, however. The pathos contained in the image of the face threatens to overtake the humanism that forms the basis of the national community. For example, the danger implicit in Birri's close-ups manifests from what Michael Chanan refers to as the "dialectic edge" in *Tire dié*'s humanist reflection on underdevelopment.[43] This is the tension between the dignified face of the downtrodden and the disfiguration of this face through the representation of pathos. In other words, we encounter the same dialectic that organizes the political genealogy of the facial close-up that I trace in this chapter. While the amplified image of the face enacts a community by establishing a humanist relation, the formal violence inscribed in the close-up, which severs the head in the frame, threatens to dehumanize this same image. In this moment, the close-up vacillates between the face and its defacement.

In the wake of *Araya* and *Tire dié,* filmmakers took up the utopian close-up in a variety of national contexts. This was not a coordinated program, as Birri affirms that the aesthetic strategies of the NLAC emerged "without any kind of, let's say, confabulation between us, but because [they were] in the air."[44] A crucial element of this shared ethos is the spirit of humanism that finds its expression in the facial close-up. Filmmakers working within the social documentary tradition experimented with the close-up as a basis for enacting the *pueblo* as a political subject. The same tactic can be seen in León Hirzman's *Maioria absoluta*

(Brazil, 1964), Mario Handler's *Carlos, cine-retrato de un caminante* (*Carlos: Film Portrait of a Montevideo Panhandler,* Uruguay, 1965), Nemesio Juárez's *Muerte y pueblo* (Argentina, 1969), and Marta Rodríguez and Jorge Silva's *Chircales* (*The Bricklayers,* Colombia, 1972), among others. In these examples, filmmakers punctuate their denunciation of social inequalities with close-ups of marginalized subjects that they suture with images of the collective. Following Carlos Ossa, the objective of the NLAC was both the denunciation of social realities and the creation of community. These films elaborated the utopian close-up in the service of political praxis: the creation of a populist utopia that would "incorporate the starless bodies of the bastards."[45] Filmmakers addressed the aporia of political cinema, whereby the construction of the *nomos* requires the filmmaker to set boundaries to the community.[46] In other words, politics requires a frame; the community must be given a form. The NLAC attempted to resolve this contradiction through the utopian close-up. Here, the image of a severed head is at the origin of the people.

While Benacerraf and Birri documented the faces of the rural and urban margins, constructing an image of the people that would include those subjects who had been cast aside in the uneven development of Latin American modernity, two filmmakers who took up the tradition of the social documentary in their wake drew on the facial close-up in reckoning with the racial politics that structured this historical process. While the Afro-Cuban filmmaker Sara Gómez and the Colombian filmmaker Marta Rodríguez have been critically overshadowed by the masculine canon of the NLAC, recent restorations of their films and attempts to correct such disciplinary blind spots have once again drawn attention to their vital contributions to Latin American cinema.[47] Working in markedly different national contexts—Gómez in postrevolutionary Cuba and Rodríguez in Colombia—both filmmakers pushed the regional tradition of the social documentary to reflect on questions of race and ethnicity through their emphasis on the marginalization of Afro-Cuban and Indigenous communities within revolutionary politics and representations of the national popular. Furthermore, both filmmakers exhibit a careful attention to cinematic form, employing the utopian close-up to humanize communities that had not only been excluded from modernization but subjected to violence for their perceived obstruction of the modernizing project. Indigenous and Afro-Cuban subjects "were deemed 'alien to modernity'" by the nation-state, a fact that motivated their dehumanization through racialized violence and marginalization since the conquest.[48] These filmmakers draw on the humanistic tradition of the close-up to subvert the racial politics that have underscored this form since Balázs. If the Hungarian film theorist associated the close-up with the supposedly universal features of the white face, an ideology that persisted in the representation of Indigenous characters in national cinema as discussed above, then Gómez and Rodríguez denounce this tradition in their close-ups of Afro-Cuban and Indigenous subjects, which they suture into critical discussions of racialized oppression.

In a powerful scene from her documentary short *En la otra isla* (*On the Other Island,* 1968), Gómez aligns a humanist politics of the close-up with a critical reflection on the persistence of racism in post-revolutionary Cuba. The film is the first in a trilogy of shorts, alongside *Una isla para Miguel* (*An Island for Miguel,* 1968) and *Isla del tesoro* (*Treasure Island,* 1969), that document the revolutionary government's efforts toward engineering social inclusion through a reeducation program on the Island of Pines, later dubbed the Island of Youth. For decades, authorities sent adolescents and young adults deemed in need of social reform to work in agriculture and other trades on the island. Through a series of interviews, *En la otra isla* documents the experiences of these young revolutionary subjects, whom authorities intend to mold into the image of the revolutionary New Man. María Caridad Cumaná has emphasized the humanism that guides Gómez's cinema, and I underscore that the filmmaker expresses a politics of revolutionary humanism through audiovisual form.[49] Among them is Rafael, a young Afro-Cuban man who studied vocal performance at the National Arts School founded by the revolutionary government in 1961. In what Cumaná calls "one of Cuban cinema's most impactful testimonies of racial discrimination," Rafael recounts his experiences with racism while collaborating on an opera in Havana.[50] He recalls that despite proclaiming revolutionary ideals, a member of the production refused to perform alongside him because "it would be anti-aesthetic for a white woman to share a scene with a Black man." Following this conflict, the singer abandoned the production and was sent to the Island of Pines, where he began training in agriculture. *En la otra isla* presents Rafael's testimony through a series of close-ups that reassert his dignity in the face of this dehumanizing experience.

Rejecting the static convention of the talking-head testimony, Gómez structures this narrative in a montage of three conversations. The first frames Rafael's face in profile in the foreground as he turns to his left and speaks to Gómez, whose head barely appears in the frame. The faces of two white colleagues appear out of focus in the background as they, like the spectator, listen to the conversation. In the subsequent shot, Gómez positions herself in profile across from Rafael in a tighter composition, with their faces positioned in the middle of the frame. Following this staging of the face-to-face encounter, the narrative culminates with a close-up of Rafael that centers his face as he recounts the effects his time spent on the Island of Pines has had on him. Rafael insists that he has not renounced art, but that through this agricultural training the revolution has taught him to overcome the shame and fear of racism. Gómez concludes the sequence with Rafael smiling and looking off into the distance optimistically, to the sound of upbeat music. Across these three shots, Gómez builds up to the cathartic image of the facial close-up through which the filmmaker reasserts Rafael's dignity following the dehumanizing experience of racism. While initially registering Rafael in profile, the testimonial narrative culminates with this humanist image.

Rodríguez's *Nuestra voz de tierra, memoria y futuro* (*Our Voice of Earth, Memory, and Future,* 1981), codirected with Jorge Silva, similarly draws on the counterhegemonic politics of the close-up while complicating the homogeneous image of the revolutionary people advanced by the NLAC. The filmmakers hybridize the social documentary and docudrama to represent the history of expropriation experienced by the Coconuco, whose ancestral territories lie in Colombia's Cauca Valley, and document the efforts of the Consejo Regional Indígena del Cauca (CRIC; Regional Indigenous Council of Cauca) to recuperate and defend the lands, language, and heritage of this community. The film opens with members of the Coconuco tracing this history from the Spanish conquest to the foundation of the Colombian state in the nineteenth century and the dominance of transnational capital in the twentieth. Throughout *Nuestra voz,* Rodríguez and Silva balance testimony, direct observation, and found footage with stylized performances by the Coconuco. This strategy questions the empirical principles of the social documentary, which privilege an objective and didactic representation of reality that often does not coincide with Indigenous epistemologies. The film's commitment to representing Indigenous beliefs, which Rodríguez and Silva suture with their documentation of Indigenous activism, bridges experimental ethnography and the militancy of the social documentary.

Rodríguez and Silva invert the racial politics of the humanist close-up in their staging of the Coconuco myth of La Huecada, in which the devil takes the form of a landowner. If members of the community heard footsteps outside their homes at night, this was a sign that the devil had come to claim their lives and their land. Terrorized by the history of violent land dispossession in the Cauca Valley, many members of the Coconuco abandoned their territories out of fear that the diabolical landowner had returned for them.[51] The retelling follows the expository tone of the film's opening sequence, which addresses the complicity of church and state in this history of expropriation. Nevertheless, following the transition to the dramatization of La Huecada, the film does not signal its abandonment of the familiar terrain of nonfiction. Instead, the filmmakers treat the myth as a form of collective memory that documents this history of colonial violence. A male voice-over recounts how he and another member of the community began to track two cows that had wandered from the herd. Following the cattle up into the mountains, the trail eventually runs cold. From atop a peak the men spot a corral that is guarded by the devil, who has stolen the livestock. Members of the Coconuco participate in the dramatization, which the filmmakers stage as if it were a documentary reenactment. The camera alternates between sweeping wide-angle shots of the Cauca Valley and close-ups of the protagonists. The faces of the two Indigenous men are juxtaposed with an eerie masked figure on horseback, who represents the devil. The landowner is accompanied by his *mayordomo,* a pale figure that resembles Uncle Sam, and another masked assistant with the features of an extraterrestrial. In their voice-over, the Coconuco recall that the spurs worn by the devil recall those used by the *carabineros.* The narrative thus relates the white landowner to the state and the neocolonial interests of the United States. At the culmination of the dramatization, the camera cuts rapidly between close-ups of the Coconuco and the menacing figures that represent the forces of expropriation. The humanizing power of the close-up is heightened from the contrast between the Indigenous faces, which fill the screen, and their adversaries, who are defaced through these stylized masks.

Narrative films similarly developed an emancipatory politics by way of the utopian close-up, while also signaling the fragility of the face. Miguel Littín thematizes the dehumanization of the most vulnerable members of Chilean society through such motifs in *El chacal de Nahueltoro* (*The Jackal of Nahueltoro,* 1969). The film re-creates a historical case in which the peasant and drifter Jorge del Carmen Valenzuela Torres murders a woman and her children in a drunken frenzy. The protagonist later repents in prison. After he becomes literate, finds religion, and learns a trade, Valenzuela petitions for a pardon. The state refuses, and the prisoner is executed by firing squad. The film emphasizes that Valenzuela's actions were the product of his upbringing and suggests that the state's exploitation of the rural poor first creates criminals by marginalizing this group and subsequently eliminates these undesirables through imprisonment and capital punishment.[52] *El chacal de Nahueltoro* thus holds up Valenzuela as the scapegoat of an exploitative society and calls on the audience to identify with his humanity through the close-up. When narrating Valenzuela's upbringing, Littín meditates on the child's face in close-up in order to capture his suffering and demand emancipation from this oppression. Littín dramatizes his execution as an act of defacement and, therefore, dehumanization. When preparing to face the firing squad, Valenzuela declares "I want to die as a man" and refuses to wear a veil. Nevertheless, his executioners force him to conceal his face (Figure 6). Through this metaphor, the film visualizes the oppression of the people through the erasure of the face. Valenzuela's effacement denies the image of the national popular and underscores the fragility of the face as a site of representative politics. This humanist politics of representation is exposed to the threat of opacity.

While the symbolism of the veil visualizes the vulnerability of populist representation, Gerardo Vallejo's *El camino hacia la muerte del Viejo Reales* (*Viejo Reales' Long Journey to Death,* 1971) addresses the fragility of the close-up's humanism even more explicitly. Vallejo moves from Littín's denunciation of effacement to a politics of defacement. A student of Fernando Birri, Vallejo shares the spirit of revolutionary humanism expressed in *Tire dié.* Indeed, *El camino* opens with an immense facial close-up of his protagonist: Gerardo Ramón Reales, known as El

Figure 6. Jorge del Carmen Valenzuela Torres prior to his execution. *El chacal de Nahueltoro,* dir. Miguel Littín, 1969.

Viejo. An elderly sugarcane cutter in Tucumán, Argentina, El Viejo testifies to the hardships of his life. Throughout, *El camino* examines the violence experienced by the rural poor of Argentina, as illustrated through the experiences of El Viejo and his family. Vallejo incorporates neorealist narrative strategies with this testimony by reenacting episodes of cruelty with members of the community. The film concludes with a final act of brutality. As Vallejo was finishing the production of *El camino,* El Viejo was murdered by a young man in a mugging attempt. Vallejo closes his film with an extreme facial close-up of El Viejo's corpse, filmed at his wake. Having begun the film with the utopian close-up, which embraced populist humanism by amplifying El Viejo's face to monumental proportions, the spectator is left with a hollow death mask (Figures 7–8). The film does not abandon the humanism of the facial close-up or its aspirations of creating a utopian community. However, it documents the violence of political repression, recognizing the fragility of revolutionary humanism, and mourns this figurative defacement of the people.

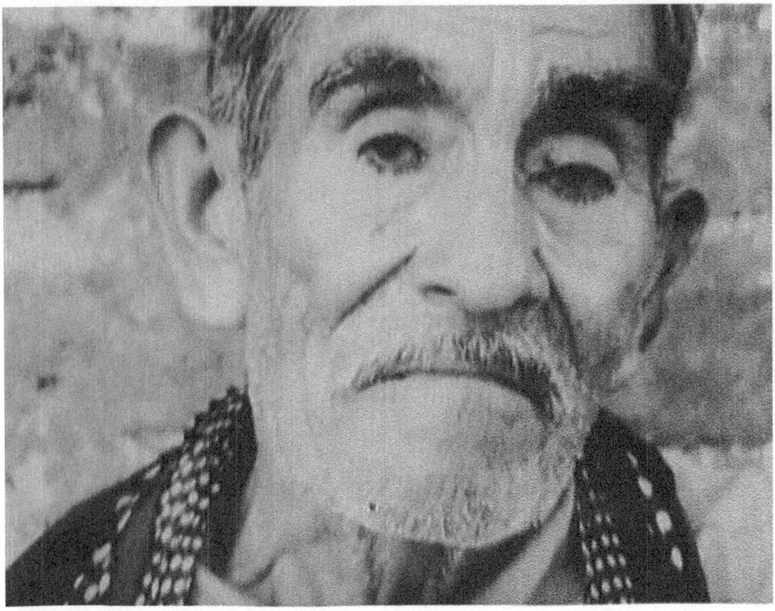

Figure 7. The face of El Viejo. *El camino hacia la muerte del Viejo Reales,* dir. Gerardo Vallejo, 1971.

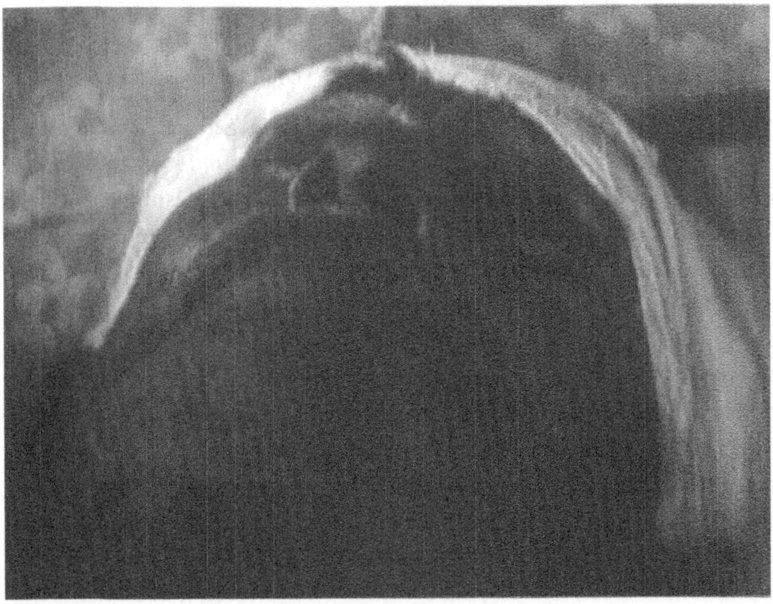

Figure 8. El Viejo's cinematic death mask. *El camino hacia la muerte del Viejo Reales,* dir. Gerardo Vallejo, 1971.

The decision to end the film with the close-up of El Viejo's corpse does not diminish Vallejo's humanism. While the majority of *El camino* bridges social documentary and neorealist narrative, the final close-up moves toward a militant mode of address. As I examine below, the turn to cinematic militancy foregrounded the violence of the close-up and shifted attention from the face to defacement in response to the repression of revolutionary movements by authoritarian governments. The long production history of *El camino* spans this gradual increase of violence.[53] Consequently, the transition from face to defacement presented in the film's narrative reflects the broader transformation of the politics of the close-up as filmmakers abandoned the social documentary for militant cinema. With this gesture, the face gives way to the death mask, and pathos reaches its limit. The utopianism identified with the facial close-up is overwhelmed by the threat against the face. This shift toward defacement characterizes the militant period of the NLAC, when the most radical of filmmakers embraced the close-up in a politics and aesthetics of defacement.

Cinematic Defacement and the Two Avant-Gardes

With *El camino,* Vallejo signals the tension between the face and its defacement in the NLAC. The severed head produced by the close-up of the deceased communicates the violence directed at Argentina's marginalized classes through cinematic form. The image recalls the infamous conclusion to Fernando Solanas and Octavio Getino's *La hora de los hornos* (*The Hour of the Furnaces,* 1968), which magnifies the face of Che Guevara's corpse in close-up and holds this image for three minutes. One of the most prominent examples of the NLAC and a masterpiece of global political cinema, *La hora de los hornos* takes the form of a revolutionary essay film on the violence of colonialism, the neocolonial exploitation of the region's resources by European and US capital, and the cultural imperialism advanced both by the lettered elites and the advertising industry. Through its formal experimentation and call to take up revolutionary struggle, *La hora de los hornos* exhibits the intersection of the aesthetic and political avant-gardes that became characteristic of the NLAC. The film opens with a dedication to Che, and its first part ends with an epic close-up of his corpse that is accompanied by a crescendo of beating drums. After nearly eighty minutes of essayistic reflection on the exploitative effects of economic dependence and cultural imperialism, the screen cuts to black and the voice-over interpellates the spectator. "What is the only thing left for the Latin American?," the disembodied voice asks. Following a dramatic pause, the screen lights up once more, this time with the image of Che's visually severed head.

The image is a close-up of the infamous photograph of Che's corpse taken by Freddy Alborta in Vallegrande, Bolivia, in 1967. Using a wide frame, Alborta's photograph registers the display of Che's corpse by the Bolivian military as part of a photo opportunity for the press to confirm the execution of the revolutionary leader. One officer points to Che's uncovered torso, which is stretched across a large stone sink, while another holds up the head of the deceased for a second photographer, who appears in the foreground with his back to the viewer. Alborta's photograph immediately circulated throughout the global press. To US and Bolivian authorities, the image signaled a victory over revolutionary insurrection in the Americas. The image took on a wholly different meaning among the international left. Such sympathetic readings of the photograph associated the display of Che's face with the face of Christ.[54] Alborta's photograph was received as a sacred image that depicted the martyrdom of a messianic figure and symbolized the ongoing struggle for liberation.[55] The body of Ernesto Guevara is defaced as his likeness is converted into an icon. No longer a subjective face expressing an inner essence, this image is abstracted and converted into a political sign of revolutionary struggle: a head severed amid revolutionary fervor. The violence underlying this close-up provokes the spectator, stirring a revolutionary affect intended to motivate the audience to take up arms. Indeed, the inclusion of Che's death mask was so controversial that Cuban authorities demanded that the image be removed before *La hora de los hornos* was screened in Havana.[56] The filmmakers thus draw on the visual guillotine to represent the defacement and dehumanization of a sacred figure by neocolonial forces. Solanas and Getino register political violence through the form of the image: by cropping Che's body in close-up, they represent the figurative decapitation of the revolutionary movements that had taken hold throughout Latin America in this decade.

As the controversial conclusion to *La hora de los hornos* demonstrates, the humanist impulse of the NLAC had begun to falter within a decade of Benacerraf's and Birri's close-ups.[57] Filmmakers faced political violence for denouncing the oppression of the social margins. Birri was driven into a period of prolonged exile after completing *Los inundados* (1961), his first feature-length film. The election of Salvador Allende in 1970 provided Littín with the creative freedom to complete a second film in Chile, but the 1973 coup d'état forced him into exile as well. Responding to the assault on revolutionary movements throughout the region, filmmakers grew increasingly militant. The brutality of state violence provoked a crisis of humanism that extended to audiovisual politics. Revolutionary filmmakers challenged the tradition of classical humanism and accused neocolonial elites of invoking the universal values of Western culture to marginalize the cultural practices of the *pueblo*. In the postcolonial context, doctrines of human essence proved oppressive. Of course, revolutionary movements did not reject humanism tout court but sought to free it of its racist and colonial baggage.[58] Nonetheless, militant cinema broke with the humanist tradition of the close-up initiated by Balázs. Filmmakers increasingly foregrounded the violence of this form as part of their anticolonial critique. They wielded the facial close-up not to create community but to represent the violence directed against the people. This represents a turn in the dialectic that has marked the close-up since the earliest experiments with this device: from the face to defacement.

As opposed to the dignified faces of neorealism and the social documentary, the close-up increasingly disfigured the face, rendering it ugly and inhuman. Militant filmmakers encoded the practices of defacement that were central to the aesthetic avant-garde with the radicalism of the political avant-garde. Even when they operated in different political registers, the films I have previously examined in this chapter ground the close-up in a humanist framework. These filmmakers understood the face as a medium for inner human expression that provides the basis of community through audience identification. Militant cinema breaks with this politics and aesthetics of the facial close-up. In his essay on *La hora de los hornos* and the two avant-gardes, Robert Stam recalls the oft-invoked simile of the camera as a gun.[59] Paraphrasing Stam, I propose a similar association between the camera and the guillotine. In these examples, politics cannot be separated from the form of the frame's cut.

Postwar European cinema had similarly challenged the facial close-up's ability to mediate human essence. A crisis of humanism provoked by the horrors of war and the Holocaust had led filmmakers to disfigure the face by experimenting with cinematic form. Following Aumont, such cinematic modernism channeled experiences of cruelty toward the face. The close-up of this period transgressed the humanist tradition initiated by Balázs and eliminated the beauty of the face. Instead, filmmakers "defaced the face."[60] In the wake of disaster, the close-up no longer represents; it decapitates. The objective of the frame in this cinema is to channel the annihilation of humanism by defacing this image. Nonetheless, Aumont's examples do not fuse this defacement with political radicalism; they remain within the realm of modernist abstraction. In contrast, the militant filmmakers of the NLAC foreground the politics of cinematic disfiguration. Fusing the two avant-gardes, the defacement of the close-up represents the dehumanizing violence of neocolonialism. Emptied of human expression, these close-ups disfigure the face to display the severed head.

In Latin America, the roots of cinematic defacement emerge from critiques of neorealism. For example, in *Los olvidados* (*The Young and*

Figure 9. The ugly face of the bull-child. *Los olvidados,* dir. Luis Buñuel, 1950.

the Damned, 1950) Luis Buñuel introduces his audience to the film's protagonists—a band of violent children who roam the streets of Mexico City—through a series of grotesque close-ups. Buñuel opens on the children playing in an empty lot. The boys simulate a bullfight, with one playing the matador and another the bull. Amid the game, Buñuel cuts to a close-up of the bull-child. He faces the camera, snorts, and twists his mouth into a snarl before charging the camera (Figure 9). The image is deliberately ugly: the boy's face is dirty, and he is missing teeth. This close-up defaces him, and he is animalized as a result of this dehumanization. After the close-up, the camera assumes the bull-child's perspective.

While *Los olvidados* has often been inscribed within the global spread of neorealism, the close-up of this ugly and disfigured face suggests that Buñuel had a more complex relationship with the humanism that defined this movement. The filmmaker rejected comparisons to neorealism and criticized the movement for its conventional and rational representation of reality.[61] Indeed, Buñuel's rejection of classical humanism has led Adam Lowenstein to theorize the hideous close-up of the bull-child as an expression of the filmmaker's posthumanist surrealism. First the exaggerated ugliness of the face animalizes the bull-child, and then the point-of-view shift forces the audience to occupy the perspective of this posthuman figure. Despite the risks of such a perverse attack on the facial close-up, Buñuel considers the humanist elevation of suffering to be even more offensive.[62] Finally, Buñuel's critique of neorealism's humanism cannot be divorced from his rejection of the aesthetic and political codes of Mexican national cinema.[63] *Los olvidados* not only mocks the folkloric costumes and repertoire of films such as *María Candelaria;* its treatment of the face also rejects the close-ups through which this national cinema imposed a false image of the people in the service of the nation-state.

Decades later, Luis Ospina and Carlos Mayolo similarly employ the close-up to disfigure the face in *Agarrando pueblo* (*The Vampires of Poverty,* 1977). Echoing Buñuel, the filmmakers satirize the social documentary tradition that emerged from neorealism's adaptation in Latin America. An early example of the Latin American mockumentary, *Agarrando pueblo* follows a team of filmmakers as they document the misery of the impoverished residents of Cali and Bogotá. *Agarrando pueblo* reacts to localized examples of the social documentary tradition in Colombia.

Documentary film production expanded significantly in the 1970s due to the financing provided by the Colombian government following the Ley de Sobreprecio (Surcharge Law) of 1972. This law introduced a box-office surcharge which then financed national productions, and it required cinemas to screen locally produced short films before features. Many of the shorts supported by this initiative addressed social themes, especially the country's alarming rates of poverty.[64] However, they often lacked the sophistication and critical framework exhibited by filmmakers associated with the NLAC, such as Marta Rodríguez and Jorge Silva.[65] A wave of hasty and uncritical imitations caricaturized the social documentary tradition, exploiting the impoverished documentary subjects and making a spectacle of the slums. Perhaps the most infamous example is Ciro Durán's *Gamín* (1977), whose representation of street urchins in Bogotá exemplifies the same elevation of human misery that Buñuel critiqued in *Los olvidados*. Durán adapts the aesthetics of *Tire dié*, particularly Birri's representation of the destitute child in facial close-up. These formal similarities are grounded in a shared cinematic humanism, but

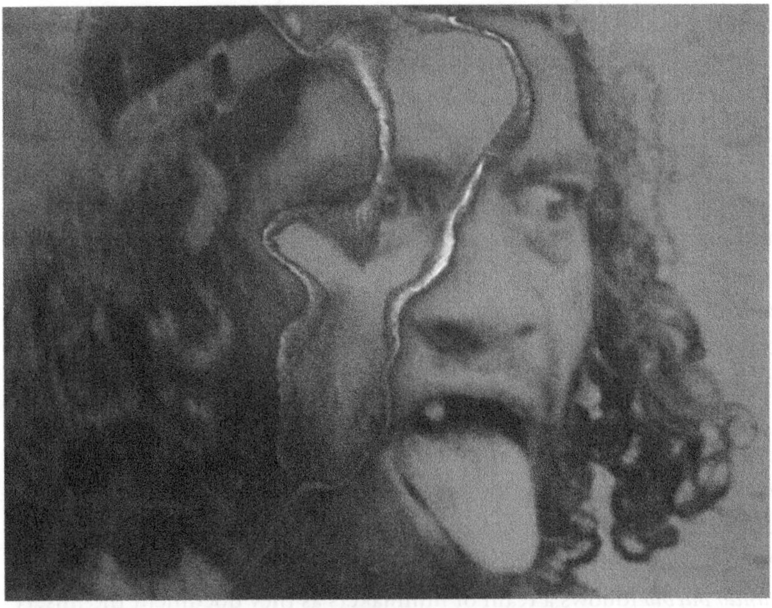

Figure 10. The contorted face of Luis Alfonso Londoño. *Agarrando pueblo*, dir. Luis Ospina and Carlos Mayolo, 1978.

by the time of *Gamín* this form had been exhausted. Ospina and Mayolo derided the miserabilist cinema that *Gamín* exemplified, which they labeled *pornomiseria* (misery porn).

Agarrando pueblo offers a fierce critique of the politics of representation by disfiguring the documentary subject through the close-up. Ospina and Mayolo themselves appear as members of a fictional film crew that is producing a documentary for German television. In the words of the director, played by Mayolo, the purpose of the project is simply to "film all these scenes of misery." The filmmakers drive around the cities of Cali and Bogotá in search of marginalized subjects for their film. Going down a list, they instruct their cab driver to take them to a neighborhood where they'll find street urchins, sex workers, beggars, and the mentally ill. Approaching a homeless mother and child, Mayolo instructs his cameraman to make sure that he captures their misery in a facial close-up: "Pan from face to face. Get the face!" As production of the film within the film reaches its conclusion, the crew occupies what appears to be an abandoned shack to film its final scene. The fictional narrator's remarks parody the rhetoric of liberal humanism: "Cases of abandonment, child urgency, juvenile delinquency, dementia, and illiteracy. On a larger scale, a gigantic mass of humanity that doesn't share in the nation's benefits or take part in political and social decisions." This caricature is suddenly interrupted by Luis Alfonso Londoño, the owner of the shack that the production has occupied without his permission. Entering the center of the frame, he sticks out his tongue and twists his face (Figure 10). Londoño's outburst marks the climax of the film, in which he verbally assaults the exploitative crew before threatening them with a machete. Londoño appears entranced, judging by his contorted expression, as he opens a film canister and wraps himself in the negative. No longer expressing any human essence, his face mediates the effects of systemic violence he has suffered. Through their framing of this disfigured face, Ospina and Mayolo transform the politics of the close-up. *Agarrando pueblo* rejects the face as the representation of human essence and basis of community. The political logic of representation and identification, by which the utopian close-up had forged the *pueblo* as a collective political agent, had lost its currency. Here, the modernist abstraction of the face that Aumont observes in postwar European cinema joins forces with the political avant-garde. Defacement becomes a symbol of radical politics as filmmakers realize the close-up's potential to function as a visual guillotine.

In joining the two avant-gardes, radical filmmakers reconceptualized the close-up in relation to political violence. Ugo Ulive's *¡Basta!* (1969) takes the metaphor of defacement to an extreme. The short film juxtaposes recordings of autopsies with a discourse by Fidel Castro to radicalize spectators.[66] In a radical departure from the humanist tradition of the close-up, Ulive compares the frame to the scalpel that literally removes the face from the body. Only bones and viscera remain for the spectator to contemplate; identification by way of the face becomes impossible. Rather than stage a face-to-face encounter with the oppressed, *¡Basta!* establishes a corporeal relation between viscera: both represented on-screen and experienced by the spectator in his embodied reaction to the film's depiction of real autopsies.

Drawing on images filmed in a psychiatric hospital, *¡Basta!* invokes the tradition of physiognomy and the progressive dehumanization of the face by disciplinary power. This marks the point of departure for Ulive's critique of the neocolonial experience of capitalism in Latin America. *¡Basta!* has gained notoriety owing to its graphic imagery. The film opens on a butchered human torso that is represented in close-up, with its viscera exposed. The image focuses on a disembodied hand holding a scalpel as it cuts the skin and pulls it over the chest cavity. As the body opens, Ulive reframes the image by widening the zoom lens to reveal more detail. With this grisly introduction, *¡Basta!* commences a dizzying collage of images taken from the psychiatric hospital, which it juxtaposes with clips of guerrillas, street life, advertisements, and pornography. These are accompanied by a soundtrack that lacks human speech and instead foregrounds the grunts and cries of the insane, the tumult of the city, moans of sexual pleasure, gunfire, marching, and the natural soundscape of the jungle. Taken together, this disorienting montage of sound and image agitates the spectator for the purpose of political radicalization. The construction of a community, in this case a militant *pueblo* that will violently resist the neocolonial threat against its sovereignty, passes not through the face but through the body. The logic of representational politics does not disappear; it shifts from the face to the viscera as Ulive establishes a relation between the spectator and the pro-filmic bodies that are violently defaced throughout the film.

The film's title is taken from the final lines of Fidel Castro's "Second Declaration of Havana" (February 4, 1962), a speech given days after the Organization of American States expelled Cuba from its ranks and approximately a year following the failed Bay of Pigs invasion. A fragment of Castro's voice is included prior to the opening credits, set to a black screen. This is the only instance of language in the film. Castro proclaims, "This great humanity has said 'enough!' [*¡Basta!*] and has begun to march." One of Castro's most famous speeches, the Second Declaration is an impassioned denunciation of imperialism that begins with the death of José Martí in the War of Cuban Independence and ends with a call to revolutionary martyrdom. Throughout, Castro denounces the experience of humiliation and dehumanization that Cubans, and by extension all Latin Americans, have experienced as integral to their shared colonial history. Both Castro's speech and Ulive's film engage the discourse of revolutionary humanism that emerged from the anticolonial movements of the 1960s. Abandoning the tradition of classical humanism imported to Latin America by creole elites, this Third World humanism centered the experience of neocolonial violence and reasserted the dignity of colonized peoples. Yet *¡Basta!* does not intend to elevate the spectator's shock by contrasting this invocation of human dignity with the image of an eviscerated corpse. Rather, Ulive's representation of dismemberment participates in the elaboration of a revolutionary humanism by identifying defacement, disfiguration, and decapitation with the violence of capital and neocolonial oppression. *¡Basta!* directs this message to the people, specifically to the worker who is alienated within neocolonial capitalism, to mobilize the spectator in defense of his dignity.

¡Basta! progressively abstracts the body through a series of cinematic and surgical cuts. Following the initial image of the scalpel, Ulive follows the remainder of the autopsy in close-up. Cutting to a different angle, we see the face of the cadaver in detail. It is lifeless and remains uncannily still as the coroner jostles the rest of the body while severing its ribs with a bolt cutter. This is followed by a collage of brief clips that identify the neocolonial institutions that stand behind this allegorical cruelty. Ulive splices in images of a nun, a woman performing a striptease, an impoverished child, the logo of a Mobil gas station, and a priest before returning to the autopsy with an extreme close-up of the face of

a cadaver. Positioned above the operating table, the camera zooms out from this still face to show the coroner removing the intestines. By reframing the shot through a zoom lens, Ulive again draws attention to the edges of the image, identifying the scalpel with the camera that fragments the body and visually beheads the corpse. After the autopsy concludes, Ulive cuts to an enormous Pepsi-Cola logo on the facade of a building, followed by a street vendor selling Schick razors. By juxtaposing symbols of religion, extractive capitalism, and consumerism, Ulive associates the defacement and dissection of the body with the violence of capital and the church. This autopsy allegorizes the violence to which neocolonial subjects are submitted. In one of the film's most gruesome images, the surgeons remove the skin from the head of a corpse and peel it back to reveal the skull underneath (Figure 11). They then saw the head open and remove the brain. Juxtaposed with the images of the razor and consumerism, *¡Basta!* implies that capitalism lobotomizes the worker. Ulive reframes the close-up as an anatomical procedure that symbolizes neocolonial violence.

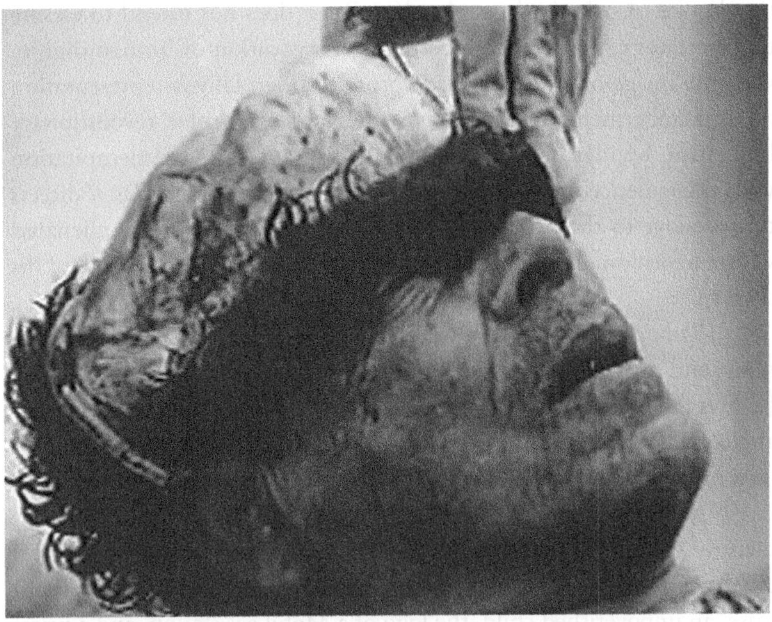

Figure 11. Surgical defacement in the psychiatric hospital. *¡Basta!*, dir. Ugo Ulive, 1969.

¡Basta! joins the two avant-gardes by grafting cinematic abstraction onto a militant critique of neocolonialism. The close-up's defacement of the body surpasses modernist self-reflection to become a tool of radicalization. Ulive's politicized close-ups frustrate a representative politics. Yet as it impedes a face-to-face encounter, the film encourages an affective identification between the audience and the corpse. Ulive's gruesome imagery draws the audience's attention to its own viscera and thus opens a relation between the spectator and the pro-filmic body on the basis of this affect. *¡Basta!* thus enacts community through disfiguration and defacement. Rejecting faciality, this visual guillotine enacts a politics through the severed head, skull, and viscera. The film's aesthetic of defacement instills a revolutionary humanism in the audience and motivates the spectator to take up arms in defense of popular sovereignty.

Ulive and the militant filmmakers of the NLAC radicalized the shock with which the close-up was first received. In these films, the close-up beheads the pro-filmic subject, disrupting the semiotic order of the body and stripping the face of human expression. The violence of framing comes to the forefront and advances a politics of cinematic form. Accounts of the early reception of the close-up underscore the repulsion of critics and audiences. Radical filmmakers channeled this affect toward politics as they joined the aesthetic and political avant-gardes. The modernist aesthetics of defacement that Aumont identifies with the crisis of humanism in the cinema of postwar Europe appear in Latin America as filmmakers responded to the experiences of a cruel modernity. Unlike the European filmmakers in Aumont's account, Ulive, Ospina and Mayolo, and others politicized this assault on the face. These films mark the cathartic culmination of a political tradition of the close-up that began decades earlier, with the national studio systems that projected the face of the nation.

Throughout the political history of the close-up that I have traced in this chapter, the face is tied to the modern concept of the people and the nation's pact with popular sovereignty. Whether by imposing a face on the political community or representing the violence to which this collective subject is exposed, the politics of the facial close-up depends on a logic of identification. With the decline of Latin America's radical filmmaking tradition in the late 1970s, this political tradition of the close-up draws to a close. The 1980s and 1990s saw the proliferation of neoliberal economic policies and accelerated globalization throughout the region. Government support of filmmaking declined, forcing filmmakers to seek out private financing. As Gonzalo Aguilar has documented in the case of Argentina, in these decades cinema's pact with the popular began to fray as a consequence of the crisis of the liberal state. The severed head produced by the facial close-up would no longer function as a political sign. While the face resurfaces at moments, notably in the talking-head compositions of documentaries that responded to the cruelties of dictatorships and authoritarian governments that suppressed the revolutionary movements of the 1960s, this form shifts from a political to an ethical register. Within the human rights discourse that determines these documentaries, filmmakers sought to stage a face-to-face encounter between the spectator and documentary subject. Following Aguilar, recent documentaries diverge from the radical tradition of the 1970s by returning to an obsession with faciality.[67] However, the emphasis on subjectivity and memory in films such as *Los rubios* (*The Blonds*, 2003) and *M* (2007) demonstrate that the facial close-up has lost the political weight assigned to it in modernity. The faces of victims or relatives of the disappeared offer evidence of state violence as they testify in front of the camera, but these images no longer represent the *pueblo*. With the decline of this collective political subject, the face loses its political resonance; the close-up no longer gives form to the people or channels its pathos. The spectator ponders the alterity present in these talking heads, but filmmakers do not construct political community through this image.

Despite this broader shift from politics to ethics, filmmakers have not completely abandoned the facial close-up as a site of political struggle. The politics of defacement continues in the expansion of audiovisual practices following the digital turn, as I discuss in subsequent chapters, though it no longer relies on the humanist logic of identification with the image of the destroyed face. Rather, in their experimentations with digital video, filmmakers such as Colectivo Los Ingrávidos (chapter 4) and Lucrecia Martel (chapter 5) channel the affect released through defacement toward disrupting the ideological operation of the moving image today. In this sense, the politics of defacement developed by the radical filmmakers of the NLAC survives the mutation of the audiovisual apparatus. This shift from a populist politics of identification, which reflects cinema's pact with the *pueblo,* to an affective politics of cinematic form begins with the decline of the NLAC. As I discuss in the next chapter vis-à-vis montage, the late 1970s saw the violent repression of militant cinema and the emergence of a new politics of the cinematic cut. While it saw the decline of cinema's commitment to the popular, the visual guillotine continued to give form to politics through the intensities released through the cut.

2

FROM THE GUILLOTINE TO THE SPLICER

MONTAGE, BEHEADING, AND THE POLITICS OF AFFECT

Though montage is most often associated with modernist practices that aim to raise the audience's consciousness of the fragmented materiality of the moving image, the concept has not always been defined in terms of rupture and self-reflexivity. In the original French, *montage* is defined as assembly, in this case the construction of a cohesive narrative from a series of fragments.[1] In this sense, montage refers to the physical labor of suturing film into a coherent sequence of images. This tradition, which shaped the style of continuity editing that has dominated cinema throughout most of its history, utilizes the cut not to shock the spectator or draw attention to the film's artifice, but instead to insert the audience into a narrative by smoothing over its assemblage of images. As I discuss in the introduction to this book, the earliest films of Thomas Edison and Georges Méliès dissimulated the cut to create a spectacle of beheading.[2] The success of this operation depended on the audience's inability to detect the substitution splice. In exploring the association between cutting film and cutting bodies, these works laid the groundwork for montage theory, which would come into its own decades later, with the avant-garde. In the Soviet Union, Sergei Eisenstein and Dziga Vertov politicized the violence of cutting, which was first theorized by Edison and Méliès. At the intersection of the political and aesthetic avant-gardes, the underlying violence of cinema soon gave way to politics. The purpose of experimenting with montage was not limited to drawing the spectator's attention to cinematic fragmentation. Modernist self-reflection became inseparable from revolution, and filmmakers invoked the cut to give form to radical politics. Yet why did this tradition of montage become one of the primary methods of the political avant-garde? In other words, what is it about the cinematic cut that placed it at the center of revolutionary aesthetics?

This chapter circles these questions as it traces the politics of montage in the New Latin American Cinema. I study a series of filmmakers who associate the force of montage with decapitation. These examples trace the revolutionary politics of montage to the guillotine. While film historians have long associated the NLAC with the concept of intellectual montage, which subordinates the affect generated by the juxtaposition of images to didactic processes, I draw attention to alternative montage strategies developed within this continental project.[3] Intellectual montage served radical filmmakers' goals of representing neocolonial violence and raising a critical consciousness among the audience. My account traces a less conventional current of montage within the NLAC. Rather than impart a political lesson, filmmakers including Fernando Birri, Glauber Rocha, and Nicolás Guillén Landrián experimented with the cut to communicate revolutionary affect, overwhelming the spectator with sensation either through an excess of cuts or their titillating delay.

Revolution was a euphoric event; driven by the pathos of the people, it resulted in an outburst of energy and sensation. The guillotine was an instrument of such revolutionary affect, and the historiography of the French Revolution has long been dominated by the trope of carnivalistic savagery. In Enzo Traverso's words, "It was an outrageous sacrificial ceremony in which blood expiated the sins of the *ancien régime,* with corpses mutilated and exhibited, then paraded through the streets like trophies. The public executions by the guillotine were not enough to satisfy the 'Dionysian impulsions' of the avenging crowds."[4] For this reason, Raymond Bellour has traced a genealogy of cinematic affect to the guillotine. The public spectacle of decapitation, which mechanized the reproduction of the severed head, hypnotized the urban masses. Bellour associates the affect produced by this visual *dispositif* to the awe attributed to cinema's first spectators.[5] Bellour's account, which is centered on the near-simultaneous emergence of cinema and psychoanalysis in the final decade of the nineteenth century, does not dwell on the political connotations of this correlation. However, I draw on his argument to relate the force of montage to the guillotine and emphasize the relation between form and revolutionary affect. In the triangulation of the cinematic cut, politics, and sensation present in these films, I identify the legacy of the guillotine. The filmmakers I examine here politicize affect through montage by joining this formal experimentation with political themes. Following the violent repression of movements with which this cinematic project had allied itself, as well as the rise of authoritarian governments throughout the region, these films underscore the violence of montage by associating the cinematic cut with the severed head. In this visual guillotine, an affect-driven montage echoes the revolutionary frenzy of beheading during the Terror.

In the context of Latin American film history, the most explicit theorization of montage occurs within the NLAC. As a regional movement allied with radical politics, the NLAC embraced an avant-garde aesthetics to encourage audiences to reflect on the material conditions of cinema and society. Filmmakers from Cuba to Argentina sought to break with the classical style that relied on linear editing and encouraged the audience to identify with an immersive narrative. Instead, they advanced their revolutionary politics through an avant-garde aesthetics. In politicizing the cinematic cut, the NLAC revived the tradition of intellectual montage originally conceived by Eisenstein and the Soviet avant-garde.[6] Eisenstein defined this concept as the most complex form of montage. Whereas rhythmic, tonal, and overtonal montage variously orchestrated the collision of shots to create a measured beat, structure the action of a scene, or achieve an emotional effect, intellectual montage placed the cut's affective force in the service of political and cinematic signification.[7] From his concept of the montage of attractions to intellectual montage, Eisenstein constantly revised his theory of the cut. This has prompted some film historians to attempt to periodize Eisenstein's theories, implying a linear development of his ideas. Nevertheless, I follow Jacques Aumont's conclusion that we cannot identify a unified theory of montage in Eisenstein's oeuvre and that it would be inappropriate to force a teleological order upon the filmmaker's writings that culminates in the concept of intellectual montage.[8] As I discuss below, Eisenstein's interest in montage shifted toward a formalist account of revolutionary affect after he completed his most famous films and texts in the 1920s and undertook his unfinished project on the Mexican Revolution.

Intellectual montage proved particularly influential in Cuba, where cinema was a critical tool in the institutionalization of the revolution. In 1959, within three months of assuming power, the revolutionary government established the state film institute, the Instituto Cubano de Artes e Industrias Cinematográficas (ICAIC; Cuban Institute of Cinematographic Art and Industry), to create and promote radical and anti-imperial cinema. The documentary filmmaker Santiago Álvarez, one of the cofounders of the ICAIC, has long been acknowledged as perhaps the most prolific heir to the tradition of intellectual montage in Latin America. Álvarez reimagined Soviet montage theory in the context of the global anticolonial struggles, and the targets of his critique ranged from the invasion of Vietnam and the violent repression of the civil rights movement in the United States to the increasingly globalized society of the spectacle that emerged from postwar consumer capitalism. Frequently drawing comparisons to Eisenstein and Vertov, in the 1960s Álvarez directed a series of experimental documentaries that sought to instill a critical revolutionary consciousness in Cuban audiences through an accelerated montage of photographs and found footage. For example, in *LBJ* (1968) Álvarez critiques the violence of American capitalism and its role in imperial expansion by juxtaposing scenes from a Hollywood Western with the machine gun scene from Howard Hawks's *Scarface* (1932) and an advertisement for Winchester rifles. Yet despite his revolutionary commitment to intellectual montage, Álvarez claimed to have encountered Soviet cinema only after he had developed this style. While his work synthesizes Vertov's commitment to avant-garde documentary with Eisenstein's intellectual montage, Álvarez explains that these resemblances were not the result of direct influence but rather a coincidence that emerged from shared revolutionary contexts.[9]

Eisenstein's montage theory also informed the work of Tomás Gutiérrez Alea, another cofounder of the ICAIC. Alea's *Memorias del subdesarrollo* (*Memories of Underdevelopment,* 1968) famously abandons conventional editing by constructing a complex collage of narrative, documentary, newsreel, television, and photography in a critical reflection on the place of the bourgeois intellectual in the aftermath of the revolution. By intercutting narrative and documentary elements, Alea's montage advances not only the action and tone of the film but also its political critique of false consciousness. While the film's modernist style has long drawn comparisons to the pantheon of European masters, particularly Antonioni, Fellini, and Godard, Alea himself cites the prewar avant-garde as his primary formal and theoretical inspiration. Eisenstein's intellectual montage organizes the overarching structure of the film. Paul Schroeder Rodríguez identifies this method with the film's production of specific ideas through the juxtaposition of images in a single sequence. Throughout *Memorias* the filmmaker encourages the spectator to practice the intellectual process of dealienation that is necessary to realize the decolonial objectives of the revolution. For example, Alea's use of repetition in his character study of the aspiring bourgeois writer Sergio operates through a dialectic of identification and alienation that leads the audience to a critical synthesis of dealienation by which they develop a revolutionary consciousness.[10] The spectator initially identifies with Sergio and sympathizes with his difficult situation, such as the argument he has with his wife that prompts her to flee to Miami and abandon her husband in Havana. The film later returns to this same scene from a different perspective, alienating the audience from Sergio by revealing that his condition results from his own childish actions and character. In his book-length essay *Dialéctica del espectador,* published in an attempt to explain the intellectual foundations of *Memorias,* Alea himself defines this intellectual practice as the viewer's dialectic and traces its roots to the thought of Eisenstein and Brecht.[11] By employing montage to alternate between identification and distanciation, Alea sought to raise the audience's revolutionary consciousness.

Outside of Cuba, the synthesis of Eisenstein's intellectual montage and Brecht's epic theater similarly informed the postulates of Fernando Solanas and Octavio Getino's militant essay film *La hora de los hornos* (*The Hour of the Furnaces*, 1968). Like the aforementioned examples from Álvarez and Alea, the film forces the spectator to engage critically with the image by constructing an assemblage of nonfictional elements including newsreel, documentary, photography, and advertising. Like Álvarez's montage from *LBJ, La hora* updates Eisenstein for the society of spectacle. In one of the most famous sequences from the film's first part, Solanas and Getino explicitly cite Eisenstein's abattoir montage from *Strike* (1925) when intercutting the slaughter of cattle with advertisements for consumer products. The filmmakers cut back and forth between grisly images of the abattoir, with the animals strung up and bleeding, and the happy faces of consumers posing with American soft drinks, cigarettes, cars, domestic products, and fashionable clothes. A butcher sharpens his blade and slits the throats of sheep before the film cuts to print ads for Champagne and brandy. As Robert Stam observes, the scene revises Eisenstein's intellectual montage in the age of Warhol. The clash that emerges from the juxtaposition of these radically different registers leads the spectator to conclude that the advertising industry constitutes its own form of class violence. This argument is reinforced by a series of title cards that summarize the state of Argentina's export economy, implying that the slaughterhouse workers whose labor drives the nation's enormous meat industry are subdued by the manufactured desire for imported consumer goods that are forced on them by the advertising industry.[12] Solanas and Getino thus revive the intellectual montage of the Soviet avant-garde amid the rise of postwar consumerism, converting this arrangement of found materials into an engine of critical revolutionary thought.

While I have limited this summary to a conventional account of the NLAC, I follow efforts by scholars to revise this historiography to recognize the complexities of a regional movement that spanned nearly three decades. As early as the 1980s, B. Ruby Rich critiqued scholars for homogenizing the aesthetics and politics of the NLAC. In subsequent decades, greater attention has been paid to the periodization of this project. Rich initiates this historiographic shift by arguing that the characteristics commonly associated with the NLAC, such as the revolutionary didacticism and populism that I have described in relation to intellectual montage, were limited to what Rich refers to as the "early" militant phase of the 1960s.[13] I heed Rich's call to complicate the historiography of the NLAC by examining the variety of its aesthetic strategies. To be clear, I am not proposing to revisit the periodization of the NLAC but rather to observe a correlation between the shift away from the didacticism of the early NLAC and transformations to the politics of montage.

Although modernist filmmakers have politicized montage throughout much of film history, this device cannot be reduced to an ahistorical feature of the apparatus. As Robert Burgoyne has observed, the concept of intellectual montage must be historicized and not applied universally.[14]

Critics must acknowledge the differences between the montage of the Soviet avant-garde and that of the political modernism of the 1960s and 1970s. For example, while the early films of the NLAC preserved the didactic objectives of intellectual montage, they updated this method in the context of decolonial movements and consumer capitalism. Yet despite these differences, the early NLAC maintained the hierarchical relation between filmmaker and spectator. Álvarez, Alea, and Solanas and Getino guided their audiences to logical conclusions on the violence of capital, alienation, false consciousness, and neocolonialism. Drawing on Burgoyne's historicism, Sarah Hamblin identifies the May 1968 movements as a watershed moment in the history of montage. Displacing the anti-authoritarian spirit of 1968 to the cinema, filmmakers abandoned the didacticism of intellectual montage. In its place, they established a horizontal politics of montage that refused the logic of mastery and efforts to predetermine interpretation.[15] Filmmakers disrupted the transparent communication of ideas between filmmaker and audience, opting instead for opaque juxtapositions that left the spectator to draw their individual conclusions.[16] My analysis of montage in the NLAC draws on Hamblin's periodization. In a break with their previous work, the late films of Birri, Rocha, and Guillén Landrián abandon reason for affect, drawing on the force of the cut not to communicate ideas but to overwhelm the spectator.

In reading form for affect in the NLAC, I draw on the work of Laura Podalsky, who first shifted critical attention away from the project's commitment to revolutionary didacticism. Podalsky argues that conventional accounts overemphasized this element, thereby painting the picture of a cerebral film movement that shunned affective modes of address. Consequently, film historians had overlooked the movement's contribution to a genealogy of political affect in Latin American cinema. Even the most militant figures of the NLAC acknowledged the importance of affect in the process of consciousness-raising and intellectual montage.[17] For example, Solanas and Getino shock their audience with the images of the abattoir to capture attention, provoke outrage, and channel this emotion toward political reflection and praxis. In contrast, the examples I consider in this chapter align themselves with the horizontality and rejection of didacticism that radical filmmakers embraced in the spirit of 1968. Furthermore, intellectual montage served a politics of representation. For example, filmmakers sought to inform the audience of the oppression of the people and identify with the victims of this violence, thereby moving the spectator to take up revolutionary praxis. In contrast, the examples I discuss in this chapter move beyond representation and instead signal a shift toward a posthegemonic politics in Latin American cinema. Rather than mobilize the audience through the image of the people, Birri, Rocha, and Guillén Landrián abandon didacticism and pursue revolutionary politics through affective registers.

Eisenstein's Mexican Guillotine

Sergei Eisenstein, the most prolific theorist and practitioner of montage, understood the power of the cinematic cut to shock his audiences and mimic the violent force of revolution. Looking back on his cinematic legacy in his memoirs, Eisenstein frames his obsession with cutting with a rhetorical question: "I wanted so much to be a part of history, but what sort of a history was it, if there was no guillotine?!"[18] Anne Nesbet argues that for Eisenstein, "history and film [were] both fundamentally indebted to relentless editorial blades: guillotine; scissors."[19] While Eisenstein is most often identified with his concept of intellectual montage, which he developed throughout the 1920s, film historians and theorists highlight a shift in the filmmaker's thought in the latter half of his career. I preface my account of the NLAC with an analysis of this turn from intellectual to affective montage that Eisenstein initiated during his unfinished film *¡Qué viva México!* (1930/1979) because this transition represents a model for Birri and Rocha, who similarly move from the didacticism of intellectual montage to an affective treatment of the cut. For Eisenstein, history and politics were not necessarily rational. The shock of montage has an electrifying effect on the crowd, similar to the turmoil of political struggle. Nesbet highlights the filmmaker's "savage junctures," or the moments in his work when modern image making and prelogical, sensuous thought come together. The guillotine was an example of a savage juncture that captured Eisenstein's cinematic imagination. His enthusiasm for the guillotine is at once revolutionary desire and cinematic metaphor. For the Soviet filmmaker, it was evident that the moving image, like modern politics, derived from the guillotine.

Cutting preoccupied Eisenstein in one form or another throughout his career. However, as Aumont notes, Eisenstein does not present a single, unified theory of montage. The late Eisenstein may indeed contradict his earlier writings because he continuously revises this concept and method.[20] Like Lev Kuleshov, Eisenstein argues that the essence of cinema resides in its power to cut: the body of the film and the performer exist to be mutilated and rearranged. Later in life, Eisenstein's fascination with the guillotine led him to explore other forms of bloody sacrifice. An extended stay outside the Soviet Union between 1928 and 1931, and especially his time in postrevolutionary Mexico, led the filmmaker to develop a fascination with avant-garde primitivism. Mexico marks a point of inflection in Eisenstein's theory of spectacle. While traveling throughout the West, Eisenstein collected an anthropological library and began to rethink his theory of montage in relation to the concepts of magic, ritual, ecstasy, and sacrifice.[21] These interests overtook his filmmaking practice not long after, when he traveled from Hollywood to Mexico to undertake *¡Qué viva México!* In what follows I survey the posthumous cut of the film—edited by Grigori Alexandrov, who accompanied Eisenstein in his travels—as well as the filmmaker's notes, correspondence, diaries, memoirs, and drawings. Fetishizing violent pre-Columbian rituals, Eisenstein elaborated a theory that associated montage with the severed head.

Eisenstein's encounter with Mexico represents a watershed moment in the filmmaker's life and intellectual trajectory.[22] In highlighting the effects of this experience on Eisenstein's thought, Peter Wollen characterizes the filmmaker's late work as attempting to synthesize "emotional saturation, ecstasy, the synchronization of the senses, myth, and primitive thought" through montage.[23] In other words, Eisenstein moved away from the didactic commitments of intellectual montage to develop an affective politics through the cut. The filmmaker initiates this shift when he leaves the Soviet Union for the West in the autumn of 1928, traveling first to Berlin and from there to Zurich, London, and Paris. In France, Eisenstein signed a contract with Paramount and set sail for New York, finally arriving in Hollywood in June 1930. When this project fell through, Eisenstein pitched his initial concept for *¡Qué viva México!*—a film on the Mexican people and their revolution—to Charlie Chaplin.[24] Chaplin turned Eisenstein down, referring the filmmaker to Upton Sinclair. Though known for his writing, Sinclair was curious about the film's potential to support the socialist cause. After a few brief meetings, the two signed a contract.[25] Eisenstein arrived in Mexico City in December 1930.[26] Eisenstein was drawn to Mexico in part because he perceived it as embodying a dialectic between the "prelogical," sensual thought of Indigenous cultures and the rapid modernization the nation was experiencing the 1930s. For the filmmaker, Mexico was montage. Eisenstein "was inspired, as he used to say, by the 'montage' of the country itself, where movement through space, from one province to another, is also a voyage through centuries of time."[27] This was Mexico *as* cinema. The rituals of the pre-Columbian past coexisted with its violent transition to modernity, and this juxtaposition was to be represented through montage.[28] Eisenstein sought to capture the cinematic specificity of this primitivism and the primitivism of cinema, which he conceptualized in relation to the severed head. Nevertheless, Eisenstein was forced to abandon the project abruptly when Stalin demanded he return to Moscow after his prolonged absence.

Through a variety of media, Eisenstein came to explore the shock evoked by montage as a form of sensuous thought he identified with Indigenous cultures. Whether reading, writing, drawing or filming, Eisenstein was always revising his ideas on montage and the powers of cinema. There is a constant slippage here between media: for Eisenstein all of these activities amounted to research.[29] Through these unorthodox reflections, Eisenstein demonstrates a sustained preoccupation with the relation between montage and decapitation, which the filmmaker related to the rituals of Indigenous civilizations. In a letter dated 8–10 May 1931, Eisenstein remarks that his encounter with Indigenous cultures in Mexico was proving fruitful for his film theory.[30] Furthermore, in a separate and undated letter from this period, Eisenstein "makes direct references to a series of pre-Columbian deities, demonstrating a high level of familiarity with the subject, and 'sadistic' pre-Columbian rituals, noting that they had triggered his theoretical work."[31] Eisenstein's ethnological fascination with bloody ritual frames his work during this period: in his rushes for Sinclair, but also in his drawings, diaries, and letters. Furthermore, in the wake of his Mexican period Eisenstein continued to articulate his theory of the prelogical forces underlying cinematic language. In "Film Form: New Problems" (1935), Eisenstein complicates evolutionary models of culture according to which magic constitutes a "primitive" practice that progresses into religion. Eisenstein extended these debates to cinema to elaborate the medium's primitive roots. Rather than evolving from ritual, premodern and modern elements coexist in cinematic spectacle. Eisenstein argues that film mechanizes prelogical (sensual) practices; in his words, "art is nothing else but an artificial retrogression in the field of psychology towards the forms of earlier thought-processes."[32] Montage was perhaps the most important example of this, as it relied on a process of violent dismemberment, as in the rituals that fascinated the filmmaker.

Another form of cutting, the close-up was also crucial to this project. For Eisenstein, this device had the power to express the type of sensual thought proper to the primordial by mutilating a body. Interested in all aspects of fragmentation in cinema, Eisenstein eventually extended his theory of montage to the composition of the individual shot. In a close-up, the frame slices off the performer's body and beheads him, just as the editor's blade dismembers the filmic body. Like the shot in the montage of the film, the head is reduced to a syntagma whose signification varies depending on how it is arranged. In his discussion of the close-up in "Dickens, Griffith, and the Film Today" (1944), Eisenstein writes, "The first factor that attracted us in the method of the close-up was the discovery of its particularly astonishing feature: *to create a new quality of the whole from a juxtaposition of the separate parts.*"[33] The late Eisenstein thus does not oppose montage and the shot but rather searches for montage within the shot. For Eisenstein, the shot fragments an object and reduces it to its basic, constitutive elements so that they may be juxtaposed with another shot through a second, higher-order montage. The camera lens has the power to create a montage of body parts by cutting them in the frame. Arms, legs, hands, heads: these become building blocks for the filmmaker, who combines the close-up with editing and arranges these elements in a symbolic order. The body in pieces mutilated by the frame is an erector set, just like the strip of film.

In *¡Qué viva México!,* Eisenstein combines his interests in corporeal montage and violent ritual. Repeatedly, he severs the Indigenous head in order to display it as an object. This gesture marks the film's prologue. Eisenstein shoots a series of landscapes featuring Mayan ruins, interspersed with close-ups of details, sculptures, and reliefs. Human figures stand motionless amid these monuments as the voice-over booms, "Stone. Gods. People." As the spectator hears these words, the head of a young man appears at the bottom of the frame (Figure 12). The stone figure of a Mayan deity towers over him. Presented in a long shot, the man is beheaded. Eisenstein frames the image as if it were a close-up but shoots from a distance. The composition plays with perspective by juxtaposing these figures within the shot and thus introducing montage into a single image. In this case, the towering statue has the potential to trick the spectator into thinking that this image is a close-up of a much smaller figure. The human head provides scale here. Decapitated by the frame, this severed head is at once a modern image of the weathered stone face and also a sacrificial offering to the deity. The interior montage of the shot—the operation of the visual guillotine—partakes in this ritual cinematic offering. Placed squarely within its stone hands, this severed head has been offered to the god. Here, Eisenstein's experiment with film form coincides with a bloodless take on a violent sacrifice and ritual offering.

As the prologue progresses, this image is followed by a series of Indigenous heads that appear motionless and in close-up. One man, in

Figure 12. A severed head sacrificed to the deities. *¡Qué viva México!*, dir. Sergei Eisenstein, 1930–1931/1979.

profile, positions his head next to the stone bust of an Indigenous figure. Abandoning the pyramids, the subsequent images follow a funeral procession. Here too Eisenstein uses the frame to decapitate the Indigenous body. A woman kneels. Facing the camera, she is beheaded by the frame; her head fills the entire image. In this procession the body of the deceased is not shown: only his head appears through a hole in the coffin. In the same image, Eisenstein also emphasizes the heads of the coffin bearers. These men are shown in profile, their faces blank. In a subsequent image, three women kneel and place their heads on the coffin with their faces partially obscured and their bodies invisible in the shot. Masha Salazkina argues that the dissection of bodies in the prologue follows the fragmentary logic of cubism.[34] Yet when placed into dialogue with Eisenstein's ethnological interest in "prelogical sensation," the fragmented composition suggests that the legacy of pre-Columbian cultures and their ritualistic relation to death passes through the severed head.[35] Eisenstein's violent framing recurs throughout *¡Qué viva México!* I highlight these elements because of the relation Eisenstein establishes between modern Mexico and its pre-Columbian past. In this prologue, Eisenstein uses the frame to abstract the bodies of his actors; he cuts the head to place it outside any temporal or spatial context. These are not faces; they are severed heads that, for Eisenstein, evoke the ecstatic energy of primordial violence.

Eisenstein's drawings from this period offered another outlet for his morbid fascination with beheading. Influenced by the representations of ritual he encountered in anthropological literature, ethnographic museums, and Mexican art, Eisenstein's drawings during this period reimagined these primitivist themes. The filmmaker took to drawing in Mexico while his production was delayed, generating an impressive body of work in a short period. Eisenstein reflected obsessively on sexualized violence, circling these themes throughout hundreds of drawings. Film historians have associated this intense productivity with his theoretical concerns, labeling them "experimental drawings."[36] The theme of decapitation stands out in Eisenstein's two series on *Salomé* (1932) and *Macbeth* (1931), in which the filmmaker returns time and again to the ecstatic and sexualized scene of decapitation. The drawings emphasize the violent rupture of corporeal unity and the display of the severed head. In one example, a beheaded John the Baptist is bound around the legs of Salomé. Both figures appear nude in a minimalist line drawing in black and red ink. Standing in profile, Salomé holds the severed head up at her eye level and gazes at it intensely. The image is spare, with no background. The black lines that give form to these figures are punctuated by the intense red of the blood that spills from the severed head, which matches the color of Salomé's lips and suggests that she has drunk the blood of her victim. Eisenstein imagines a similar scene of eroticized beheading in his *Macbeth* series, in which the filmmaker obsessively depicts the murder of Duncan. In one entry from this series, a black-and-white line drawing, two bodies are intertwined in what suggests a scene of sexual passion. Both figures appear in profile. King Duncan is decapitated, and a line of blood trickles from his severed head. As in the *Salomé* drawing, this violence culminates in ecstasy. Duncan's body is contorted, his limbs stretched out. The severed head is held up on display, its eyes closed and mouth gaping open in an expression of pain and pleasure.

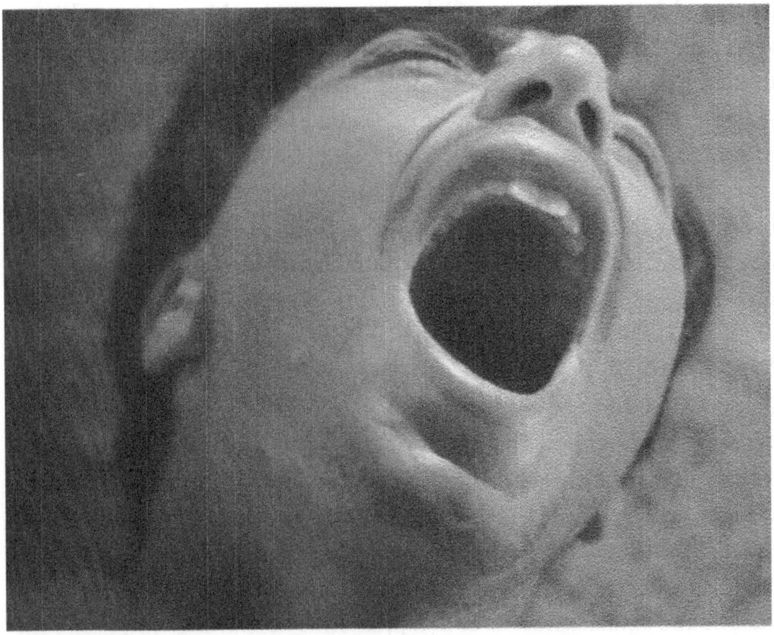

Figure 13. The death of a campesino on the maguey plantation. *¡Qué viva México!,* dir. Sergei Eisenstein, 1931–1932/1979.

The fascination with the ecstatic violence of beheading exhibited in Eisenstein's drawings informs a later sequence from *¡Qué viva México!* To represent the origins of the Mexican Revolution, the filmmaker reimagines the violence suffered by peasants on a Porfirian hacienda. In this narrative, a young peon presents his betrothed to the owner of the estate. After a drunken guest of the landowner accosts the young woman, the peasants rise up to defend her. A fight ensues with their overseers, and the rebels flee into the maguey fields. A group of charros capture, torture, and eventually kill them. Once captured, the peasants are buried up to their necks in dirt with only their heads visible. The tension builds rapidly as the horsemen trample the campesinos in a frenetic montage. Punctuating this moment of catharsis, Eisenstein cuts to an extreme close-up of one of the victims. The young man's decapitation is twice displaced: with only his head protruding from the earth, the frame cuts his body at the neck. Eyes closed tightly and mouth gaping, his face is contorted in ecstasy (Figure 13). This blurring of eros and thanatos resembles the expression of Duncan's severed head in the sexualized *Macbeth* drawing discussed above. While Eisenstein maintains a realistic tone throughout the sequence, his interest in ritual violence informs this image. Drawing on accounts by Eisenstein's student Jay Leyda, Salazkina argues that the images of the peon's death were to be intercut with "scenes of the ecstasy of a peon in a Corpus Christi festival which took place in Tetlapayac, thus linking the peasant's death—and visual decapitation—with an ecstatic religious experience."[37] To return to Nesbet's account of Eisenstein, this image of the peon's severed head is an example of a savage juncture in his cinema. Eisenstein depicts the intense cruelty at the origin of the Mexican Revolution through the symbolic violence of the cinematic cut. The image both represents and communicates the affective force of revolutionary struggle through the cinematic legacy of the guillotine.

Fernando Birri's Montage of Excess

¡Qué viva México! had a profound and immediate impact on Mexican cinema and visual culture.[38] Outside the country, different cuts of the unfinished film went on to circulate throughout Latin America's cine-clubs after Eisenstein was suddenly forced to abandon Mexico and return to Moscow by order of Stalin. The film had a ripple effect on the region's

cinema and offered a model for a subsequent generation of filmmakers who, in the 1960s and 1970s, combined cinematic modernism with a regional project of decolonial politics spurred by the Cuban Revolution. Fernando Birri—one of the most influential figures of this period—likened *¡Qué viva México!* to a seed planted in the soils of Latin American cinema that germinated in the form of the NLAC.[39] Decades earlier, Birri had followed in Eisenstein's footsteps when he undertook an overwhelming political and aesthetic experiment with montage that nearly failed. After being forced to resign from his position as director of the Documentary School of Santa Fe in 1963, he abandoned his native Argentina and entered what would become a long exile. Upon returning to Italy, where he had studied a decade earlier at the Centro Sperimentale in Rome, Birri began work on his colossal film *Org* in 1968. Though filming lasted only fifty-nine days, Birri edited the three-hour film obsessively over a decade, until its debut at the 1979 Venice International Film Festival.[40] "I shut myself in and worked for eleven years," he wrote, "making and unmaking the film, cutting and re-cutting."[41] While the average feature-length film contains between 600 and 800 cuts, Birri's finished film includes an astounding 26,625. Birri himself admits that he had become so consumed with editing *Org* that his friends began to think he had gone mad.[42]

Just as this excessive montage drove the filmmaker to the limits of reason, so too does it overwhelm the spectator. *Org* rejects standards of continuity editing, which rely on match cuts that suture shots to economize spectatorship and immerse the audience in the illusion of spatial and temporal cohesion. As a result, the film favors rupture and shock over a coherent narrative. Though it maintains a playful tone, *Org* frustrates traditional modes of reception and refuses to be easily consumed. Birri does away with intellectual montage through his strategy of excess: the number and pace of cuts often prevent the spectator from identifying the images, forming an association, and synthesizing an idea. Birri's excessive display of montage draws attention to the function of the cinematic apparatus that most spectators take for granted. In this respect, it echoes the formal experimentation of the counter-cinemas of this time, which sought to dispel the illusionism of psychological realism and the classical style of narrative.[43] However, my reading of *Org* does not reduce its excessive montage to a Brechtian strategy of distanciation.

In highlighting the structural presence of the cut through such exaggeration and associating this necessary violence with beheading, Birri's cinematic politics derive from his stimulation of revolutionary affect. Birri constantly interrupts *Org*'s loose narrative frame, a fetishistic tale of severed heads, with an unrelenting sequence of cuts. As we will see, the filmmaker openly recognizes his debt to Méliès and continues the tradition, established in cinema's first decade, of theorizing the relation between cinema and decapitation. Birri grounds this visual guillotine in a politics of montage influenced by the political strategies set in motion by the global 1968 movements and the modernist cinemas they inspired.

While *Org*'s aesthetics radically depart from Birri's prior work, the film is similarly located at the intersection of the cinematic and political avant-gardes. Birri's conceptualization of politics shifts dramatically between his early productions in Argentina and *Org.* Influenced by his studies under Cesar Zavattini in Rome, and later through his work at the Documentary School of Santa Fe, Birri first set out to construct a national popular cinema grounded in documentary realism. These efforts culminated in two collectively produced manifesto films. *Tire dié* (1958/1960), takes the form of a social survey on child beggars and the working poor in rural Santa Fe, featuring extensive interviews. The film's documentary practice also included surveys of audience feedback. After screening a rough cut in the working-class neighborhood in which it was filmed, the film's subjects commented on the accuracy of this representation. Birri then made changes to the film based on this data in order to remain as faithful as possible to reality.[44] With *Los inundados* (1961) Birri took up narrative fiction while maintaining a documentary neorealism. Featuring nonprofessional actors, the film follows a poor rural family as it is displaced by flooding. As opposed to either industrial or art films—the two modes available to filmmakers in Argentina at the time—Birri's early films developed a "realist, critical, and popular" cinema.[45] Through an empirical image of underdevelopment, the filmmaker sought to create community among the oppressed and mobilize political praxis. The power of this early work offered a model for other filmmakers of the NLAC. However, in Birri's own words, *Org* marks a watershed moment in his filmography.[46] Not only does it represent a departure from documentary didacticism to the intensity of spectacle, it also marks a shift from the national popular politics of Birri's early period to the global revolutionary discourse catalyzed by May 1968. Both the film's production and reception thus channel a sense of rupture that coincided with the political fractures this movement introduced. Crucially, Birri communicates the political intensities unleashed by 1968 by associating the severed head with an excessive montage.

In a manifesto titled "For a Cosmic, Delirious and Lumpen Cinema," presented at *Org*'s premiere in Venice, the filmmaker calls for a new language of political cinema. Birri rejects the hegemonic politics of his critical popular cinema and adopts the language of molecular revolution, writing, "madness and rigor go hand-in-hand there won't be a long-lasting revolution without a revolution of language *tablula rasa:* cinema from nothing in order to experience ORG as a non-film in other words an experience for each individual spectator ('only for the crazies')."[47] By *Org*'s premier in 1979, Birri had distanced himself from the concept of the revolutionary *pueblo.* Rather than represent an image of the people in order to construct this community among the audience, *Org*'s politics relies on the resonance of affective intensities released through montage. Like its accompanying manifesto, *Org* undoes conventional language. Opposing the dialectics of intellectual montage, Birri embraces the power of the cut to provoke a collective delirium that characterized the spirit of 1968. Nevertheless, he did not see this madness as divorced from reality. Rather, he considered it a political affect that could be channeled outside the movie theater, toward horizontal social movements.[48] This was not the psychedelic escapism of the hippies, but an embodied spectatorship that captured the revolutionary spirit of the time. This affective state was meant to move the audience to political action.[49]

Birri defines *Org* as an experience, not a film. This work resists analytical summary by design. However, to frame this formal experimentation Birri adapts a story from an Indian oral tradition.[50] In the original narrative, a man falls in love with a beautiful woman and marries her. The couple travels to a religious festival, accompanied by the brother of the groom. While worshipping at a temple, the husband enters an ecstatic fit and sacrifices himself by severing his own head. When the brother discovers the headless corpse, his grief leads him to follow these actions. Searching for the two men, the wife then comes across their severed heads and decapitated bodies. As she too is about to commit suicide, the goddess of the temple intervenes and grants her the ability to revive her husband and brother-in-law. Yet in her hurry to do so, the woman mistakenly reattaches each head to the wrong body. The story ends with a riddle posed to the king: which of these hybrid forms may claim to be the woman's husband? The king concludes that human identity lies in the head, and that therefore the figure with the brother's body and husband's head ought to be the woman's lover.[51]

Birri sets his adaptation in a postapocalyptic future, after nuclear war has ravished the Earth. A love triangle emerges between a woman named Shuick and two men, Grrr and Zohoom. Though Grrr initially helps his friend woo Shuick, he eventually strikes up an affair with her. When Zohoom discovers Grrr's betrayal, he beheads himself out of guilt and grief. Upon discovering the headless corpse, Grrr decapitates himself as well. Shuick happens upon the remains of her friends but manages to revive them (Figures 14 and 15). Nevertheless, she too attaches the heads to the wrong bodies and a debate emerges regarding these hybrid forms to determine who may claim Shuick. To resolve the issue, the three consult the Illustrious Commander, who takes the side of Zohoom, whose head finds itself attached to Grrr's body. Zohoom and Shuick live happily, while Grrr exiles himself to another planet. After Shuick gives birth to a child, her desire for Grrr returns and she leaves in search of him. Zohoom secretly follows her and discovers their affair. The three search for a solution to their love triangle but decide that the only way to avoid the unhappiness of a member of the group is to commit mass suicide, leaving behind their child in hope of a better future.

Birri extends this narrative over three hours, engaging political digressions along the way. In keeping with the film's psychedelic aesthetic, he saturates the images with bright colors and interrupts the narrative with startling visuals, from flicker effects to kaleidoscopes of dancing heads. Furthermore, the film intermittently abandons its campy science fiction frame for long stretches of time to meditate on cinematic politics. *Org* engages the aesthetics of collage, weaving together interviews with Godard, Rossellini, Julio García Espinosa, Glauber Rocha, and Fernando Solanas. Birri juxtaposes these clips with reflections on revolution, featuring passages from or recordings of Che Guevara, Malcolm X, Mao, and Lenin, and literature, referencing Borges, Walt Whitman, and William Blake. Furthermore, Birri splices in an overwhelming amount of found

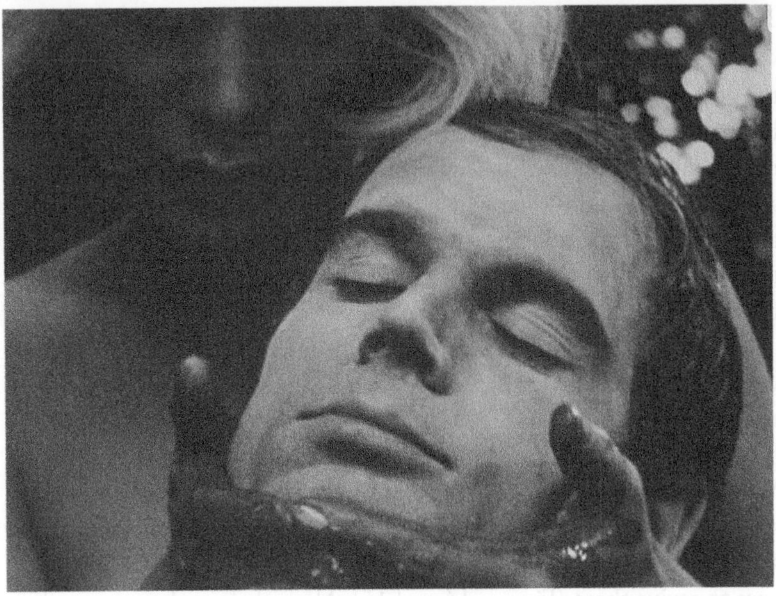

Figure 14. Shuick attaching Zohoom's severed head to Grrr's dismembered body. *Org,* dir. Fernando Birri, 1978.

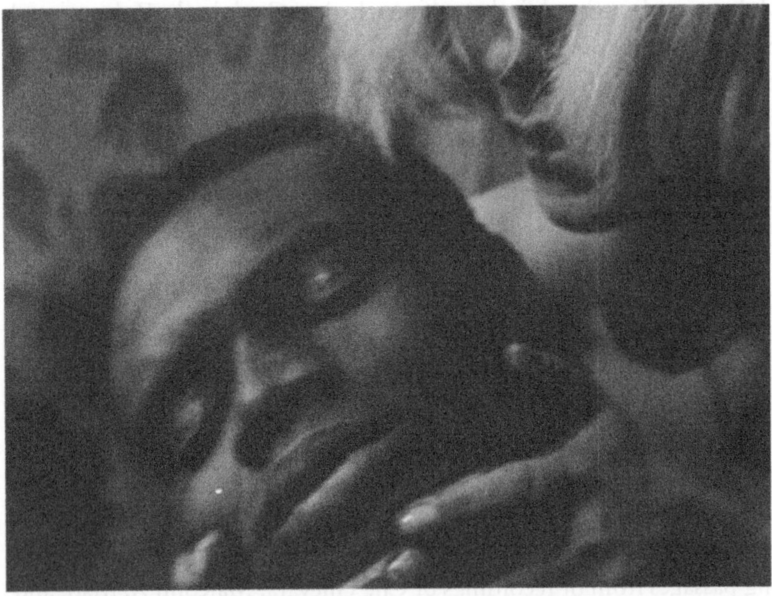

Figure 15. Shuick attaching Grrr's severed head to Zohoom's dismembered body. *Org,* dir. Fernando Birri, 1978.

objects, including films, television broadcasts, radio recordings, music clips, paintings, comics, cartoons, pamphlets, newspaper clippings, animations, photographs, and quotes from a variety of texts. These reference the Vietnam War, the May 1968 movements, Nazism, the Ku Klux Klan, the civil rights movement, and global anticolonial struggles. Thus, while the semblance of a narrative exists in *Org,* its hold on the spectator is weakened through the sheer number of extradiegetic references and digressions. This overwhelming montage discourages a cerebral spectatorship and privileges affect over representation. Rather than communicate with the audience on an intellectual level—imparting a lesson that will inspire political action—Birri does so by means of revolutionary affect.

Birri's experiment with montage echoes the political and formal concerns of filmmakers and theorists in the late 1960s and 1970s. Fusing accounts of literary modernism, Lacanian psychoanalysis, Althusserian Marxism, deconstruction, and semiotics, the discourse of political modernism interrogated the relations between cinematic signification, spectatorship, and ideology.[52] This entailed drawing attention to elements of the cinematic apparatus that held political potential but had become so normalized as to go unnoticed by spectators. Birri's experimental montage in *Org* operates in this vein. By taking the cinematic cut to an extreme, Birri draws the spectator's gaze to the violence of montage within the structure of the moving image. Yet despite these parallels, *Org* is an eccentric work that does not fit neatly within a programmatic account of political modernism. D. N. Rodowick argues that within this discourse, montage is one strategy through which the countercinema of the avant-garde dispels the illusion of film's organic unity. Through such formal experimentation, montage becomes a didactic tool for revealing the ideological conditioning of cinema.[53] Hamblin critiques this conclusion, maintaining that the didacticism Rodowick attributes to montage in this context contradicts the nonhierarchical politics that overtook the radical imagination in 1968. In the wake of 1968, radical filmmakers such as Birri enacted a horizontal form of montage that would level the field of cinematic signification. In Hamblin's words, "Whereas Eisenstein's montage was a 'tractor over the psyche,' a form aimed at pushing the spectator to decode a specific, pre-determined message, the cinemas of '68 rejected this authoritarian model in which the filmmaker is positioned as the master who aims to impart specific wisdom to an unaware audience."[54] I follow Hamblin's argument but note that Eisenstein's influence is more nuanced here.

By the time he abandoned Mexico in 1932, Eisenstein had begun to distance himself from the intellectual montage of *Strike* (1925) and *Battleship Potemkin* (1926). Instead, as I have explained, he shifted his attention to the political potential of montage as an affective device. While Birri abandons the stultifying pedagogy of intellectual montage, *Org* echoes Eisenstein's approach to political affect in *¡Qué viva México!* They trace the political affect of montage back to the collective delirium of the guillotine. The politics of the cut thus go beyond an ideological critique of the apparatus. Abandoning a stultifying didacticism, Birri embraces spectatorial agency in the process of signification. Each spectator will create their own associations, rather than be guided to them through obvious juxtapositions. The number and pace of cuts contributes to this by overwhelming the spectator with images. *Org*'s politics therefore derive from this excess.[55] This revolutionary excess of montage, and its affective resonance, derives from the influence of three figures, to whom Birri dedicates his film: Che Guevara, Wilhelm Reich, and Georges Méliès. Together, these referents help unravel Birri's unorthodox political modernism by orienting the film's commitment to radical politics, sensation, and formal experimentation, respectively. By triangulating these themes, Birri strives to generate revolutionary affect through cinema.

Of course, Che's influence accounts for the film's commitment to revolution. The affective dimension of this politics, however, derives from the legacy of Reich. A student of Freud, Reich sparred with institutional psychoanalysis over its ignorance of social issues. In the 1920s and 1930s he emerged as one of the earliest psychoanalysts to explore the intersection of Marxist and Freudian thought. Reich remained convinced that modernity's social ills—crime, poverty, capitalist exploitation—resulted from untreated neuroses. Furthermore, he tied alienation to sexuality and argued that the repression of sexual desire impaired the lumpenproletariat's class consciousness. Consequently, Reich advocated for the liberation of the senses by means of sexual revolution. The release of orgasmic energy, he believed, would lead to political transformation. Reich referred to this affective potential as the *orgone,* from which Birri derives the title of his film. Reich's theory of sexual politics had a profound impact on the filmmaker, as this homage suggests.[56] Birri reaffirmed his commitment to this theory of political affect when presenting *Org* at the Festival of New Latin American Cinema in 1982. Speaking in Havana, Birri echoed Reich and critiqued Latin America's institutional left for repressing the senses. The revolution could not succeed through purely rational and empirical means. In a text read at the screening, Birri declared, "We will not subordinate, nor will we oppose, orgasm and revolution, revolution and orgasm. We have not come to this earth . . . to decide between orgasm and revolution, but to live in Revolution and Orgasm: Revolution and Orgasm."[57] This digression now leads me back to Birri's visual guillotine. The filmmaker's homage to Reich—his theory of a sexualized political affect to be achieved through cinema—ties the violence of montage to the *petite mort* of the orgasm. In other words, the cathartic energy released in the instant of the cinematic cut mimics the orgasmic force that would stir revolution. Though he did not specify his theory in such detail in his 1982 speech, Birri's project involves a third category: orgasm, revolution, and montage.

This discussion of the pleasure of the cut brings me to Birri's third reference: Georges Méliès. As I discuss in the introduction to this book, Méliès theorized montage through the severed head. Following Tom Gunning, this strategy constituted a cinema of attractions designed to agitate the audience by provoking an emotional and psychological shock.[58] Like Méliès, Birri awes his spectator through the exhibition of the cut and its conceptual link to decapitation. Indeed, Méliès pioneered the devices at Birri's disposal, such as the substitution splice and double exposure. Throughout *Org,* Birri acknowledges the debt avant-garde cinema owes to Méliès. For example, he includes a clip of Méliès's *Le voyage dans la lune* (1902) and, more obliquely, references Méliès by splicing in—seemingly at random—close-ups of a magician. He also frames the pioneering filmmaker as a theorist of montage and demonstrates the political consequences of his early cinematic experiments. Like Méliès before him, Birri highlighted the violence of montage and associated the cinematic cut with beheading. Birri's excessive montage breaks the illusionism of narrative cinema by exhibiting the cinematic apparatus and reminding the spectator that cinema is constructed from cuts. Indeed, *Org* is constructed almost exclusively through jump cuts. Figures do not move smoothly through the frame, of their own volition. Instead, the rapid displacement of images animates these forms in a manner similar to stop-motion. This creates an unnatural movement that fragments gestures through montage. Furthermore, combining this tactic with a narrative of severed heads lost and found heightens the audience's attention to the violence of this process. The explicitly political references in the film link Birri's film theory to the revolutionary legacy of the guillotine. Not only does *Org* thematize the visual guillotine, but the film's disorienting effect also mimics the rapturous state that the severed head provoked in the crowd.

The combined influence of Che, Reich, and Méliès in *Org* thus unites the political and cinematic legacies of the guillotine and embraces the affective power of both the cinematic cut and the severed head. Through an excess of cuts, Birri thematizes the relation between montage and decapitation—in other words, the visual guillotine. Beheading drives *Org*'s narrative frame. However, I propose that the decapitation of Grrr and Zohoom, followed by Shuick's reassembly of their severed heads and dismembered bodies, becomes a metaphor for montage. Like Birri's characters, the body of the film is mutilated by the editor's guillotine, only for these fragments to be rearranged. Just as the mismatched heads and bodies provoke a crisis of meaning in the diegesis, the product of montage—specifically *Org,* which self-consciously presents itself as a Frankensteinian assemblage of fragments—overturns epistemological and phenomenological models familiar to the audience.

The Titillation of the Delayed Cut and Glauber Rocha's Violence of the Long Take

Like Birri, the Brazilian filmmaker Glauber Rocha shifted his political aesthetic from a didactic to an affective register following the reorientation of revolutionary politics in 1968. Critics have traced this shift when noting the disparity between Rocha's earlier manifesto, "An Aesthetics of Hunger" (1965), and its subsequent revision in "An Aesthetics of Dreams" (1971). The former responds to an overarching concern within Brazil's Cinema Novo and NLAC more generally, namely, How can a political cinema be sustained in a context marked by underdevelopment?[59] Rocha grounds his response in documentary realism, arguing, "What has given *cinema novo* its singular international importance is precisely its heightened commitment to portraying the truth."[60] In this regard, "An Aesthetics of Hunger" exhibits NLAC's early debt to neorealism. Rocha argues that a hungry, low-quality, and militant cinema offered a path forward. Brazilians, who were all too familiar with this condition, were best situated to transform hunger into revolutionary violence.[61] Nevertheless, Cinema Novo's failure to transform an aesthetic of hunger into revolutionary praxis—in the context of the 1964 coup d'état in Brazil—provoked a break with this militancy and ushered in a self-reflective phase.

Presenting "An Aesthetics of Dreams" at Columbia University in 1971, Rocha renounces the empiricist impulse espoused in his earlier manifesto. The filmmaker had hinted at such a rupture in "An Aesthetics of Hunger" when he wrote, "We know—we who make these ugly, sad films, these screaming, desperate films, *in which reason hasn't always taken center stage*—we know that hunger will not be cured by government plans" (emphasis added).[62] The neocolonial burden of reason, a source of epistemic violence directed at the traditional beliefs of Indigenous and Afro–Latin American communities, becomes the target of an attack that Rocha intensifies in "An Aesthetic of Dreams."[63] He opens his polemic by relating his rejection of rationality to the events of 1968. The filmmaker embraces the anti-authoritarianism that marked the student protests and critiques the institutional left for relying too heavily on a didacticism rooted in a patronizing image of the people. Rocha advocates for the abandonment of such strategies, which characterized the earlier films of the NLAC. Rather than represent the people, filmmakers should politicize the forces of unreason and affect. Put differently, they must pursue politics by posthegemonic means. In the filmmaker's words,

> The dominant *reasoning* classifies mysticism as *irrational* and it represses it at gunpoint. According to such reasoning, everything that is *irrational* must be destroyed, whether it's religious mysticism, or political mysticism. Revolution, as the possession of a man who follows an idea, is the highest point of mysticism. Revolutions fail when such a possession is not complete, when the rebel doesn't free himself completely from repressive reason, when the signs of the struggle are not produced at a level of stimulating and revealing emotion. . . . A liberating irrationalism is the revolutionary's most powerful weapon.[64]

I align Rocha's political antirationalism—achieved, as we will see, by inducing oneiric and hallucinatory states in the audience—with a revolutionary affect provoked by montage. Whereas Birri embraced excess, disorienting the spectator through rapid and unremitting cuts, Rocha takes up an inverse strategy. In *Terra em transe* (*Entranced Earth,* 1967) and even more so in *Cabezas cortadas* (*The Severed Heads,* 1970)—released in the years between "An Aesthetics of Hunger" and "An Aesthetics of Dreams"—Rocha prolongs takes and relies on the anticipation of the cut to communicate violence. Breaking with the politics of montage elaborated by the historical avant-garde, he combines sequence shots with jump cuts to charge his film with revolutionary affect—the legacy of the guillotine—through a titillating delay of the cut. Through these strategies, these films mimic the shock of political revolt through the power of the cut, as if cinema and guillotine were analogous as violent political spectacles.

Terra em transe marks the transition from an aesthetic of hunger to an aesthetic of dreams in Rocha's cinema. The film presents a political allegory of the 1964 coup: in the fictional republic of Eldorado, the poet and journalist Paulo Martins abandons his support for the newly elected conservative senator Porfirio Díaz in favor of Felipe Vieira, a populist candidate for governor of the rural region of Alecrim. However, after winning the election the progressive Vieira becomes beholden to his financial backers and fails to fulfill his campaign promises. Disenchanted, Paulo solicits the support of media mogul Julio Fuentes in attacking Diaz, who is preparing a coup with the backing of the multinational EXPLINT (Company of International Exploitation). Though Fuentes initially agrees, he later betrays Paulo and sides with Diaz and EXPLINT. Paulo becomes increasingly frustrated with the political establishment and insists on the need for armed struggle. The film begins at this moment. Vieira, now governor of Alecrim, represses the dissidents. Shortly after, Paulo is wounded by the police and dies. Paulo then narrates *Terra em transe* in the form of a flashback chronicling the events leading up to his death.

The structure of Rocha's film places the spectator into the subject position of a delirious man on the verge of death. Cinematically, this is achieved through the techniques of free indirect discourse conceptualized by Italian filmmaker and film theorist Pier Paolo Pasolini. For Pasolini, this modernist mode of narration offers a means of elaborating a cinema of poetry, through which the filmmaker sought to access not only the sphere of dream and imagination, but a primitive state that anticipates the division of real and unreal.[65] Pasolini held that cinema is poetic by nature because its reliance on images resuscitates the irrational, brute, and instinctive character of visual expression that anticipates the elaboration of language and writing.[66] While this is the basic condition of cinema, Pasolini understood that it was not immune to violation. With the consolidation of narrative montage, the cinema of poetry was converted into a cinema of prose. As an alternative to this dominant aesthetic, Pasolini embraces free indirect discourse to "liberate the expressive possibilities stifled by narrative conventions by a sort of return to their origins, which extends even to rediscovering in the technical means of cinema their original oneiric, barbaric, irregular, aggressive, visionary qualities."[67] Pasolini himself cites Rocha as an example of the cinema of poetry. The influence is reciprocal, and Rocha pays homage to Pasolini in his final film, *A idade da terra* (*The Age of the Earth,* 1980). Critics have made this connection as well, highlighting Rocha's extensive use of free indirect discourse in *Terra em transe* to induce in the audience the narrator's disoriented, ecstatic state.[68] In my reading I emphasize the film's formal elaboration of this style through montage. The visual guillotine makes this oneiric state possible by disjoining time and space. The rapid and shocking cinematic cut—like the fall of the guillotine's blade—forces the spectator into a momentary trance. These visions mimic the protagonist's ecstatic experience in the throes of a revolution that ultimately fails. The cinematic cut approximates the affects released in the throes of political violence.

On a formal level, Rocha achieves this effect by alternating between dizzying sequence shots and jump cuts. When the protagonist returns to the capital of Eldorado after his disappointment with Vieira's politics, the audience is offered a glimpse of his troubled state in an orgiastic scene. The sequence opens with an abrupt transition. In the previous scene, the camera walks calmly through the arcade of a shopping mall and out onto the street as Paulo narrates, "When I came back to Eldorado, I don't know when . . . When I saw once again the same landscape, nature, the same people lost in its impossible splendor, I brought the sadness from lost encounters and once again I got lost in the depths of my senses. Only my flesh could burn and there I could find myself." In this subdued long take, the camera proceeds slowly from the dark and cavernous shops into the intense brightness of the street. The transition from the shadows into a blinding light—captured in a washed-out, overexposed image—leads into Paulo's trance. Rocha cuts to the orgy with a burst of energy. The spectator is immediately disoriented by both sound and image. From a quiet street, the audience is overwhelmed by blaring saxophones. Spatial orientation is disrupted. The audience finds itself in a dark room with few clues to anchor the action in time or space. Two bodies devour each other in close-up. They kiss, baring teeth, before the woman's ecstatic smile twists into a devilish grimace. The sequence shot surveys a mass of contorted bodies throughout a party. Women dance in and out of the frame, consumed in ecstasy. Bodies enter and leave focus, many of them dismembered by the frame. The camera approaches a couple before a saxophonist jumps into the shot and distracts the viewer. Characters are dimly lit in chiaroscuro, and bodies emerge from or disappear into the darkness. Rocha amplifies the disorientation by suddenly ending the long take and introducing a jump cut. Eventually, we hear a voice proclaim, "I, Julio Fuentes, declare a permanent state of joy in Eldorado and I greet Paulo Martins, poet and patriot." As Fuentes speaks, the image cuts again to introduce Paulo grabbing a woman by her neck and kissing her forcefully in extreme close-up. Cut again to the heads of Paulo and Fuentes with hypnotized expressions, swaying in a close-up. Cut next to Paulo with two women, and again to a man crawling on the floor. In the midst of the chaos, Fuentes laughs maniacally and proclaims, "The people! They should invade the palaces! The people, Paulo! The guerrillas! The guerrillas!" At this point, Paulo staggers over to Fuentes, who holds him upright. The scene ends with a close-up of the protagonist's severed head, his eyes closed, lost in trance (Figure 16).

Rocha's montage yields a dizzying stream of images that mimics Paulo's entranced state by alternating between duration and the swift fall of the editorial blade. This material fragmentation of the film coincides with the visual dismemberment of bodies throughout the scene. Because the sequence shot follows the pro-filmic event, it establishes continuity of time and place as the spectator witnesses the action unfolding in front of the camera. The jump cut suddenly breaks this temporal and

Figure 16. Paulo in trance, his severed head capturing this ecstatic state. *Terra em transe,* dir. Glauber Rocha, 1967.

spatial duration. David Bordwell observes that the visibility of the jump cut and its power to disturb are contextual. Whereas the use of the device proved provocative within postwar cinematic modernism, jump cuts were much less controversial in Soviet montage precisely because they became so prevalent; more than just the sheer shock of the cut, it was the intellectual power of montage that drew the attention of these filmmakers.[69] In other words, the jump cut is powerful because it interrupts continuity, and this power becomes muted when there is little continuity to interrupt. Rocha's use of sequence shots throughout *Terra em transe* thus amplifies the shock of the jump cut. Furthermore, when juxtaposed with the duration of the sequence shot, the rupture of montage creates a rhythm alongside the energetic jazz soundtrack. Combined with the handheld camera that weaves through this Dionysian scene, the spectator assumes the perspective of the entranced revelers. Rocha politicizes this affect through a free indirect discourse. In "The Aesthetics of Dreams," the filmmaker writes, "The vanguards of thought can no longer support the hollow victory of responding to *oppressive reason* with *revolutionary reason.* Revolution is the *anti-reason* which communicates the tensions and rebellion of the most *irrational* phenomena which is *poverty.*"[70] The visual guillotine, through which Rocha induces this cinematic trance, evokes the irrationality of revolution. As Bellour argues, the guillotine hypnotized its audience.[71] The fervor of revolution threw the crowds surrounding the scaffold into ecstasy. In Rocha's cinema, the visual guillotine—as expressed in the jump cut—mimics this affect through the formal and material practice of cutting. Rocha captures revolution as trance, and the political potential of trance.

Rocha continues to refine his aesthetics of dreams with the return of the allegorical figure of Porfirio Díaz in *Cabezas cortadas*. Produced in Spain during Rocha's exile, the film presents the dictator as an aging lunatic exiled from Eldorado. Here, Rocha further radicalizes his use of the sequence shot and jump cut to mimic an altered state in the spectator. The film proceeds largely through long takes separated by narrative, spatial, and temporal ellipses. For example, after an establishing shot of a crumbling castle, the film opens with a nine-minute sequence shot of Díaz under a fading tapestry. The protagonist talks on two phones simultaneously—a receiver up to each ear—with a former official and an ex-lover. The camera slowly approaches Díaz until the frame decapitates him in close-up. He is disheveled, and alternates between the two conversations. These shift abruptly, and the spectator is left wondering whether the interlocutors exist at all, or if these are the ramblings of a madman. Following the phone calls, the sequence shot continues as Díaz embraces a dog and begins to sing. Without further explanation, this sequence shot suddenly cuts to a rocky hillside. A bearded young man with long hair, dressed in white and carrying a scythe over his shoulder, climbs upward toward the camera. This character, referred to as the Shepherd, combines allegorical embodiments of Death and the Messiah, since soon after his introduction he bends down to heal a blind man. Rocha transitions from the close-up of a visually beheaded Díaz to this image with the Shepherd carrying his scythe, creating an association between the severed head and death. In "Observations on the Long Take" (1967), Pasolini identifies the cut with death. If the sequence shot captures a subjective gaze, montage is violent, immediate, and definitive. Pasolini compares the long take to the present tense because this device registers the pro-filmic event directly. In contrast, montage complicates this temporality and allows the filmmaker to communicate with greater nuance. From here, the filmmaker observes that life resembles a single, ongoing long take interrupted only by death. In Pasolini's words,

"*It is thanks to death that our lives become expressive.* Montage thus accomplishes for the material of film (constituted of fragments, the longest or the shortest, of as many long takes as there are subjectivities) what death accomplishes for life."[72] The sequence shot, which in its duration appears to be the negation of montage, in fact depends on it. Without the cut, the sequence shot cannot achieve the expressive power of free indirect discourse. Instead, as we have seen, the cinema of poetry in Pasolini and Rocha relies on a dialogue between montage and the sequence shot. Without montage, the filmmaker cannot achieve a free indirect discourse that places the spectator into the subject position of the character, because the sequence shot alone merely reproduces the perspective of the camera. The decisive intervention of the cut—the visual guillotine—makes a cinema of poetry possible. Returning now to Rocha's opening sequence in *Cabezas cortadas,* Pasolini's comments on death and montage gain new resonance. This cut refers to a special kind of death: the impending decapitation that haunts the paranoid dictator who is exiled from El Dorado.

Thrown into Díaz's hallucinations, the audience witnesses his inner paranoia. Militants arrive from Eldorado in an attempt to assassinate Díaz, though they are captured, executed, and beheaded. In one scene,

Figure 17. Díaz's prisoners are decapitated. *Cabezas cortadas,* dir. Glauber Rocha, 1970.

three militants, tied together at the neck, approach the camera. Dulcinea —Díaz's love interest—enters the frame with a sword held above her head. A fixed camera films her dancing with the sword, in a reference to Salomé. Rocha then cuts to another static long take, with Díaz covered in mud as he proclaims the beheadings of each militant. After he signs the decree of execution on a piece of parchment, Díaz gestures, twists his head, grunts, and mimics the expression of a corpse. Dulcinea then crosses the frame holding the severed head of a statue, which represents one of Díaz's victims (Figure 17). This action repeats in a long take until Rocha cuts to Díaz and a woman we have not previously seen dancing salsa as drums blare behind them. Again, the jump cut disorients the audience by introducing a temporal and spatial shift. In this transition, as well as the transition following the opening sequence that I describe above, a severed head anticipates an uninterrupted and confusing cut. In the first example, this beheading is visual: Díaz is decapitated by the frame. Rocha holds the sequence shot on the aging dictator's severed head as he raves into two telephones. This disembodiment signals that Díaz has lost his head figuratively as well; in other words, he has lost his mind. Beheading and montage thus coincide as Rocha theorizes the visual guillotine as a tool to achieve his aesthetics of dreams. By disorienting the spectator, Rocha provokes an affective response. Through this seemingly senseless montage, he seeks to drive his spectator mad.[73] The ellipsis created by montage disorients and induces madness in the audience, putting the spectator in Díaz's position. The spectator is figuratively beheaded.

Nicolás Guillén Landrián and the Montage of Madness

The delirious montage of Rocha's aesthetic of dreams is anticipated by a less canonical filmmaker of the NLAC, Nicolás Guillén Landrián, who has been largely absent from Latin American film history until only recently. Landrián had been censored by the Cuban government for thirty years, and a new generation of filmmakers rediscovered his experimental documentaries after his death in 2003. Guillén Landrián began his career forty years prior, directing a total of eleven short documentaries for the ICAIC. However, the Afro-Cuban filmmaker's political and aesthetic nonconformity provoked reprisals during this period that ultimately led to his expulsion from the ICAIC in 1972 and exile to Miami in 1989. In 1966 the government sent Guillén Landrían to the reeducation camp on the Isle of Youth. This attempt at enforced reform ended approximately a year later with the filmmaker dousing a brood of chickens with gasoline, setting them on fire, and burning down a farm. The authorities determined he had gone mad, institutionalized him, and subjected him to electroshock treatments.[74] After his influential family intervened, the government permitted the filmmaker to return to ICAIC but assigned him to the division of instructional cinema, where it was presumed that he would have little freedom to create subversive films.[75] Nevertheless, Guillén Landrián directed two of his most influential films during this second stint at the ICAIC: *Coffea arábiga* (1968) and *Desde La Habana ¡1969! Recordar* (*From Havana 1969! To Remember*, 1970). These works defy the didacticism that defined much of ICAIC's documentary production and instead privileged affective force, which it developed through a dissonant montage. Indeed, Julio Ramos defines Guillén Landrián's work as the displacement of Pasolini's cinema of poetry to the domain of nonfiction.[76] Documentary has long been conceptualized as a "discourse of sobriety" that assumes a direct and transparent relation with reality.[77] To this end, its montage privileges intelligibility. However, Guillén Landrián embraced the potential of montage to overwhelm the spectator and affect their embodied state over the indexical or didactic value of the image.

For his critics, the delirious montage of Guillén Landrián's poetic documentaries—filmed after his psychiatric institutionalization—was only further evidence of the filmmaker's insanity. Based on a series of interviews with those closest to Guillén Landrián during this period, Ramos concludes that the filmmaker undoubtedly did suffer from mental illness. However, what is at stake in approaches to Guillén Landrián's legacy is the critical framing of his madness.[78] While the revolutionary government took advantage of the filmmaker's illness to discredit him, Ramos frames his insanity as a point of entry into his cinema. Whereas the revolutionary didacticism of a filmmaker such as Álvarez drew on the Soviet tradition of intellectual montage, Guillén Landrián experiments with the cut to create a manic cinema that unsettles the spectator's consciousness.

Filmed after the filmmaker's psychic break on the Isle of Youth, *Coffea arábiga* experiments with the aesthetics of educational cinema produced by the revolutionary government. The point of departure of this short documentary was the promotion of El Cordón de la Habana, Fidel's initiative to mobilize the citizenry to utilize the nation's capital to produce coffee and other agricultural products. The ICAIC commissioned Guillén Landrián to advertise the campaign, which ultimately failed, and teach audiences to plant coffee. Nevertheless, the filmmaker subverts these objectives and instead offers a cinema of poetry grounded in Afro-Cuban experience that critiques the revolutionary government's labor policies. A discontinuous and affective montage is Guillén Landrián's primary tool in this subversion. In the opening sequence of *Coffea arábiga,* Nicolás Guillén, Cuba's national poet and the filmmaker's uncle, reads from his poem "Un largo lagarto verde" to an image of the sun in the center of the frame. From here, the film traces the history of coffee cultivation on the island to its origins in slavery through a rapid succession of photographs of a colonial coffee plantation. Guillén Landrián intercuts these images with intertitles that read, "Los negros en el cafetal como mano de obra. Los negros. ¿Cómo? ¡¿Los negros?! Sí, los negros." This text, which is paired with a subdued soundtrack, ends with an image of chains and then explodes to the sound of chants and drums with a clip of Afro-Cuban women dancing in a *santería* ritual. The opening sequence then ends with the repetition of Nicolás Guillén's recitation of his poem, after which the film's titles emerge to the fast pace of a jazz bass line.

As a framing device, this sequence fails to achieve the film's expository purpose. Apart from a historical reference to the origins of coffee cultivation in slavery, there is no way for spectators to orient themselves as to the thematic and practical concerns of El Cordón de la Habana, which the film was commissioned to promote. However, these seemingly random associations constitute a poetic critique. Ramos defines Guillén Landrián's cinema as an assemblage of countercultural experimentation, Afro-Cuban poetry, and political discourse. With this opening sequence, Guillén Landrián frames *Coffea arábiga* as a cinematic expression of *afrocubanismo,* a poetic movement—spearheaded by the filmmaker's uncle—that drew on oral, musical, and performative traditions within Afro-Cuban culture. The documentary abandons indexicality, propaganda, and pedagogy and leaves its audience suspended in this poetic montage. The inclusion of the *santería* ritual announces that *Coffea arábiga* will construct a cinematic trance through a rhythm of cuts.[79] As Ramos argues, Guillén Landrián roots his experimental montage not in the European tradition of the avant-garde, but in the historical trauma that characterizes the Afro-Cuban experience.[80] Just as the Afro-Cuban poets mimicked the beat of drums in rituals and traditional performances, so too does Guillén Landrián's montage match the rhythm of these songs on the soundtrack. *Coffea arábiga* not only criticizes the continuation of racist colonial legacies in revolutionary policies, it also cinematically emulates the cultural forms that arose in response to this violence.[81] Like the *santería* ritual, Guillén Landrián's cinema provokes a state of trance in the audience through his manipulation of the visual guillotine.

The poetic opening of *Coffea arábiga* sets the tone for Guillén Landrián's cinematic and political critique. The film does its best to destabilize language within the film's institutional restraints. Following the opening credits, a voice-over reads from a manual on coffee cultivation as words flash onto the screen against a backdrop of jumbled letters that appear and disappear at random. The words on-screen do not coincide with the text of the voice-over. Following this deliberate confusion, the filmmaker sarcastically includes the intertitle, "¿Está claro?" The film impedes visual intelligibility through rapid montage. When showing workers planting coffee, the filmmaker fragments their gestures and cuts away before the audience can comprehend the action performed. Educational films—a cinema of prose by design—rely on the durational or sequential presentation of labor to reinforce legibility; audiences need simply to repeat the steps seen on-screen.[82] This model captures the root of Jacques Rancière's analogy between conventional spectatorship and stultifying pedagogy. Traditional models of exhibition rely on the separation of the audience and performance (in the case of theater) or image (in cinema). Pedagogy, Rancière argues, similarly operates according to a gap in knowledge between the teacher as master and student as ignoramus. Even though the teacher's duty is to diminish this divide, their very presence paradoxically reinforces it. In response, Rancière proposes an emancipatory pedagogy that converts the student from a passive receiver into an active creator of knowledge by inverting this intellectual hierarchy. Analogously, the spectator must be activated as a participant in order to be emancipated from passivity.[83] Guillén Landrián accomplishes this effort through his poetic montage in *Coffea arábiga.* As a genre, the educational film makes the analogy between spectacle and pedagogy explicit because it approaches the spectator as the ignorant student, while the filmmaker takes on the role of the stultifying teacher. Guillén Landrián abandons his position of authority and undoes the conventions of cinematic didacticism by attacking filmic language and undermining efficient communication. In another example, the film presents an ironic take on the social documentary when Guillén Landrían asks a woman on the street about her opinion of El Cordón de la Habana. The woman answers in Bulgarian, and the film generates confusion by leaving her response untranslated. This is followed by a rapid series of extreme close-ups that fragment her face. The interview has no explicit bearing on her response or the theme of coffee production. Once these images disappear as suddenly as they interrupted the film, Guillén Landrián cuts to images of coffee plants growing. As these examples demonstrate, the film's montage embraces an aesthetic of digression that privileges an audiovisual dissonance and provokes a trance-like state the filmmaker likens to Afro-Cuban dance and ritual.

Throughout this chapter, I have examined the affective force of montage and its political potential. Yet behind each of the more than twenty-six thousand cuts in *Org,* to take the most extreme example, is the violent material process that Teo Hernández and Walter Murch highlight in their studies of editing that I discussed in the introduction to this book. Cinema cannot exist without this guillotine, though the disruptive force of the cinematic cut is suppressed in the continuity editing that dominates narrative cinema. I have opened this dialogue between Birri, Rocha, and Guillén Landrián, who share Eisenstein's commitment to the prelogical and antirational logic of montage, because these filmmakers identify what I term the visual guillotine: the political power of the cut, and the affects inscribed within it, which may be traced back to the intensities of revolution. Their pursuit of cinematic politics rejects the representation of the people and embraces the affective force of the cut. In privileging affect over representation, they elaborate a posthegemonic aesthetic that diverges from the populism traditionally associated with the earlier films of the NLAC. Following the decline of this regional project in the late 1970s and 1980s, the political commitments of Latin American cinema shifted from a commitment to the revolutionary *pueblo* to identity-based movements and a politics of memory. At the same time, the transition from film to electronic and digital media has transformed the material conditions of the audiovisual apparatus. Yet while the cut dematerializes in the process, as I discuss in the next chapter, the visual and symbolic violence of the visual guillotine survives in the present. The cut continues to give form to politics, though the political register of the visual guillotine undergoes a dramatic transformation.

3

CINEMATIC CRIMES

THE DECAPITATION VIDEO AND COUNTERMONTAGE

In his lecture "Politics as a Vocation," Max Weber observes, "Politics is made with the head, not with other parts of the body or the soul."[1] Of course, Weber here refers to the head figuratively, as a symbol of reason. Yet, in the case of Mexico today we might take his statement literally. A quantitative analysis is far from my intention here, though to contextualize the prevalence of decapitation as an act of symbolic violence within Mexico's ongoing narco-conflict I cite a report by the Procuraduría General de la República (Mexican Attorney General's Office) from 2012, which estimates that between January 2007 and September 2011 approximately 5,323 people were "decapitated or dismembered" in Mexico.[2] This figure is underestimated, of course, given that these are only those mutilated corpses registered by the authorities. The performance of decapitation still overshadows the armed conflict more than a decade since this report. Noting that Mexico continues to experience its most intense violence since its revolution, author Juan Villoro captures the contemporary political currency of decapitation when he describes Mexico as "a tower of severed heads."[3] Critics have understood these crimes as a form of symbolic violence that both communicates a specific message to rival forces and terrorizes the public.

Scholars such as Rossana Reguillo have understood the uncanny return of the severed head as a performative act of political violence. I displace Reguillo's observations from performance studies to the realm of the moving image by focusing on the videos that have also sustained this conflict. In addition to their macabre displays of necropower, criminal organizations have produced and circulated dozens of graphic videos exhibiting beheadings, mutilations, and dismemberments. In this chapter I reflect on the emergence of these images amid the mutation of politics and audiovisual practices in the present. The decapitation video is the product of the crisis of sovereignty provoked by the hollowing of the state's institutions and the fraying of the social contract in the wake of neoliberalism and globalization. Patrick Dove has revived Gramsci's concept of interregnum to describe this state of affairs, in which the political institutions and conceptual vocabulary of modernity—the modern nation-state, popular sovereignty—have exhausted their interpretative capacity.[4] Cinema studies has also had to reckon with the critical anachronisms that result from the continued insistence on modernist concepts. The digital apparatus has introduced an untimeliness akin to interregnum as new media remediate the old in a context that theorists have termed postcinematic. The decapitation video synthesizes the transformation of these two categories—cinema and politics—and the pact that they established in modernity. In other words, the decapitation video represents a new union of the political and aesthetic avant-gardes. I approach these videos as a site of audiovisual politics today, and conclude that the politics of the cinematic cut—the visual guillotine—has been weaponized by reactionary forces in the twenty-first century.

The decapitation video tends to be recorded on a cheap compact camera or smartphone and subsequently circulated on the internet. It often includes the interrogation and torture of the victim, who gives a confession and names individuals from rival organizations or the government who are being targeted by the producers of the video. Yet in many cases it is not apparent who the victims in the videos are, and instead all that matters is the capacity of the severed head to horrify.[5] Such videos address a general audience: to all who might interfere in the operations of the business, you may be next. Despite their precarious production quality, these videos participate in a media apparatus governed by a politics of fear. The decapitation video intends to intimidate rivals and pacify the public. Typically, the group producing the video identifies itself clearly, and often states a motive. There may be a group of armed and masked men standing behind the victim, and they may announce their organization, hang a banner with its name behind them, or identify themselves through insignia displayed on paramilitary uniforms. Kneeling or sitting in front of this group is the victim, bound and typically naked. Signs of previous torture are legible on his body. The videos are shot in secluded and unidentifiable settings, often outdoors and with the help of artificial lighting. Some contain *norteño* or *narcocorrido* music in the background.[6] Others are silent, with no audio at all. The image's subjective angle and shaking frame reminds the viewer that a human being is indeed the author of this video.[7] Some examples, as we will see, also include editing in postproduction, giving them an even more cinematic quality. In other cases, they also take advantage of the camera's digital zoom to behead the victim in close-up. The authors of these rudimentary yet horrifying films exhibit their audiovisual politics by joining real and symbolic violence. As in the examples studied in previous chapters, the cinematic cut of montage and the close-up coincides with the cutting of a human body. Yet while the visual guillotine is a political device, its operation is not a priori tied to any specific politics. While in previous chapters I have examined how filmmakers exhibited the visual guillotine's force for the purposes of revolutionary politics, here we witness its weaponization by reactionary forces. The purpose of the decapitation video is to generate even higher profits for criminal organizations by ensuring their operations continue smoothly as the result of a horrified public. Horror, Adriana Cavarero reminds us, induces a state of paralysis.[8] This is the legacy of the Medusa: the severed head that paralyzes the public sphere to prevent any resistance to the criminal politics of what Reguillo calls the parallel state.[9]

The decapitation video continues the genealogy, which I have traced throughout this book, that correlates cinematic cutting and the severed head. The grisly moving images produced within the narco-conflict have not abated after fifteen years. The political power of the decapitation video in part derives from its unwatchable character. Having been reduced to a specter of barbarism haunting Mexico from the ether of the internet, they exert their power with impunity. They have scarcely been subjected to aesthetic critique. The authors of these crimes intuitively theorize the visual guillotine by exhibiting the relation between the moving image and beheading. These cinematic crimes stage the visual guillotine with jarring literalism by adapting audiovisual form to make a spectacle of decapitation. The videos appropriate the digital apparatus and constitute a hypercontemporary form of cinema that is governed by the logic of snuff. Though they have been derided as barbaric, these videos exhibit contemporary audiovisual practices, experimenting with the most advanced forms of neoliberalism and adapting to trends in digital production, exhibition, and spectatorship. While their authors are not consciously media theorists, these amateur productions represent the cutting edge of audiovisual politics in the age of what political philosopher Carlo Galli calls Global War.[10] My intention is to pull back the curtain to reveal how the decapitation video appropriates the cut to provoke horror. By examining the recordings of beheadings produced and disseminated by criminal organizations, I reconsider the relation between violence and the moving image today.

Navigating these materials—both viewing them for the purposes of this research and explicating them here—poses unique difficulties, the most obvious and disturbing of which is their content. How do we reckon with the image of the decapitated and destroyed body? How does one write about these images if, following Reguillo, the objective of their authors is to paralyze the public sphere by nullifying language? More importantly, *why* would we look at the decapitation video? Why not avert our eyes from what is clearly meant to be a spectacle of barbarity? Does viewing these videos not erase the subjectivity and dignity of the victim, effectively reenacting the crime? My argument originates in an insistence on the gaze, however unconformable this may result for the spectator. I maintain that it is necessary to look, and in so doing to respond, despite the difficulty of viewing or discussing these videos. To do otherwise would be to condemn the memory of these images to the abyss.[11] Despite the fact that they constitute one of the most reactionary examples of audiovisual politics in contemporary Latin America, critical engagement of these videos has been largely absent. It is necessary to respond, despite the challenges, and in the process forge new approaches to the representation of violence in the moving image.

In addition to the graphic content of the decapitation video, the framing of these images poses a challenge to any responsible viewer. Sergio González Rodríguez identifies in the visual culture of violence what he terms "the anamorphosis of the victim."[12] If we were to derive pleasure from these videos or view them as a form of entertainment—

the most common mode of reception, judging by how they have circulated on social media and by the comments viewers have left below the videos—then the victim disappears. Yet if we shift our critical position then the victim becomes apparent. The trouble for the viewer is to circumnavigate these objects, determining from which angle to disarm the videos and render them critically legible. We must displace these images from the sphere of gore entertainment and study them as documents of the conflict and products of the new pact between politics and the moving image. To achieve this, and thus to demonstrate the survival of the visual guillotine today, I rely on a critical practice of montage. Though I summarize the gruesome contents of these videos, my intention is not to titillate the reader but to provide flashes of insight. My descriptions are brief and technical. My intention is not to aestheticize, though clinical representation won't do either. First, these are moving images, and I am limited to the format of the page. I cannot faithfully represent the visceral charge of this montage—the interval between images—nor would I intend to serve the interests of the criminal authors by burdening the reader with their weaponized affect. Discussing these images requires an intervention. My experiment in countermontage, both written and visual, attempts to sketch such a possibility.

The decapitation video weaponizes the cinematic cut, including montage. My practice draws on a tradition of critical and historical montage that lies outside the formal or material scope of cinema, though of course it shares affinities with the moving image. The primary representative of this tradition today is the French art historian Georges Didi-Huberman, who revives the method of historical montage developed by Aby Warburg in dialogue with the modernist tradition of political aesthetics that includes Walter Benjamin, Bertolt Brecht, Ernst Bloch, and Harun Farocki.[13] In *Images in Spite of All,* Didi-Huberman argues for both the political urgency and the necessity of imagining the horrors of Auschwitz by looking at the disturbing photographs that survive. "In order to know," he begins, "we must imagine for ourselves."[14] To imagine, we must look. Didi-Huberman's intervention relies on the montage that he creates from these images and on the insights he draws from this practice. His method has been deeply influential in Latin American cultural studies.[15] Of course, a major difference between my reflection on the decapitation video and Didi-Huberman's montage of the surviving photographs from Auschwitz is that the latter possesses the critical distance permitted by the passage of time. Some may disagree with the decision to address violence while we are still in the midst of it because this temporal proximity inhibits reflection. In other words, without this critical distance, it becomes impossible to escape the trap of spectacle. I respect the intellectual and ethical impetus behind this position, though I still insist that we cannot simply ignore the weaponization of moving images in Mexico. Montage allows me to navigate this impasse. The anachronisms I introduce through juxtaposition simulate such distance by estranging images that have become too familiar.

In the montage of screen captures presented in this chapter, I construct a grammar of cuts that undoes the formal language of the videos from which I extract them. I reappropriate the language of montage, which these videos have weaponized. This archive exists online, and it can say many things. But to those who close their eyes to them, these images will only remain within the power of their authors. By extracting these images through screen captures and rearranging them, I use the tools of digital media and the legacy of montage to activate new meanings that were unintended by their original authors. Nevertheless, in my attempt to disarm the imagery of these videos, the risk of collateral damage will always persist. Farocki sought to address this danger of political aesthetics in *Inextinguishable Fire* (1969), his cinematic response to the horrors of the Vietnam War. Farocki suggests that it can be difficult to divorce the critique of violence from its redirection toward the spectator. The filmmaker asks,

> How can we show you napalm in action? And how can we show you the injuries caused by napalm? If we show you pictures of napalm burns, you'll close your eyes. First, you'll close your eyes to the pictures. Then you'll close your eyes to the memory. Then you'll close your eyes to the facts. Then you'll close your eyes to the entire context. If we show you a picture of a person with napalm burns, we will hurt your feelings. If we hurt your feelings, you'll feel as if we'd tried napalm out on you at your expense. We can give you only a hint of an idea of how napalm works.[16]

Farocki, like Blanchot vis-à-vis writing, wrestles with the limits of representing violence and the transference of affects. Is every representation of violence merely its repetition? By discussing the details of decapitation videos, am I subjecting the reader to their cruelties? The reader will likely be affected by this material. However, my objective is to contest the affective politics that emerge from the decapitation video's place in the reactionary realm of spectacle through a countermontage. If the decapitation video weaponizes the visual guillotine through a reactionary use of montage and the moving image, then my objective is to deconstruct this process.[17] By juxtaposing these documents with images taken from the canons of Mexican and global cinema, I highlight the confluence of postcinema and necropolitics in these videos. With this gesture, I encourage the reader to reflect on how the decapitation video opens a new chapter in the history of audiovisual politics.[18]

Sovereignty and Expressive Violence in the *Necromáquina*

While it is easy to dismiss the return of the severed head as an exceptional and anachronistic expression of barbarism, theorists have framed its symbolic crimes as a crisis of sovereignty. Rather than an uncanny return to primitivism, these decapitations reflect the reconfiguration of politics in the present. Drawing on the work of Rita Segato, Reguillo has consistently critiqued the political and economic logic of the conflict since rates of symbolic violence first flared with former Mexican president Felipe Calderón's declaration of a war on the *narco* in 2006. Reguillo has proposed a series of new concepts to account for the erosion of the social contract and crisis of the nation-state, which can no longer guarantee the sovereignty of its territory or the safety of its citizens. As the conflict continues to unfold, Reguillo has further revised her own ideas to address the interconnectedness of neoliberalism, gender, necropolitics, and expressive violence in twenty-first-century Mexico.

Reguillo's framework departs from her concept of paralegality, which signals the exhaustion of the state of exception as a cornerstone of the modern state. From Carl Schmitt to Giorgio Agamben, political theorists have employed this concept to theorize the sovereign's ability to supersede the law in times of crisis.[19] In this case, the rise of expressive violence would constitute a political crisis that necessitates the declaration of the state of exception to reassert the state's authority. Yet Reguillo observes that the state of exception has become the norm, and as such this concept has lost its currency. Expressive violence has reached such a level of excess that it now constitutes a parallel order. If the state of exception rests on the temporary suspension of the law in times of crisis, Reguillo observes, this parallel order systematically obscures distinctions between legality and illegality, filling a void left by the hollowing of the state under neoliberalism. Legality, Reguillo notes, rests on the foundation of a social contract that decades of economic reforms have eroded.[20] The distinction between state and nonstate actors becomes obscured in this context. Paralegality, therefore, constitutes a third space "that emerges in the border zone opened by violence, generating not an illegal order, but a parallel order that produces its own codes, norms, and rituals which, by ignoring institutions and the social contract, paradoxically represents an even greater threat than illegality."[21] This order exists alongside the state; it displaces the sovereign as the locus of power and inaugurates sociabilities that are grounded in expressive violence. As I will discuss in greater detail, the decapitations that represent the excesses of this conflict are not merely crimes; rather, they are both a performance of sovereignty and symbolic form that consolidates power. The concept of the state of exception is insufficient to account for the operation of sovereignty in this context. The *narco* is not a barbarian at the gates of the law. As the tragic events of Ayotzinapa have shown, the state is implicated in this paralegal order and cannot overcome it by invoking a state of exception.[22]

Shunning the term *cartel,* which not only has proven to be imprecise but also has been appropriated by the state and the culture industry to mythologize organized crime, Reguillo initially refers to the apparatus that governs this paralegal order as the *narcomáquina* (narco-machine) to express how, in the context of the neoliberal transformation of Mexico, drug trafficking adopted the same entrepreneurial logic as legal sectors of the economy. The hollowing of state institutions under neoliberalism empowered criminal organizations to pursue their financial objectives with even greater impunity. The mechanical metaphor in Reguillo's concept expresses the systematic character with which the *narco* employed violence to increase profits. Echoing Blanchot, Reguillo observes that language fails to adequately describe the disaster that overtook Mexico. Faced with the proliferation of severed heads and mutilated bodies, our interpretative systems collapse.[23] The *narcomáquina* supplants language with its own forms of communication to consolidate its power. In this apocalyptic landscape, sociability depends on forms of expressive violence that abolish the possibility of understanding. A rhetoric of violence emerges, and decapitation becomes its most powerful expression. The dissolution of both language and humanism in these processes serves to increase the profits of the *narcomáquina.* To capture the neoliberal logic of this parallel order, Reguillo refers to decapitation and mutilation as "the labor of violence [el trabajo de la violencia]." However, as the conflict deepened, Reguillo revises her concept of the *narcomáquina* to account for the *narco*'s more profound challenge to the modern concept of sovereignty. The *narcomáquina* does not cease to function amid these transformations, but rather expands its objectives beyond the accumulation of wealth to greater control over territories and bodies.[24] In other words, as the crisis of sovereignty deepens throughout the conflict, the parallel state takes on a necropolitical function.

If the concept of the *narcomáquina* addressed the use of expressive violence to maximize profit, Reguillo observes that the events of Ayotzinapa in 2014 mark a watershed moment in the development of this parallel state and its symbolic strategies. For her part, Reguillo has updated her theory over the years and proposed a third concept, the *necromáquina* (necro-machine). On one hand, the change in language reflects the development of the conflict as criminal organizations sought out new markets. From drug trafficking, the agents of violence expanded to other illicit goods and services, most notably human trafficking. Nevertheless, Reguillo has maintained the metaphor of the machine, proposing a rhizomatic movement from the *narcomáquina,* dedicated to increasing profits from drug trafficking through expressive violence, to a *necromáquina* governed by unprecedented cruelty.[25]

Before I proceed to my visual analysis of the decapitation video, I briefly turn my attention to the forms of symbolic violence that gave rise to it in the Latin American context. A wave of similar recordings in the early twenty-first century—authored by terrorist organizations and religious extremists in Afghanistan, Pakistan, and Syria—undoubtedly influenced the rise of the decapitation video in Mexico. However, critics such as Jean Franco have traced a genealogy of this expressive violence, especially the public display of the body in pieces, to a regional history of political violence. Franco underscores the legacy of expressive violence that emerged during La Violencia, the period of intense civil conflict in

Colombia between 1948 and 1963, survived in the country's guerrilla conflict and drug wars, and finally made its way to Mexico following the transfer of power in the drug trade in the mid-1990s.[26] In her study of La Violencia, Colombian anthropologist María Victoria Uribe highlights the importance of decapitation and dismemberment as a form of expressive violence within the conflict. In the massacres perpetrated in the rural state of Tolima, gangs and paramilitary groups allied with either liberal or conservative political parties decapitated their victims post mortem and symbolically staged the corpses as a message to their opponents. In these rituals, the specific cuts to which the victim was submitted and the subsequent reorganization of the body formed the basis of a communicative system. Uribe summarizes the cultural logic of these political crimes:

> First, the victims generally killed by means of a gunshot wound, which caused biological death by acute anemia. Next, they were killed again [se las *contramataba*] by decapitation, only to be killed a third time [*rematándolas*] by subjecting the corpse to a series of *post-mortem* cuts that ultimately dismembered the body. . . . This yielded a carefully ordered display, a true *mise-en-scène* in which the perpetrators would arrange the corpses in a row, seated or reclining, with their severed heads between the legs or on the abdomen.[27]

In these cases, the perpetrators submitted the body to a series of macabre modifications. Their actions reduced the severed head and other limbs to individual syntagmas that they subsequently recodified in a gruesome new syntax. Following Uribe, this hijacking of the body's expressive power depended on the spatial rearrangement of its members. Limbs were inverted from top to bottom and vice versa, as in the "Florist's Cut" (Figure 18), or from inside out in the case of disembowelment, which was also a common element of such scenes. The symbolism of these crimes implies that the perpetrators' objective in these cases was to deface the corpse and rob the victims of the trace of subjectivity their bodies retained in death. In these examples, sovereign power not only controls life and death, but also life-in-death.

Departing from Uribe's theory of decapitation, I observe that the act of cutting the corpse and creating an expressive and communicative schema by reordering its fragments as syntagmas resembles the process of montage. Determined to identify the source of cinematic signification, the Soviet filmmaker and theorist Lev Kuleshov first identified cinema's medium specificity with montage. In his experiments, Kuleshov dissected films for analysis as a coroner might break down a corpse. Reflecting on his practice, Kuleshov writes, "In order to determine the main strength of the cinematographic effect, we took one strip of film, cut it apart into its separate shots and then discussed where the very 'filmness' which is the essence of filmic construction lay."[28] The roll of film provided Kuleshov and his students with a series of building blocks that simply needed to be cut and rearranged accordingly. The cinematic body, a long strip of film, must be immobilized and guillotined to fragment the stream of images into syntagmas. The body of the actor represented in this film has likewise been mutilated in the process of filming. Limbs and organs are torn from the actor's body through the close-up. On their own, they signify little. However, through montage they are cut and rearranged to communicate meaning. The body in pieces thus offers the discrete, minimal units for constructing cinematic signification. For

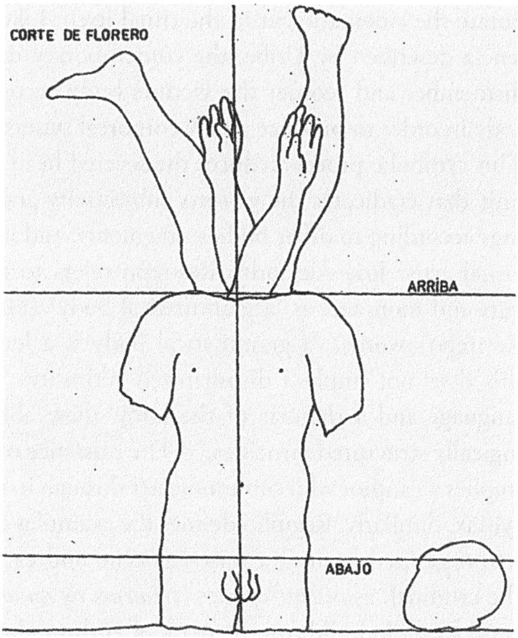

Figure 18. "The Florist's Cut." Illustration from María Victoria Uribe, *Matar, rematar y contramatar: Las masacres de La Violencia en el Tolima, 1948–1964* (Bogotá: CINEP, 1996), 186.

example, Kuleshov celebrated the construction of a fictitious woman from a Frankensteinian assemblage of severed body parts. The filmmaker took the lips of one woman, the legs of another, the back of a third, and the eyes of a fourth.[29] By associating these individual organs and limbs with one another, Kuleshov led the spectator to believe that they belonged to the same fictitious woman. Underlying this appearance of unity is a practice of mechanized mutilation. In his experiment, Kuleshov fragments the bodies of his actors just as he slices the filmic body that contains these images. Like the examples from Edison and Méliès examined in the introduction to this book, Kuleshov theorizes montage through the body in pieces.

Returning to Uribe, I identify an affinity between these macabre displays and the logic of montage. I thus refer to these beheadings and symbolic mutilations as *cinematic crimes.* Their authors establish the analogy between cinema's structural violence—the necessity of cutting—and criminal politics. These examples of expressive violence generate meaning through the cutting and rearranging of syntagmas, as in montage-driven cinema.[30] This makes them an antecedent to the contemporary decapitation video. By recording their actions, the perpetrators incorporate the cinematic cut in the ritual itself. Like the crimes of La Violencia described by Uribe, the contemporary decapitations in Mexico dismember and reorder the victim's body according to an established code in order to produce a new corporeal syntax by means of montage. This symbolic process reduces the severed head to a minimal symbolic unit that eradicates the victim's subjectivity and generates new meanings according to other bodies, fragments, and images. The Colombian visual artist José Alejandro Restrepo refers to this body, subjected to cuts and montage, as "a grammatical body" (*un cuerpo gramatical*). In Restrepo's words, "a grammatical body is a loquacious body, though this does not imply a disorganized verbosity. . . . Through symbolic language and a rhetoric of the body, these abhorrent rituals become logically structured atrocities."[31] The existence of the grammatical body implies an author who communicates through it, reconfiguring the body's syntax. Similarly, Reguillo defines the examples of decapitation in Mexico, organized around a mise-en-scène and carrying a calling card of the criminal, as *auteur*-crimes (*crímenes de autor*). In coining this concept, Reguillo builds on the work of anthropologist Rita Segato, whose influential study of femicide in Ciudad Juárez identifies, in many cases, a stylistic crime that carries an authorial signature.[32] Following Segato, Reguillo suggests that the body in pieces carries the calligraphic mark of power on the body, functioning indexically in relation to the *necromáquina.* Through their affinity with cinema, these crimes exhibit both the symbolic violence that structures the moving image as well as the conditioning of visual culture by criminal politics in the twenty-first century.

The Gore Culture Industry

The acceleration of image production in the twenty-first century has coincided with the emergence of new, perpetual global conflicts dependent on digital technologies. Recent decades have witnessed the continued advancement of what Jonathan Crary has termed 24/7: ceaseless accelerationism as a consequence of neoliberal globalization that has resulted in, among other things, a nonstop network of digital images that is structurally necessary for the function of contemporary capitalism.[33] These forces have radically reorganized our conceptions of violence, space, and time vis-à-vis the digital apparatus. The criminal organizations producing decapitation videos in Mexico share the same structure, objectives, and (increasingly) methods as the multinational corporations that drive 24/7. Emphasizing the corporate structure of the *necromáquina,* Sayak Valencia refers to its violent interpretation of neoliberalism as "gore capitalism."[34] Valencia emphasizes that the organizations commonly referred to as cartels effectively operate as transnational corporations, taking the violent logic of neoliberalism to its most extreme conclusion by converting death, torture, and decapitation into an engine of capital. The videos they produce—like the twenty-four-hour news cycle, social media, or viral marketing campaigns—contribute to the "immense incapacitation of visual experience" that is the hallmark of the uninhibited and uninterrupted pursuit of global markets.[35] Though more gruesome, these videos are products of the same digital apparatus that produces a persistent onslaught of images that direct the spectator's gaze to electronic devices.[36] I argue that these videos are emblematic of media practices in the age of gore capitalism; they are the logical outcome of contemporary global conflicts that rely on the production, circulation, and consumption of screen violence.[37]

It might appear at first sight that the act of decapitation and the public display of a mutilated body expresses a premodern form of violence. Adriana Cavarero suggests that contemporary decapitations represent a regression to primitivism because they reject the guillotine—its industrial efficiency a symbol of modernity—and instead commit the dreadful act with a knife, axe, or saw, as if butchering an animal.[38] Yet this argument ignores the technology of the digital apparatus that makes these videos possible, as well as the hypercontemporary reinterpretation of capitalist violence in which they participate. While performing the primitive, these videos depend on our most contemporary forms of audiovisual production, exhibition, and spectatorship. As products of gore capitalism, they contribute to the theorization of the moving image and its relation to capital through violence. The *necromáquina* appropriates digital technology and the moving image in its pursuit of financial gain by any means. These conflicts overwhelmingly rely on images and information as they tap into new digital networks to weaponize vision.

I open a dialogue between the reconceptualization of sovereignty by Segato and Reguillo and film and media theory to consider the aestheticization of politics in this conflict. Cinema similarly faces exhaustion in the wake of political modernism. As an intermedial category, postcinema designates the proliferation of aesthetic strategies, materialities, and modes of production and exhibition that mark the dissolution of cinema's medium specificity.[39] These moving images inherit cinema's aesthetic forms, modes of subjectivization, and affective force.[40] However, they are transformed through algorithmic, networked, and interactive processes that determine digital media today. As the decapitation video demonstrates, postcinema does not designate a rupture with the form and politics of cinema. Postcinema is also a product of the contemporary interregnum, situated in the awkward historical transition between modernity and the radically new aesthetic and political forms that have yet to be born.

The decapitation videos that have emerged in this conflict are symptomatic of recent trends in digital media production and consumption, which has seen a surge in the distribution and spectatorship of snuff films and other extremely violent content. The emergence and acceleration of the digital apparatus has made recording devices more accessible.

The production of images has been facilitated by media convergence—in recent decades any digital camera or mobile phone has also been configured to shoot video—and the ubiquity of cheap technology. Likewise, the digital networks have made the circulation of moving images instantaneous and inexpensive. In the age of digital video, every aspect of production has been streamlined. For these reasons, among others, "an unprecedented amount of documentary death footage [has reached] the public" in recent years.[41] Even though decapitation had already been used as a gore tactic in Mexico, with criminal organizations displaying heads in public spaces, its practice increased exponentially after a recording of a beheading first went viral via YouTube. Furthermore, the neoliberal model that transformed film production in the last twenty years—forcing filmmakers to abandon analog film for video—has been taken to its extreme in the form of gore capitalism. Boris Groys observes that the traditional separation of labor in representations of war—the division between warrior and artist—has been done away with in the twenty-first century. The collapsing of these roles follows a neoliberal logic of downsizing and professional flexibility that requires the individual to take on additional roles without compensation. Video has become the default medium within the aesthetics of terror, in which "terrorists and warriors themselves begin to act as artists nowadays."[42] Just as we cannot distinguish between state and criminal actors in the *narcomáquina,* we cannot always differentiate between those who exert violence and those who represent it.[43] Furthermore, the production of moving images has been delocalized in the *narcomáquina.* While these groups produce their own movies, they are set in non-places: back roads, empty fields, bare rooms. This dispersion of image production follows the logic of neoliberal capital and contrasts sharply with the monumentality of the traditional film studio under an industrial model of image production.

Not only does the visual production of global conflict capture the neoliberal logic of postcinema's streamlined infrastructure, it also makes explicit the metaphoric violence of digital dematerialization. In his influential text "Dispersion," contemporary artist Seth Price reflects on a 2002 video created by members of a Pakistani fundamentalist organization that shows the beheading of the corpse of American journalist Daniel Pearl. In that same year, the CBS network received strong criticism after it aired the video as part of a news program. Yet, Price observes, "one of the video's most striking aspects is not the grisly, though clinical, climax . . . but the slick production strategies, which seem to draw on American political campaign advertisements."[44] Since the death takes place off-screen, the focus of the video is on the post-mortem act of decapitation entirely. Price analyzes the video as a work of conceptual art in dialogue with contemporary political and aesthetic discourses. His account emphasizes how the image's content reflects its digital modes of distribution. "One question," Price writes, "is whether it has been *relegated* to the Internet, or in some way created by that technology. . . . The video's deplorable content is clearly bound up with its extraordinary routes of transmission and reception."[45] These are uniquely digital forms of images that theorize their own modes of representation. Their digital condition allows these videos to perform their own dematerialization, especially through the disarticulation of the body. These are what Hito Steyerl calls "poor images," subject to continued degradation by the digital apparatus through nonstop copying, resizing, uploading, downloading, and compression. In its active dismemberment of a human body, the decapitation video thematizes the ontology of the poor image. These recordings have an affinity with conceptual art and digital media through their tendency to dematerialize. Citing Félix Guattari, Steyerl argues, "Capital's semiotic turn . . . plays in favor of the creation and dissemination of compressed and flexible data packages that can be integrated into ever-newer combinations and sequences."[46] Like the fragments of information that compose the digital image in their constant rearrangement, in this example the content of the image is itself a fragmented body. Through decapitation and dismemberment the *necromáquina* reduces the body to its basic units (head, arm, torso), which are then rearranged and exhibited on the internet to communicate meaning. In so doing, these poor images also merge death and the act of representation. This process mirrors the dematerialization of the image and its reduction (also spurred on by the forces of capital) of the body to basic units of information. Steyerl highlights the emancipatory power of the poor image when she aligns it with Cuban filmmaker Julio García Espinosa's 1969 manifesto, "For an Imperfect Cinema."[47] Yet *unlike* the poor image defined by Steyerl, the decapitation is not emancipatory. This is not agit-prop; it is pastiche. The decapitation video is the poor/imperfect image that has been co-opted by the neoliberal logic of the *necromáquina.*

Unlike a civil war or insurgency, the criminal organizations producing these images are not just challenging the state's monopoly on violence. They are also theorizing—through the severed head—the monopoly of gore (and capital) held by Hollywood. There is a short circuit between the violence we are accustomed to seeing in today's industrial cinema and the decapitation videos produced by the *necromáquina.* Following Valencia, we must keep in mind that these crimes rely on an aesthetic referent: gore cinema, an uncommonly bloody variant of Hollywood horror film.[48] Valencia reflects on decapitation videos, analyzing them as examples of how narco-corporations draw on gore cinema when marketing their brand:

> Within the logics of profitability and exclusivity that the market uses to drive consumption, international mafias have created their own *individual trademarks, offering a personalized product.* In the case of Mexican organized crime, this trademark is developed through the deployment of gruesome, sensationalist, and bloodthirsty practices of violence: gore violence, which seems to be inspired by Hollywood movies but ends up being a specific brand for each cartel.[49]

The videos themselves are in direct dialogue with cinema and push to its logical conclusion the connection between cinema's (implicit and explicit) violence toward the body and commercial gain. These are amateur movies, and they establish a feedback loop of gore imagery between popular media that disperse and circulate back to the screen in the form of the decapitation video. In part these videos are unbearable for the spectator because they serve as a mirror of mediated societal violence that is otherwise easily and uncritically consumed.

The weaponization of the moving image by the *necromáquina* echoes past appropriations of media for violent ends. In the twentieth century, fascism included cinema, photography, and spectacle in its political arsenal. In response, the Frankfurt School elaborated a theory of media to counteract these efforts by making explicit the aesthetic and political logic of this appropriation. Walter Benjamin's seminal essay "The Work of Art in the Age of Its Technological Reproducibility" became a political manual for decoding this aestheticization of politics. Beyond Europe, the consolidation of audiovisual industries likewise provoked the theorization of mass culture as a political tool. These are preconditions of gore capitalism. Indeed, Valencia's concept refers to the influence of cinema—one of the largest modern industries—by theorizing contemporary violence and capital in relation to the Hollywood genre of gore. The twenty-first century has witnessed a parallel weaponization of new media with the expansion and politicization of the digital apparatus. A similar theoretical manual is necessary today to decodify this violent appropriation of the digital within contemporary global conflicts and gore capitalism. We must urgently develop a visual pedagogy so that these images do not paralyze us. We must be able to disarm these images. Responding to the 9/11 attacks and the rise of Global War in the twenty-first century, Galli writes, "Indeed, there is a real need for imagination and for the production of new concepts; today, we need *to relearn how to look*—seeing, the Idea, is a problem once more."[50] My countermontage takes a step in this direction by laying bare the aesthetic and political logic of the decapitation video in Mexico. I draw on my theory of the visual guillotine, outlined in the first two chapters of this book, to study the role of the moving image within these conflicts. In the twenty-first century, new audiovisual industries have emerged in tune with global conflicts to create a hyperviolent and ongoing war of images. Paraphrasing Valencia, we are witnessing the consolidation of what we might call gore culture industries. If in her account Valencia analyzes the ways in which agents of the *necromáquina* theorize capital through violence, then I respond to its parallel theorization of the moving image.

The Political Aesthetics of Snuff

In analyzing the aesthetics of the decapitation video, I turn to the first production to go viral in Mexico, in 2006. The five-minute-and-sixteen-second video, recorded in Acapulco, was uploaded to YouTube with the title "Be a patriot, kill a Zeta" (Figure 19). The camera opens on a visually beheaded but still living body of a middle-aged man. Stripped to his underwear, the victim is seated in a chair with his arms tied behind his back. In the center of the image is his torso, which contains a number of marks made in black ink. On his chest is a large Z, branding him a member of the criminal organization Los Zetas. Below this the spectator can make out two phrases: "Welcome woman- and child-killers" and "You're next, O$tion." Ostión, the recipient of this message, was the alias of a high-ranking member of Los Zetas.[51] On the victim's left thigh is written Z-14, referring to his rank within the organization. The video opens with the man confessing his membership within Los Zetas and detailing attacks carried out by this organization against the producers of the video in Acapulco. Following this confession there is a pause. Two disembodied hands wearing surgical gloves enter the frame and place a wire in front of the man's neck. As his body stiffens in anticipation of the beheading, the video suddenly cuts to a display of the mutilated body. The act of decapitation itself is not represented; rather, it coincides with the splice. The physical cutting of the head remains obscured within this cinematic logic. The video demonstrates the operation of the visual guillotine, which still survives, even after the transition to video. It is not just that the cinematic language of the apparatus expresses this morbid crime; it too exerts a symbolic violence by substituting this literal and figurative cutting.

The first decapitation video in Mexico spawned dozens of imitations, and new videos continue to circulate on blogs and message boards.

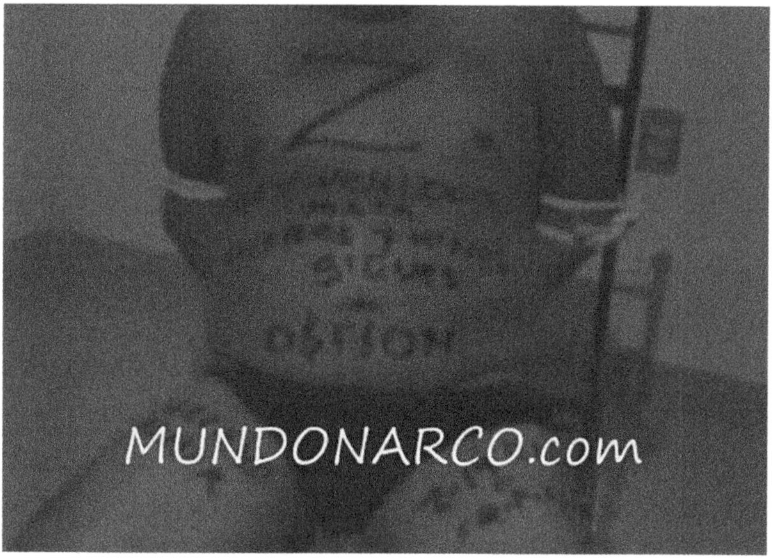

Figure 19. The body of the victim decapitated in the frame, prior to its beheading. *Haz patria, mata un Zeta.* Author unknown, undated, *El Blog del Narco.*

To describe their contents without falling into the trap of spectacle, I adopt González Rodríguez's practice of textual photographs. Facing a similar dilemma on the politics of representation when discussing femicide, González Rodríguez opts for distanced descriptions rather than visual reproductions.[52] These short texts, which draw on documentary images such as photographs and surveillance footage, introduce critical distance. González Rodríguez offers flashes from the victims' lives and the cruelties to which they were submitted, and then arranges these fragments in a montage.

> Two shirtless men sit against an exterior wall with the sun beating down on them. The shot is composed in a close-up, cutting off their bodies at the shoulders. The image cuts to a wider shot. A man dressed in military fatigues, his head cropped out of the frame, approaches with a chainsaw. The muscles in the shoulder and neck tense as the machine makes contact with his skin, but the victim does not scream.
>
> "The calm, the burn of the holocaust, the annihilation of noon—the calm of the disaster."[53]
>
> A man kneels in a field at night. Silhouetted by artificial lights, the mise-en-scène resembles a movie set. The hood of his sweatshirt is pulled down over his face and duct-taped in place, anticipating his imminent defacement. The gruesome act is committed with a machete, the camera's frame mimicking these cuts as it registers the crime in extreme close-up.
>
> "How does the camera operator compare with the painter? In answer to this, it will be helpful to consider the concept of the operator as it is familiar to us from surgery. The surgeon represents the polar opposite of the magician. The attitude of the magician, who heals a sick person by a laying-on of hands, differs from that of the surgeon, who makes an intervention in the patient. The magician maintains the natural distance between himself and the person treated; more precisely, he reduces it slightly by laying on his hands, but increases it greatly by his authority. The surgeon does exactly the reverse: he greatly diminishes the distance from the patient by penetrating the patient's body."[54]
>
> A young man stands outside at night, centered in a medium shot. He appears as if in an abyss. The light design illuminates his upper

torso in chiaroscuro, cutting him off from the surroundings. The executioner enters the frame and the image cuts to the dismembered corpse. The interval between these images becomes charged with gruesome force. The form of the audiovisual cut substitutes the heinous act.

A gruesome mise-en-scène. After a shirtless adolescent is dismembered, his limbs are rearranged, and head placed on his back. The camera moves in for a close-up.

A bound man lies face down on a patch of dirt, his head cropped out by the edge of the frame. The stillness of this body, and the blood caked to his forehead, suggests he is already dead. At first, only his blinking confirms that he is still alive. The man's eyelids open and close, cutting the images in his retinal feed.

"Look at that lamp across the room. Now look back at me. Look back at the lamp. Now look back at me again. Do you see what you did? You blinked. Those are cuts. After the first look, you know that there's no reason to pan continuously from me to the lamp because you know what's in between. Your mind cut the scene. First you behold the lamp. Cut. Then you behold me."[55]

A man lies face down on the ground in a forest, his hands tied behind his back. A group of men surrounds him. They wear uniforms and brandish military weapons. The decapitation is imminent; a handheld camera comes in for a close-up. The movement provokes a lens flair from the bright light filtering through the canopy.

"The sun has also been mythologically expressed by a man slashing his own throat, as well as by an anthropomorphic being deprived of a head."[56]

The opening credits superimposed on the video denounce traitors and threaten the enemies of its authors. Four veiled men kneel in front of a band of criminals in uniform and pose with long rifles. Blue and red lights flash in the background. Cut: the scene erupts in violence, with half a dozen figures attacking the men with machetes. The handheld camera floats through the scene, inserting the spectator into the chaos through a sequence shot.

"The refusal to see, on the other hand, is the spectator's freedom. . . . A choice that I understand, even if it is not mine. I think, on the

> contrary, that it is necessary to see one or more of these short films firsthand, to endure the images of the violent death given by an executioner and relayed by a screen, not only to see that the ignominy of showmen can go beyond abjection (and this is not a useless lesson), but, I do not hide it, in the hope of saving the cinema from what sullies it."[57]

Within the archives of gore cinema, the snuff film hovers like a phantom. Conventional definitions associate snuff with two traits. Most importantly, the snuff film must depict the death of its (traditionally female) protagonist on-screen and in real time.[58] No makeup or special effects may be used; the death must be authentic. Second, the film must be produced for commercial ends. As a generic category, the existence and definition of snuff has been debated since the term was introduced in the 1960s. Lisa Downing observes that snuff is a discourse of cultural anxieties and fantasies without a proper object: much is said of snuff, but no true snuff films exist. Furthermore, Downing identifies Latin America as the origin of this genre.[59] Yet despite snuff's phantasmatic character, many recordings of deaths exist, including those produced by police, military, and paramilitary organizations. Paul B. Preciado's definition of snuff is looser than Downing's; Preciado defines the genre as a moving image that transforms death into "public, marketable representation."[60] Broadening the concept of snuff to include gore and mondo films, Preciado relates the cultural fascination with the hyperrealistic representation of death to the brutalism of contemporary politics, concluding, "Politics has become snuff: extermination by and for representation."[61] As a form of marketing for criminal organizations, following the logic of gore capitalism, the decapitation video does just that: promote its brand and ensure that the horror generated by making this act visible guarantees that the public does not interfere in its operations.

The decapitation video is a cultural product of gore capitalism that serves the ideology of the parallel state. These messages generate greater profits for criminal organizations by pacifying the population through horrorism and intimidating competitors. The young men who commit the crimes and produce the videos, who are themselves low-ranking employees within the corporate structure of the criminal organization, represent workers in a gore culture industry. As I have already mentioned, snuff is a traditionally gendered genre. To capture the patriarchal character of gore capitalism, Valencia refers to its agents—the assassins and gangsters who produce these images—as *endriago* subjects.[62] Conditioned by the neoliberal mentality of entrepreneurship, these young men embrace violence as a means of economic agency, or what Valencia calls "capitalist necroempowerment."[63] Excluded from the spectacle of consumer capitalism that is aggressively marketed to them, young men who inhabit the social margins turn to violence to satisfy their desire to fulfill the role of male provider.[64] Put differently, the *endriago* subject reflects the mutation of the traditional pact between capital and patriarchy. In the realm of gore capitalism, the *endriago* accumulates wealth through the exercise and display of extreme violence. The decapitation video is one form through which these entrepreneurs realize this gendered division of labor, in which the victim is often female or feminized. In numerous videos, the victims are identified as sex workers, migrants, or women accused of being romantically or sexually involved with members of rival organizations. In addition to its political and economic functions, the decapitation video fulfills a ritualistic function as a tool of male sociability.

Videos in Spite of All

The ongoing conflict in Mexico is a shadowy affair. It often takes place out of sight and out of mind for those not immediately affected by its violence. Its victims disappear and cannot call attention to the crimes committed against them. Their families are persecuted by both government and criminal forces for drawing attention to unsolved murders or disappearances. In this political context, it becomes urgent to witness the images of this history. We must open our eyes. This may be difficult, given the extreme nature of this content, but that makes it no less necessary to do so. Returning to Farocki, the problem underlying the decapitation video (and the violence of the *necromáquina* more broadly) is *how* to render this violence intelligible. One strategy I adopt is to extract screen captures and treat them as photographs so that they may speak against the *necromáquina*. This allows me to rearrange images in a process of montage that undoes the logic of the original video. The objective is to allow these images to speak by erasing the authorial mark of the *auteur*-crime (as analyzed by Reguillo, Segato, and Valencia). Together they elaborate a countermontage, a *contramáquina*. I read these videos against the intent of their authors and analyze how this work of found footage might *betray* the *necromáquina.*

When analyzing the decapitation video, it is necessary to consider this object in relation to the new modes of spectatorship opened up by digital technologies. Prior to the last decades of the twentieth century, the movement and speed of the image was entirely outside the control of the spectator. With the arrival of video and home entertainment, and later online streaming, audiences were granted immense power over the moving image. My reading of the decapitation video is made possible by the very digital apparatus that allows me to halt the movement of the images and extract the frozen frame before me. As a result, I now interact with the image as if it were a photograph and not the fragment of a video. What I intend to do here is, to quote Laura Mulvey, "touch the point between the aesthetic of photography and the cinema."[65] This operation corresponds to the new forms of viewing moving images that arise with cinema's digital turn, the mode of digital spectatorship in which the *necromáquina* participates. Borrowing Mulvey's framework, I observe that the same digital infrastructure that makes possible the production and distribution of the decapitation videos that empower the *necromáquina* also contains methods for their subversion. Freezing the frame allows the spectator to return to the scene prior to the beheading, and from there to meditate on the victim prior to the crime. This decelerates the *necromáquina* and allows us to make the apparatus visible. Furthermore, by intervening in the continuum of the video—the perpetual "now" of the moving image—the spectator is able, through the still image, to instead bring to the fore the "then" of the victim. "Out of this pause," Mulvey argues, "a delayed cinema gains a political dimension, potentially able to challenge patterns of time."[66] Of course, we know that the represented is not alive. I am not suggesting, naively, that by meditating on these images we can reverse the horrific actions of their murderers. What we are observing in these images of the victim before her beheading is, instead, the image of the victim's living corpse.

In broad terms, montage refers to the juxtaposition of two elements using a logic that is extrinsic to them. While it is most often associated with cinema, modernist aesthetics converted montage into an intermedial practice spanning theater, opera, dance, collage, painting, photography, and literature.[67] Rather than a medium-specific device, montage thus constituted a cultural discourse that reacted to the transformation of visuality in modernity. Aesthetic fragmentation captured the acceleration of urban life. The shock of the cut mimicked the overstimulation of the senses amid a barrage of ephemeral experiences. Thus, across disciplines and media, montage has been understood as "a consequence and perceptual correlate of modernity."[68] I link this obsession with cutting the aesthetic object, understood as an expression of modern experience, to another trope that has been tied to debates on modern visuality: the mutilated body and, specifically, the severed head. Montage is a critical development of Linda Nochlin's concept of the body in pieces. Though Nochlin limits her scope to nineteenth-century art, montage radicalizes her theory of the bodily fragment as metaphor of modernity when, as the materials in this chapter demonstrate, the film is to be understood as a cinematic body.[69] Exploring montage therefore requires us to position cinema within a broader "culture of dismemberment."[70] With the global acceleration of industrialization in the fin de siècle, the culture of fragmentation identified by Nochlin only intensified. Both T. W. Adorno and Peter Bürger identify montage with the modernist rebellion against the organic unity of the work of art.[71] By cutting up the image or text, the author exhibited its artificial construction; art and assemblage became inseparable. Despite the intermediality of montage as an aesthetic practice, the moving image became the preferred medium for theoretical reflection on the cut in modernity. In cinema, cutting is a technical process that is materially necessary for the medium's operation.[72] While we may theorize montage in modernist poetry or fiction, the literary manifestations of this process are conceptual.[73] Even when the work is the product of a material cut, such as in collage or photomontage, the cut is artisanal and not industrialized as it is in cinema. In most films, whether narrative or avant-garde, the sheer number of cuts becomes overwhelming. Consequently, cinema quickly mechanized this process in the service of efficiency and scale. Nevertheless, cinema occupies a paradoxical space in montage's wider cultural discourse. Though it is not always explicit, the visual guillotine is a structural feature of cinema.

Though they appear alive in the recording, we know they have since been condemned to death. This is especially important in the context under consideration here, in which the authors of the videos in fact seek to annihilate the image of the dead. In reasserting the image of their body and subjectivity, we are negating the attempts by the *necromáquina* to rob them of their life-in-death by means of symbolic violence. While we cannot revive the victims, looking at them does bring them back from the higher-order death of decapitation—the erasure of the life-in-death that the untouched image of the corpse preserves. In the case of the decapitation video, the digital apparatus opens up not just new perceptual possibilities but also new political and ethical strategies. Mulvey remarks that the stillness induced by halting the film creates a pensive spectator who, in a moment of heightened consciousness given the pause from perceptual movement, reflects on the image in a manner similar to the photograph.[74] In this moment, the spectator is able to recognize the victim, to make her present, and negate the intentions of the video's authors to annihilate any trace of her subjectivity through extreme violence, mutilation, and decapitation.[75] Nevertheless, it would be naive to pretend that an aesthetic practice, even if it rescues the final moments of dignity in the face of disaster, will make these victims reappear. The second step in this operation, then, is to elaborate a montage with other images of cinematic violence culled from film history that, despite their anachronism here, make possible unforeseen temporalities. Montage can produce flashes of insight, and anachronisms permit historical connections otherwise unthinkable within the disciplinary restraints of historicism. I acknowledge that such associations might provoke polemic but am confident in their political, intellectual, and creative potential. I leave the reader to make their own associations.

The executioner converts the body of the decapitated victim into a synthetic material through which he attacks the viewer's body affectively. The effect is worsened through the oversaturation of the viewer with such images. These videos take the logic of postcinematic affect to an extreme, reflecting what it feels like to view violent imagery under gore capitalism. In this context, decapitation videos are akin to what Steven Shaviro terms "*machines for generating affect,* and for capitalizing upon, or extracting value from, this affect."[76] The horror evoked in the spectator paralyzes her and allows the *necromáquina* to continue operating with impunity. The affective flows generated by the videos, then, parallel the flows of information that structure the digital apparatus and the flows of

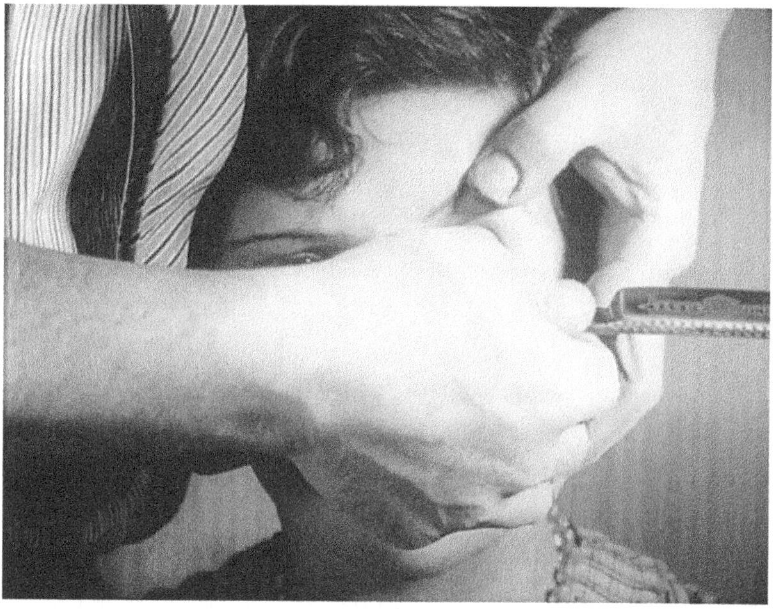

Figure 20. The avant-garde assault on the gaze. *Un chien andalou,* dir. Luis Buñuel, 1929.

Figure 21. The victim of a criminal organization, prior to his murder and decapitation. Untitled decapitation video, author unknown, undated, *El Blog del Narco.*

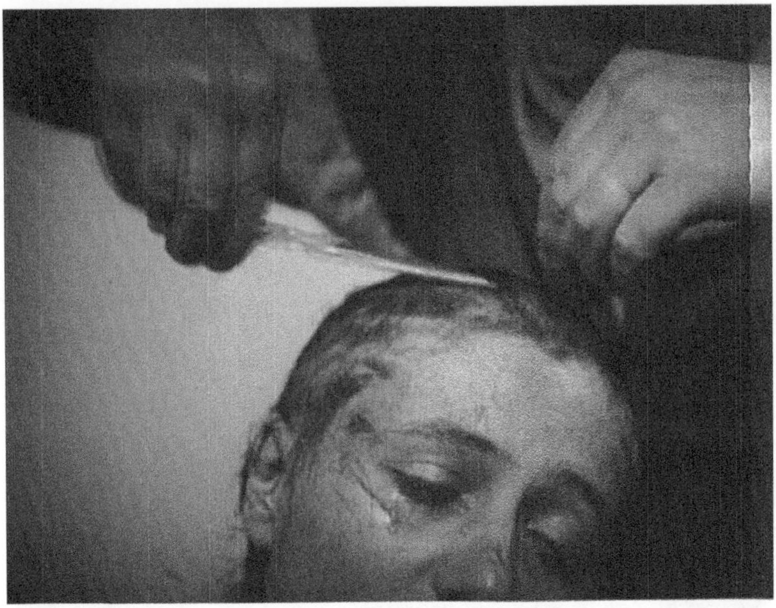

Figure 22. The torture of Joan of Arc, prior to her execution. *La Passion de Jeanne d'Arc,* dir. Carl Theodor Dreyer, 1928.

capital. The decapitation video is an emblematic example of postcinema: intended to horrify the spectator, it guarantees impunity and generates financial gain by paralyzing the public sphere.

This photographic approach to the moving image, made possible by a pensive spectatorship, opens a space for civil action that subverts the power that the *necromáquina* holds over these images. For the purposes of this argument, it is necessary first to understand the video not as an isolated object created and viewed in isolation, but as a videographic event—to paraphrase Ariella Azoulay's theory of the photographic event—that opens a space within the apparatus between technology, videographer, victim, executioner, and viewer.[77] By extracting these still images from videos, I convert the videographic event into a photographic one. Each time we view such a video, we are repeating this event and opening this matrix of relations again. It is within these relations that the *necromáquina* exerts its violence, unless we are capable of disturbing this balance of power. By extracting these still images from their videos, I am circumventing the authors' control over this event. This does not erase the horrors of decapitation. However, by focusing on a single image at a time I avoid the power of decapitation to obscure the rest of the image. By suspending videographic time, I delay the severed head long enough to draw the spectator's attention to other visual elements that would go unnoticed in the reception of this image as spectacle. Furthermore, as Azoulay suggests of photography, reading the injury inscribed in these images is a civic skill. By reading these images as photographs extracted from video, we take the images outside the control of the sovereign. Doing so opens a space in which to freely read the image and recognize the victims' presence, both in the original videographic event and in the current iteration of it made possible when my gaze meets the victims'. Following Azoulay's framework, viewing these images allows the victims to address us and for our gaze to recognize their political rights as citizens.[78] While the image cannot revive the victim, re-creating the mise-en-scène prior to the crime at least preserves their memory as a person and not a body in pieces whose syntax has been rearranged to communicate the power of the *necromáquina.* The authors of these videos, in turn, intend to prevent this by rendering the image of the victim illegible within a gore spectacle, thereby concealing the victim's gaze and maintaining the necropower of the sovereign.

Like the camp in Didi-Huberman's account, the visual logic of these videos (and of the *necromáquina* broadly speaking) relies on the unimaginability of the violence depicted. When a teenager hacks off a head with an axe and holds it up for the camera to zoom in, or when a chainsaw enters the frame to cut into a man's neck and sprays the lens with blood—when a spectator views such images on his screen, the same device on which he consumes Hollywood gore—the violence doesn't appear real. This sows terror and guarantees that the videos remain wholly within the domain of their authors. I propose that critical representation may still offer the possibility for resistance by taking these images seriously and displacing them from spaces of circulation and modes of spectatorship dominated by the *necromáquina.* Any attempt to do otherwise—to banish these videos, to close our eyes—would be to accept the concept of the unimaginability of the violence that supports the position of *necromáquina,* dependent as it is on the image that exceeds critical thought, and thus to cede their power to criminal politics. These images, to paraphrase Didi-Huberman, are sites of *possibility.* They allow us an opportunity to understand the visual operations from which the *necromáquina* derives power and to listen to the images themselves, which may betray the messages the perpetrators intend to communicate. Yet as Didi-Huberman is careful to note, we cannot ask too little or too much of such images: we may neither demand the whole truth nor reduce them to simulacra. Likewise, we cannot convert them to icons of violence or reduce them to purely objective documents of horror: they always carry a mark of subjectivity. The status of these videos lies in between these poles, and only the images themselves can tell us where they stand. We cannot know or experience where they come from. In that regard they are imperfect, but they are all that we have.

The Imperfect Image in the Eye of History

When news reports of decapitations flooded digital and print media alike, the images were often blurred, pixelated, or censored. Though headlines constantly appeared, announcing the presence of the severed head, the images themselves did not. While the images are reproduced and viewed online en masse, they are at the same time suppressed in public debate. In this removal they are mythologized and pushed to the darker corners of the internet. Yet they are still readily available, and continue to circulate on social media. One does not have to learn to navigate the dark web; a quick search will suffice to uncover this archive. The logic of videos such as these is that they are perpetually visible in the twenty-four-hour news discourse, but illegible because they cannot be seen or analyzed on their own terms, thus yielding all power the image might convey to the *necromáquina.* Despite the scale of its audiovisual production, the *necromáquina* thrives when these images are censored and converted into discursive phantoms: the public is aware that these gruesome videos exist somewhere in the cloud, and in the absence of any object, they inspire even more fear. It is in the interest of the *necromáquina* to oversaturate the population with references to these crimes and thus desensitize it so that these actors may continue to operate with impunity.

As I have discussed, the digital apparatus exerts control by incapacitating vision through ceaseless visual acceleration and a homogenization of visual experience. We consume too many images to adequately process them. Spectators are inundated and overstimulated. By reintroducing the temporality of the still image to our reading of these videos, we might begin to look in another way. Rather than economize our attention to maximize visual consumption—viewing the video uncritically and moving on to the next spectacle—stopping to meditate on a single image within it is already an act of resistance, however small. And doing so will allow me to reflect on the role of space and landscape in these images.

Having considered these videos from the perspective of the victim and spectator, I turn now to the third actor involved: the perpetrator. Who is behind the camera here? Where are they? Under what conditions are these videos produced? These documents are imperfect in part because the videos are subjective: recorded with handheld cameras, they only tell us a partial truth of the event because they pan, zoom in, zoom out, focus on some objects and not others. Images become blurred from

Figure 23. The ghostly form of the *necromáquina*. Untitled decapitation video, author unknown, undated, *El Blog del Narco*.

Figure 24. The majestic Mexican landscape. *Pueblerina,* dir. Emilio Fernández, 1949.

Figure 25. The ruins of the national landscape. Untitled decapitation video, author unknown, undated, *El Blog del Narco.*

an unsteady hand, or framing is disrupted as the camera is jostled in the havoc of the scene. The images may be out of focus or pixelated, yet such imperfections do not disqualify their capacity to speak. To the contrary, I wish to highlight their imperfect character here because they reveal much both about the event of beheading and the *necromáquina* more broadly.[79] The blurred image of a group of masked men dressed in military uniform expresses the uncertainties that are proper to this conflict (Figure 23). This fuzziness captures the imprecise borders between State and criminal actors that come to define the structure of the *necromáquina*. We are left wondering whom this figure might represent: the military, a paramilitary force, the police, or a cartel. A perfect (high-resolution) image could not represent this effect of doubt and thus, paradoxically, would not be as accurate a document.

An important formal element in many of the videos, as evidenced in Figure 23 and Figure 25, is the blurring of the image. While this effect is, in practical terms, a condition of the digital apparatus captured on cheap cameras amid much commotion, it also inscribes in the image the condition of the *necromáquina* as an ambiguous actor in Mexican politics that blurs institutions and legality. A similar effect of obstruction is created when the finger of the image's author enters the frame (Figure 25). This partially blocks the victim's corpse and impedes the spectator from perceiving the victim. Critics might dismiss the blurred or obstructed image as evidence of the document's imperfection and, thus, deny its ability to bear witness to the events. Yet these imperfections are themselves meaningful in communicating the horror of the historic moment.[80] The blurred image and the incursion of the videographer in the frame—such as when, in the panic of the moment, a finger covers the lens—remind us who is behind this horror. These imperfections represent moments when the slick propaganda machine of the *necromáquina* breaks down and the spectator catches a glimpse of the human cruelty behind the images.

These videos are filmed in a variety of spaces: often outdoors, in daylight, but also in interiors (in basements, garages, or warehouses) and at night. The emphasis on rural locales, however, communicates a deliberately masculinized primitive violence that is performed for the cameras.[81] What these settings have in common is a negation of landscape as place or agent. They are shot in unremarkable locations, with no interaction between the action and its immediate environment. These are "foreclosed or trivialized images of rurality" following "the exhaustion of landscape" in contemporary media.[82] They could take place anywhere. We are never given an image devoid of actors; the landscape itself never takes on agency. The tradition of the monumental landscape in Mexican cinema—best exemplified in the classic cinematography of Gabriel Figueroa (Figure 24)—contributed to the institutionalization of the revolution by representing the grandness of the Mexican nation. In contrast, here we have the image of a dilapidated landscape drained of any grandeur. In the videos there is no interaction with the environment; there is no concept of place in these recordings. The violence exhibited before the camera thus occurs in non-places.

The lack of landscape in the videos also visualizes the spatial reconfiguration proper to image production and violence in Global War.[83] The decapitation video is suddenly everywhere all at once: shot in rural Mexico, hosted on a server abroad, streamed to a device in the United States. This is the global digital infrastructure on which the *necromáquina* relies. Despite the parallels with Didi-Huberman's analysis of the Shoah, it bears mentioning that we are no longer in the camp. There is no need to construct a darkroom. These videos, following a neoliberal logic, take advantage of the media infrastructure already in place for commercial use via YouTube and other streaming platforms in a paramilitarization of re-creation. The erasure of modern spatiality that digital apparatus implies parallels other deterritorializing processes in the wake of globalization. When present, physical infrastructure is crumbling in these images (Figure 25). If we think of these digital productions as amateur movies, we must then consider them in the postcinematic landscape amid the dispersion of audiovisual production and the dismemberment of the traditional studio system. These recordings are emblematic of the postcinematic apparatus that has replaced the traditional studio system and streamlined production and distribution over digital networks.

In previous chapters I have traced my concept of the visual guillotine to account for the political force of the cinematic cut. The corpus of films I have organized while elaborating this argument have seized on the power of montage and the close-up to stir political affect, theorize the dehumanizing forces of both cinema and industrial capital, and interrogate the spectator's role in these processes. In this chapter I have shifted the tense of this argument from the past to the present perfect. The politics of the visual guillotine have transformed; the cinematic cut has been appropriated by reactionary forces. I have attempted to chronicle a history of this present, registering the disaster without empowering its agents. Beyond documentation, I have sought to identify and disarm the aesthetic practices of these videos so as to open a critical discourse. My strategy has been not to reproduce these videos but to fragment them. These interventions hope to produce flashes of insight into the ongoing conflict and its audiovisual politics. In adapting this unconventional approach, my aim has been "to brush history against the grain."[84] Put differently, my intention has been to contradict the framing of these images by the *necromáquina* to undo their audiovisual practice through a countermontage of my own. The next chapter continues this reflection on the potential to reclaim the radical politics of the cut by examining the *contramáquinas* proposed by Mexican filmmakers who have seen the politics of moving images weaponized in this ongoing conflict.

4

CONTRAMÁQUINAS
THE VISUAL GUILLOTINE AND THE CRISIS OF CINEMATIC POLITICS

In Mexico, the return of the severed head to political aesthetics reflects the transformation of sovereignty and the mutation of the moving image in the present. The decapitation videos discussed in the previous chapter capture the logic of the visual guillotine as I have defined it throughout this book. These gruesome amateur productions relate formal elements of the cut to the violence of decapitation by staging beheadings using close-ups and splices. In their manipulation of the corpse, which is fragmented into syntagmatic units and rearranged according to a new symbolic grammar, what Rossana Reguillo terms the *necromáquina* resuscitates the relation between cutting bodies and cutting film first established by Thomas Edison, Georges Méliès, and Lev Kuleshov. The decapitation video weaponizes the visual guillotine and appropriates the affective force of the cinematic cut. As I discuss in chapters 1 and 2, the cinematic cut that decapitates the body in the frame or dismembers the body of the film in editing gives form to politics. The act of cutting, the effects of the cut on perception, and the image of the dismembered body produced in the process all release political intensities. In the postcinematic present, the decapitation video displaces the politics of the cinematic cut from the tradition of radical cinema to the *necromáquina*.

In this chapter I interrogate audiovisual politics in contemporary Mexico by surveying responses to the decapitation video across narrative, documentary, and experimental modes. By appropriating the visceral politics of the cinematic cut, the *necromáquina* interpellates filmmakers and forces them to reevaluate the radical legacy of this visual guillotine. A strategy that once lay at the heart of avant-garde cinema is not only neutralized by one of the most violent and advanced forms of contemporary capitalism, it is also turned against filmmakers who oppose the *necromáquina*'s audiovisual regime. By considering the work of Carlos Reygadas, Amat Escalante, Everardo González, and Colectivo Los Ingrávidos, I demonstrate how these filmmakers identify the operation of the visual guillotine in the narco-conflict. Through their attention to audiovisual form, especially the relation between cutting images and cutting bodies in the context of brutal violence, these works decode the formal logic of the decapitation video. These materials frame such terrifying imagery not as an act of barbarism but as cinematic crimes that appropriate the visual guillotine in the service of a sinister politics. Because the culture industry and the Mexican security state continue to rely on a political narrative that centers the *necromáquina*'s violence as primitive and exceptional, it is difficult to understate the political importance of this critical gesture. By unveiling the performative primitivism that surrounds the decapitation video, these meditations on the weaponization of the visual guillotine aspire to what Reguillo terms a *contramáquina.* If the *necromáquina* functions as an apparatus that converts symbolic violence and the methodical reproduction of severed heads into an engine of capital, as discussed in chapter 3, then by identifying the cinematic logic behind these processes the *contramáquina* "deciphers a power that is based in the work of violence and the systematic production of horror."[1] In other words, the filmmakers analyzed in this chapter demonstrate that the shocking violence of the decapitation video is not exceptional. Rather, it appropriates a violence that is already inscribed within the audiovisual apparatus—what I have termed the visual guillotine—and pushes it to a new political register.

The decapitation video, and filmmakers' responses to its weaponization of the cinematic cut, arise from the transformation of audiovisual politics following the eclipse of cinema's commitment to the *pueblo.* In the twentieth century, Mexico's postrevolutionary state invested heavily in its national film industry. Beginning with the Golden Age of Mexican cinema of the 1930s and 1940s, cinematic politics centered on the imagination of the national subject through the construction of *mexicanidad*. Mexican cinema's commitment to popular representation continued throughout the 1950s and 1960s, reaching a breaking point with the 1968 massacre at Tlatelolco. Funded by the government of Luis Echeverría (1970–76), the auteurist New Mexican Cinema reacted to this political crisis with a melancholic revision of the national subject. Simultaneously, countercultural filmmakers and collectives experimenting with small-gauge cinema imagined utopian national communities that might replace the repressive Partido Revolucionario Institucional, which had produced the cinematic nationalism of previous decades. In sum, Mexican cinema from the 1930s to the 1970s created and then reimagined the national subject. Yet the hegemonic representation of the popular lost its political currency in the economic and political model of neoliberalism.[2] The neoliberal policies enacted in the 1980s weakened the nation-state and provoked a crisis in this modern political vocabulary. This model intensified in the wake of NAFTA, leading to a decline of the Mexican film industry in the 1990s. Production and exhibition infrastructures, long bolstered by the state in the service of cultural nationalism, withered with the privatization of culture.

Following the suspension of modern forms of sovereignty and the subjugation of the political to the extreme violence of narco-capitalism, the decapitation video represents the reconfiguration of audiovisual politics after the eclipse of cinema's pact with the *pueblo*. Furthermore, in the decapitation video we witness the transformation of the visual guillotine's political affect. As we saw previously, the New Latin American Cinema had understood revolution as the expression of popular sovereignty in response to neocolonial oppression. Through their treatment of montage and the close-up, radical filmmakers seized on the cinematic cut to create revolutionary subjects. Such strategies are no longer available to filmmakers. The *necromáquina* challenges the state and popular sovereignty as the organizing forces of politics. Nonetheless, the consolidation of power in the *necromáquina* does not eliminate the role of the state; furthermore, certain parallels still exist between modern and contemporary models of sovereignty. Sovereignty continues to be employed in the service of capitalism, as the *necromáquina* exists to facilitate the accumulation of capital through violence. Similarly, the moving-image apparatus continues to serve both capital and ideology by creating audiovisual subjects. What changes, however, is that this visual guillotine no longer functions as a form of critique or a representation of the *pueblo*. Rather than move spectators to take up political struggle, the political affect of the cut in the decapitation video is dominated by what Adriana Cavarero calls horrorism. Cavarero distinguishes horror from terror by defining the latter in terms of an impulse to mobility. Synonymous with fear, terror acts on the body of the witness by moving them to flee. In contrast, horror suspends this survival instinct.[3] This shocking imagery no longer galvanizes the spectator as a political actor but instead paralyzes them so that the economic activity of the *necromáquina* may continue uninterrupted. The tools of critique previously available to radical filmmakers—namely, the cinematic cut—have now become subsumed within a new repressive apparatus that creates subjects through the affective force of the visual guillotine.

Theories of cinematic politics have long interrogated the ideological processes of subject formation implicit in moving-image spectatorship. Perhaps the most prominent example, apparatus theory critiqued cinema's role in the reproduction of ideology, which served both capital as well as the state that ensures favorable conditions for capitalism. Under the banner of political modernism, theorists and filmmakers examined how ideology determined the material and formal elements of film, from the spatial arrangement of the projection to the structuring of audiovisual narrative through the classical Hollywood style. Furthermore, cinematic form and materiality conditioned the spectator as an ideological subject. The semiotic analysis and audiovisual disturbance of the political and aesthetic system inscribed within the apparatus, intended to disrupt this process of subjectivization, became the objective of political filmmaking and film theory.

The political modernism of apparatus theory has receded significantly since its heyday in the 1970s, though its legacy survives in our postcinematic times, as we will see later in this chapter. Concerns with the politics of spectatorship have shifted toward new theoretical frameworks. Beginning in the 1990s, affect theory began to displace the ideological critique at the heart of apparatus theory to emphasize the spectator's embodied response to the moving image instead. This continued well into the twenty-first century, when the proliferation of documentary images of graphic violence in the wake of 9/11 and the war on terror drew attention to the visceral politics of visual culture. In this decade, European filmmakers began to address the proliferation of screen violence through the transgressive aesthetics associated with the new extremity. As we will see, this transnational aesthetic blends cinematic modernism with shocking images that engage lowbrow body genres such as porn, gore, and melodrama. Critical responses to new extremity have privileged affect theory to explore the spectator's position in the audiovisual landscape of our necropolitical present, dominated as it is by images of horrifying violence. By centering the audience's visceral response, accounts of cinematic affect in the new extremity reject the ideology critique of political modernism, which privileged semiotic analysis over the emotional intensity of moving images.[4] In contrast to the political semiotics of previous generations, they propose an ethics of spectatorship that examines the affective bonds tying the spectatorial self to the projected other.[5] The ethical concerns that mark much work in theories of cinematic affect nonetheless risk two blind spots. On one hand, I join Eugenie Brinkema in her critique of affect theory's dismissal of the formal rigor of apparatus theory and find her formalist account of affect generative for advancing my concept of the visual guillotine.[6] On the other, both new extremity and the theories of cinematic affect that have arisen from it participate in a wider ethical turn that risks displacing the category of politics.[7] Examining the responses to the weaponization of the moving image by Mexican filmmakers in this chapter, I synthesize the preoccupation with the spectator's embodied response in affect theory—and in particular the visceral politics of violent imagery explored by new extremity—with the formalist treatment of affect in Brinkema's critique.

This intersection of apparatus theory and affect theory helps clarify the political function of the visual guillotine in the *necromáquina*. In this context, the politics of the decapitation video center on the transformation of the spectator into a necropolitical subject through post-cinematic form and affect. These images reconfigure the cinematic cut to serve an apparatus of horrorism. Rather than produce revolutionary subjects, this *dispositif* petrifies the public in horror to guarantee the uninterrupted flow of transnational narco-capital. The spectator metaphorically loses his head, and in this way the *necromáquina* creates what I term "acephalous subjects." The *necromáquina* appropriates the visual guillotine—the violence implicit in the cinematic cut—to govern by affect. Therefore, a response to this transformation of cinematic politics—in other words, a *contramáquina*—requires filmmakers to revive debates familiar to apparatus theory and integrate modernist formalism with accounts of postcinematic affect.

The synthesis of affect and apparatus that I identify in the decapitation video and its *contramáquinas* reflects a broader instability of the conceptual vocabulary of politics and culture in the present. If the political and cinematic foundations of apparatus theory have lost their currency, why continue to insist on this modernist framework? The short answer is that a new model has yet to emerge. Addressing similar concerns in his account of politics and contemporary Latin American literature, Patrick Dove revives the Gramscian concept of *interregnum* to describe the conceptual indeterminacy that characterizes the cultural present. Dove's reflections on literary responses to the crisis of political aesthetics are helpful in orienting my discussion of cinematic politics. In an age when the old is dying and the new cannot be born, the modern definition of literature and the aesthetic ideologies born of it exhaust themselves.[8] Neoliberalism has eroded the modernist framework that defined literature and politics as autonomous spheres, having subordinated these categories to the logic of capital. As with cinema, literature no longer serves the state by representing the national subject. It is no longer an "exemplary form for the production of citizenship," but has instead been suspended in a state of uncertainty in which the economic, political, and cultural cannot be easily separated.[9] Of course, neither literature nor sovereignty have disappeared in the twenty-first century. Dove's analysis traces the returns, repetitions, and reenactment of these concepts in the present to understand the workings of power when a new order has yet to emerge. The gaps that remain in our political and aesthetic vocabulary have yet to be filled. There is no clean break between modernist definitions of cinema, literature, or sovereignty and their postautonomous forms. Instead, we witness a series of mutations. It remains the work of the critic to parse these materials and determine what remains of modern aesthetics and politics, and how these discourses have transformed in this period of interregnum.

Acephalous Subjects

Carlos Reygadas's *Post Tenebras Lux* (2012) sparked polemic from the moment of its premier in competition at the Cannes Film Festival.

Reception was immediately polarized. While the film was met with boos and negative reviews, the jury bestowed upon Reygadas its award for Best Director. The mixed response to the film can be credited in no small part to its power to agitate the spectator. Reygadas has long courted controversy. From *Japón* (2002) and *Batalla en el cielo* (*Battle in Heaven,* 2005) to *Stellet licht* (*Silent Light,* 2007), the filmmaker has woven together a modernist transcendental style with a commitment to transgression. With *Post Tenebras Lux,* Reygadas continues to explore the political and ethical concerns that emerge from this intersection of formalist precision and affective force. Given the shocking representations of violence and explicit sex in his early films, as well as his self-identification with the canon of modernist cinema through citation and intertextual reference, critics have inscribed Reygadas within the global aesthetic of new extremity.[10] Exemplified in the provocative work of Bruno Dumont, Catherine Breillat, Gaspar Noé, Michael Haneke, and Lars von Trier, the new extremity interrogates ethical and aesthetic concerns related to spectatorship, transgression, and representation. Crucially, critical accounts of the new extremity tie the rapid expansion of its aesthetics at the beginning of the twenty-first century to a cinematic reckoning with the severe violence that conditioned (audio)visual culture amid the war on terror.[11] While it risks overlooking the subtleties of his national references, this association with the global aesthetics of the new extremity is nevertheless productive to contextualize the *contramáquina* Reygadas elaborates in *Post Tenebras Lux.* As an elliptical response to the narco-conflict and its visual guillotine, the film exhibits the new extremity's reckoning with the politics of spectatorship in a context of weaponized screen violence.

Reygadas sets a dark tone in the film beginning with the opening sequence, in which he introduces themes of animality and primal violence. Throughout its seven minutes and forty-five seconds, the camera captures the transformation of light at dusk. The landscape begins with the sky glowing red at sunset. Wide-eyed and smiling, a blond girl named Ruth toddles toward a herd of livestock, eagerly cleaning herself off as she falls along the way. German shepherds bark as they circle the girl and the cattle. Ruth's expression turns cautious as she approaches. Her face fills the center of the frame, registering her growing anxiety. Ruth's fair complexion and blond hair reflect the light of dusk and draw the spectator's gaze. The scene cuts to a medium-length shot of a black cow with menacing horns standing next to its calf. In the corner of the subsequent shot a bull mounts another cow, which flees. As the moments pass, the spectator watches as the sky slowly transforms from its previous orange-red hue to a deep purple as night falls. The camera pans over the scene, with Ruth's small figure occupying the middle ground while horses stampede behind her. Reygadas cuts back to a close-up of Ruth surrounded by the dogs, seemingly protected (Figure 26). Yet these German shepherds and pit bulls appear equally menacing; a pack quickly surrounds a horse, which attempts to kick them as it is driven off. The sequence intermittently cuts to a handheld camera, shot from a low angle to capture Ruth's gaze as the dogs bark and whirl around her. "No, perritos!," she exclaims, as the animals come too close. After the fourth minute of the sequence, the sky appears black. Night has fallen, and thunder can be heard in the distance. The spectator realizes that the pastoral landscape from the beginning of the scene has within minutes transformed into a menacing and dangerous space. "Papi?," Ruth asks. "Casa?" Reygadas now cuts to the film's title, which appears word by word against the black sky, separated amid flashes of lightning. Though

Figure 26. The innocent and vulnerable face that anticipates a narrative of cinematic defacement. *Post Tenebras Lux*, dir. Carlos Reygadas, 2012.

it begins with this idyllic sequence, *Post Tenebras Lux* ends with a disturbing scene of self-decapitation. Just as the atmosphere surrounding Ruth quickly turns threatening, this illuminated face eventually leads us to a severed head. By the end of the film, the face will be destroyed. In this narrative of cinematic defacement, Reygadas traces the effects of the *necromáquina* on visual culture.

The film's title sequence introduces the threat of primal violence and engages the charge of primitivism that characterizes discourses on violence in Mexico today. Simultaneously, it introduces metacinematic concerns. At once a reference to the Book of Job, the film's title, which translates as *Light After Darkness,* is also a cinematic metaphor that refers to the darkness of the movie theater and the light of projection. Reygadas begins his film interpellating the audience, exposing its presence in the world of animalistic violence represented throughout. Throughout *Post Tenebras Lux,* Reygadas explores the limits of cinematic production and the role of the spectator in Mexico today, reflecting on his own position as filmmaker as well. In this scene, the filmmaker identifies the spectator with the child: bourgeois, of European appearance, naive, innocent to the dangers that surround her, and above all out of place in this naturalistic state of exception.[12] Reygadas himself might best be identified with the dogs. The filmmaker is our guardian as we enter the dark and menacing space of *Post Tenebras Lux,* yet like these animals, Reygadas can also make us uncomfortable. Throughout the remainder of the film, he guides the audience through a sequence of images that abandons causal narrative. Reygadas's focus on a bourgeois Mexican family organizes these oneiric associations. The patriarch, Juan, lives on an estate in rural Mexico and experiences marital trouble. The film offers glimpses of Juan's intimate life with his wife, Natalia, as the two visit a French bathhouse and engage in group sex. Back in Mexico, Juan attends a meeting of an informal alcoholics anonymous group with one of his employees, El Siete. While Juan confesses to a pornography addiction, El Siete admits that he has struggled with drug abuse. This relationship later turns violent when Juan discovers El Siete robbing his home, presumably to feed his drug habit. El Siete shoots Juan and flees, eventually learning from Juan's young daughter Ruth that he has killed her father. After hearing the news, Juan walks into a field and beheads himself.

Following the interpellation of the audience in the opening scene, *Post Tenebras Lux* returns to questions of spectatorship in the bathhouse sequence. Here, Reygadas centers his gaze on a visually dismembered female body in an atmosphere charged with sexual violence and voyeurism. The transition to the image is abrupt: from a conversation on Russian literature in a restaurant, Reygadas cuts to the image of a female nude decapitated by the frame. Immediately preceding this shot, a man in a dark suit, smoking a cigar, faces the camera and remarks hollowly, "Truth be told, I prefer Dostoevsky. Tolstoy is too intense, but honestly Chekhov is the greatest. Or are you only reading contemporary writers?" This juxtaposition of satirical bourgeois pretension—with which we might identify Reygadas's cosmopolitan audience—and sexual baseness further serves to unnerve the spectator. This female body is motionless and takes on the aspect of a cadaver, bathed in a red light that evokes blood (Figure 27). The soundtrack, which never coincides with action on-screen, reinforces the Bataillean atmosphere of violent sexual transgression as screams of pain blend with cries of sexual pleasure. In the absence of language, the only comprehensible phrase, the imperative "Suck him off!," reinforces the voyeurism and sexual aggression present in the mise-en-scène. From the image of the beheaded nude Reygadas cuts to a series of men observing public sex in the bathhouse. With a steady camera, we see this spectator's eyes follow a naked body that passes in front of him. In the subsequent shot, a man appears from the waist up, staring directly at the camera. Behind him a series of men, blurred by the steam of the baths, stare off at a sex act that we can only hear. More reclining nudes are depicted until the camera moves out to a medium-length take of the entire room that shows a small crowd of nude spectators sitting patiently.

The bathhouse becomes a metaphor for the cinema in which the spectator has been sitting, consuming images of sexualized violence. On-screen, the anonymous bodies are seated in darkness, observing—motionless—the transgressions that surround them. The scene reflects viewers' own condition of spectatorship and complicity in the visual discourse of violence as consumers of macabre images. This critique of visual pleasure reiterates classic theories of spectatorship. Laura Mulvey's account of the apparatus is pertinent here given the traditional interpretation of decapitation as castration within psychoanalysis. Mulvey argues,

Figure 27. Visual pleasure and the decapitated female form. *Post Tenebras Lux,* dir. Carlos Reygadas, 2012.

"An idea of woman stands as linchpin to the [cinematic] system: it is her lack that produces the phallus as a symbolic presence, it is her desire to make good the lack that the phallus signifies."[13] In the image of the decapitated nude, we can interpret the beheaded body along psychoanalytic lines; it is representative of the woman's castration, the lack of her subjectivity in a sexually hostile environment. However, Reygadas's critique goes beyond psychoanalysis; it is political and cinematic commentary—by means of a severed head—on the representation of violence in Mexico today. The bathhouse sequence criticizes representations of the *necromáquina* in the media, which create a spectacle of violence. Again, the filmmaker interpellates the spectator. Reygadas denounces—or at least exposes—the scopophilic impulse of the spectator, who consumes violent media and has been enjoying similarly disturbing images throughout the film.

Reygadas returns to the theme of decapitation at the end of *Post Tenebras Lux.* The sequence begins with a body, shot from the waist down, walking through a clearing toward a forest. The field resembles the one through which little Ruth ran in the film's opening sequence. Reygadas *cuts* to a close-up of the side of the man's head, with his ear centered on-screen, bobbing up and down as the body continues in motion. *Cut* next to the opposite side of the body, shot from the waist down as before. The man's arm swings from one side of the frame to the other like a pendulum, reminding the spectator of the cinematic temporality Reygadas constructs here through montage. *Cut* again to the front of the torso from the stomach down, walking toward the camera. Suddenly the figure stops, and the camera holds steady. The spectator can observe that the lowest button is missing from the man's shirt. Perhaps here Reygadas ominously foreshadows the man's missing head; the slit of the buttonhole is evocative of the orifice created by his impending decapitation. Throughout the duration of the shot, the spectator's mind wanders. The shape of the round button that is enlarged through this decapitating close-up further evokes a series of cinematic associations: the roundness of the camera-eye, the film reel, the projector's wheel, the severed head.

Abandoning the shot, the camera cuts to a landscape of the countryside at dusk. The time and location evoke the opening sequence, suggesting a circular logic of violence in Mexico today. Reygadas cuts back to the man from the front, identifying him as El Siete, and then to a medium shot from behind so that his entire body is visible in the frame. Both shots pause at length to meditate on his body. Suddenly, in silence, the man raises his arms to his head. Bending his neck toward the ground, he fidgets. As we hear a grunt rising in a crescendo, the man raises his shoulders, lifts his arms, and beheads himself. In an act that mimics Georges Méliès's fantastic self-decapitations, the severed head flies upward and falls to the ground with an audible thud. Blood gushes from El Siete's neck onto the grass, while the roll of thunder is heard. Reygadas holds this shot for over a minute. The only visible movement in this long take comes from the rain that begins to fall. After it pools on the ground, the spectator slowly realizes that it is raining blood. Reygadas then cuts to other shots of the field where the blood has collected in large puddles; a cow approaches one and begins to drink.

As a filmmaker, Reygadas has been identified with a protracted temporality that permits critical reflection and resists the accelerationism characteristic of our era of neoliberal capital. Consequently, the fact that he employs a comparatively fast-paced editing as he cuts from one part of El Siete's body to the next warrants attention. In the fragmentation of the body that anticipates this self-decapitation, the filmmaker reverts to the foundations of cinema in Lev Kuleshov's experiments with montage. As a theorist and filmmaker, Kuleshov's contribution to cinema lies in his discovery that cinematic signification depends not on representation but on the ordering of the image through editing. Kuleshov recounts:

> By montage alone we were able to depict the girl, just as in nature, but in actuality she did not exist, because we shot the lips of one woman, the legs of another, the back of a third, and the eyes of a fourth. We spliced the pieces together in a predetermined relationship and created a totally new person, still retaining the complete reality of the material. This particular example likewise demonstrated that the entire power of cinematic effect is in montage.[14]

I am not suggesting that Reygadas's editing performs a similar operation whereby he constructs a fictitious body from several real ones. However, in his treatment of El Siete, Reygadas returns to the relation between the dismembered body and montage that has been present since cinema's infancy. In so doing, he does not just foreshadow another operation of fragmentation—the decapitation at the climax of the scene—but underscores its cinematic character. Reygadas's language suggests that the decapitations that overshadow audiovisual politics in Mexico today are themselves cinematic crimes.

The pools of blood that flood the landscape following El Siete's decapitation invoke the *necromáquina*'s political grip on Mexico. Furthermore, the juxtaposition of Reygadas's formalist meditation on the cinematic body in pieces and El Siete's spectacular beheading signal the relationship between cutting images and cutting bodies that the decapitation video weaponizes. These references may not be immediately apparent to his international audience, yet Reygadas himself asserts that *Post Tenebras Lux* interrogates the visual culture of Mexico's narco-violence. When asked by Mexican critic Fernanda Solórzano if he believed that the film's polarized reaction may be attributed to the complexity of its national references, Reygadas reflects on the clarity of his allusions and ultimately stands behind them: "The theme of decapitation, for example, is very close to us [Mexicans], but not necessarily for everyone else. On the other hand, any moderately informed person would know that decapitation is something unique to Mexico, just as any Mexican will know that in Japan someone may commit *seppuku.*"[15] Though this sequence of *Post Tenebras Lux* opens a dialogue with the severed head in Mexico today, Reygadas estranges the scene of violence depicted in popular media.

While *Post Tenebras Lux* shuns the stereotypes that the culture industry has associated with narco-violence, its most striking defamiliarization of the *necromáquina* emerges from the reflexive character of this beheading. This act references the cinematic crimes and the affective governmentality of necropolitics. That El Siete learns of the consequences of his drug-related violence immediately prior to this sequence suggests that the loss of his head represents an affective response to his actions. In other words, this self-decapitation represents the horrorism that affects both actors and spectators of the *necromáquina.* The decapitation video's weaponization of the visual guillotine plays an important role in the creation of such acephalous subjects. Overwhelmed by affect, they are interpellated by the second state, whose horrorism continues to guarantee optimal conditions for capital.

To account for the *necromáquina*'s political manipulation of affect, I invoke the transcendental figure of the *acéphale* that Georges Bataille embraced in opposition to fascism.[16] Between 1936 and 1939, Bataille proposed the headless figure of the *acéphale* as the organizing force of the avant-garde journal and secret society of the same name. Famously illustrated by Georges Masson in *Acéphale*'s first issue, the decapitated man stands with arms and legs outstretched. Clutching a dagger in one hand and a flaming heart in the other, a skull covers his genitals. Through the metaphor of decapitation, this mythic figure represents humanity's liberation from the shackles of enlightenment rationality. In a manifesto published in the first issue of *Acéphale,* Bataille proclaims, "Man will escape his head like a condemned man escaping from prison."[17] The acephalous subject's headlessness thus symbolizes a Bataillean transcendence of reason that has been weaponized by the sinister politics of the *necromáquina.* Reygadas's *contramáquina* thus signals both the perversion of the visual guillotine and the radical potential of its affective force within the narco-conflict. El Siete literally loses his head when confronted with the consequences of his own irrational violence. As a subject of the *necromáquina,* his position in a system of drug-fueled horrorism paralyzes him.

Another Mexican filmmaker and Reygadas's protégé, Mexican filmmaker Amat Escalante, similarly examines the status of the acephalous subject in his third feature, *Heli* (2013). A year after the success of *Post Tenebras Lux* at Cannes, Escalante also received the festival's award for Best Director while polarizing critics with his meditation on the *necromáquina.* Yet while audiences largely criticized Reygadas for the obscurity of his modernist style, Escalante provoked controversy for the brutal realism with which he depicts explicit violence. Grounded in a critique of the spectacularized representations of narco-violence in the press, negative reviews nevertheless mistook this unembellished style for morbid fascination. As in the case of Reygadas, critics have associated the explicit treatment of violence throughout Escalante's filmography with the new extremity. Indeed, the polemic provoked by *Heli* resembles those that followed many other films affiliated with this global aesthetic. Critics objected to the filmmaker's decision to oblige the spectator to view such explicit violence, going so far as to dismiss the film as "one of those exploitation films that sells its violent goods with art cinema pretension."[18] Yet *Heli* seeks to decode the uncritical representations of the *necromáquina* that are ubiquitous in the culture industry and reinforce its horrorist governmentality.

Unlike Reygadas, Escalante's narrative approaches the topic of narco-violence directly. Heli lives outside Guanajuato with his father, his twelve-year-old sister, Estela, his wife, Sabrina, and his infant son. Both Heli and his father work in the nearby auto parts plant, while Estela often skips school to spend time with her older boyfriend, Beto, an adolescent training at a local police academy. In a plan to fund their marriage and escape from the bleak landscape of rural Guanajuato, Beto steals a few packages of cocaine that were likely withheld by his commander during a seizure by the police. Needing a safe location to hide the stolen drugs, Beto stashes the packages in a cistern on the roof of Estela's home. Heli discovers them the next day after they clog the plumbing and—panicked—discards them. Not long after, the police break down the door to Heli's home, kill his father, and kidnap him and Estela. In the film's most controversial scene, Heli and Beto are then tortured gruesomely. These images capture the brutal violence committed by the *necromáquina* without recurring to spectacle and exhibit the structure of the audiovisual apparatus on which it relies. During the torture, Escalante stages a mise en abyme when a boy observing the violence with titillation reaches for his phone and begins recording a video that will subsequently circulate online. By exhibiting the *necromáquina*'s process of audiovisual production, *Heli* overcomes the voyeuristic spectacle of torture porn and instead proposes a *contramáquina* that visualizes the production of the acephalous subject.

Following the graphic torture scene, the film exhibits Heli's own interpellation within this process of subjectivization. Escalante begins with the image of Heli sitting on the couch and watching television. The camera is located behind him so that only his head is visible in the foreground while an old cartoon plays on the television. We see a tiger stalk Mickey Mouse and lick its lips, ready to pounce. These images ironically invoke the trivialization and spectacularization of violence in popular media. The scene then cuts to an image of Heli from the front, from the perspective of the television. Shot from just below his shoulders, he wears a neck brace that serves as a visual index of the violence inflicted on his body. In this image, Heli is figuratively decapitated, his head severed from his body by this prosthesis (Figure 28). Like the victim of a decapitation video, he sits motionless, facing the camera with a blank stare. Escalante holds this shot. Heli continues to channel surf until he suddenly stops and sits up, his head still immobile. The voice of a newscaster can be heard: "Three severed heads were found abandoned in the municipality of Piedra Parada, placed on the hood of their own patrol vehicle." After holding the camera on Heli's expressionless face, Escalante cuts to a close-up of the television (Figure 29). The news broadcast displays the heads from different angles as the voice continues: "According to authorities, the macabre scene could be a settling of scores between criminal organizations. At the moment, the identity of the severed heads is unknown." In the center of the image the severed head of Beto's commander, who originally stole the drugs and whom we presume was beheaded by the *necromáquina* for failing to have delivered the shipment to a client, rests on his policeman's pickup truck. The image then cuts back to Heli, who sits still in his prosthesis.

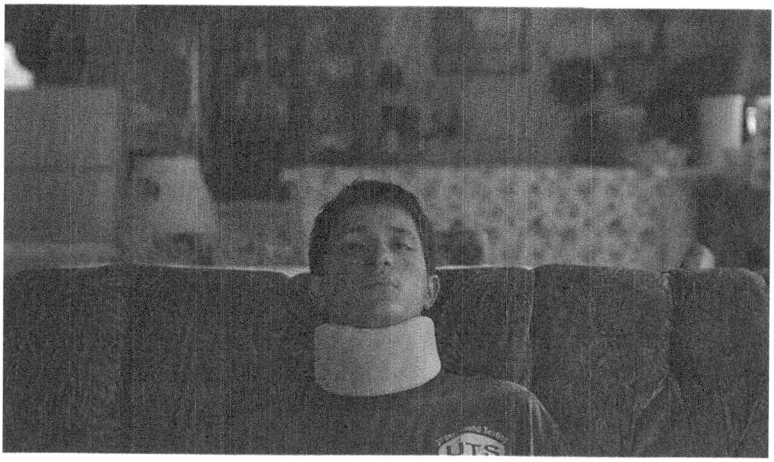

Figure 28. Shot: the acephalous spectator. *Heli,* dir. Amat Escalante, 2013.

Figure 29. Countershot: the severed heads of Heli's kidnappers in close-up. *Heli,* dir. Amat Escalante, 2013.

The scene stages the postcinematic structure of the horrorist apparatus and represents Heli's interpellation as an acephalous subject. Formally, this occurs through a conventional shot/countershot. Through this juxtaposition of close-ups, Heli's visually severed head mirrors the images on-screen. This strategy suggests a macabre mutation of the semiotic process of identification in cinema. Apparatus theory scrutinized how cinema produced subjects by suturing them into filmic narrative. Despite the cinematic and political mutations that have taken place since such theories were first elaborated, the concept of audiovisual identification is still helpful for understanding the production of acephalous subjects in the *necromáquina*'s audiovisual apparatus. The horrorism which grounds its structure of power depends on the spectator's identification with the victim's severed head. With the knowledge that they too could suffer this fate if they interfered in its operations, the public enters a state of political paralysis. The spectator is overwhelmed by horrorist affect and loses their head. Escalante's staging of this subjectivization draws attention to the role of audiovisual technology and cinematic form in the process. The image is mediated through a precarious television: taped up, with wires dangling, and flanked by cheap DVDs. Heli's use of the television remote draws our attention to this detail even further. The scene thus triangulates the relation between the media apparatus, the (figuratively) severed head of the spectator, and the severed head of the victim.

Documentary Defacement

On the evening of September 26, 2014, Julio César Mondragón survived the initial attack on a caravan of buses carrying a group of students from the Escuela Rául Isidro Burgos in Ayotzinapa to a protest. Overcome by fear, Mondragón fled the scene but did not survive the night. His corpse appeared the next morning horribly disfigured, and photographs of his mutilated corpse went viral on social media. Though unknown, the photograph's author is present in the image. The shadow of the photographer enters into the frame, leaving a mark of authorship. The ambiguous figure of the *necromáquina* is embodied quite literally: from this form alone, we cannot tell if the author of the crime was a member of the police, the military, or a criminal organization. The photographs show a body lying face up in the sun, arms stretched out, with its face and eyes removed. The gruesome act was carried out post mortem: a team of international forensic analysts determined the cause of death to be "the consequence of a traumatic brain injury caused by a blunt object," confirming a previous autopsy by local authorities.[19] The removal of Mondragón's face was, furthermore, the culmination of a lengthy process of torture, legible from the trauma recorded on the rest of his body. In the case of Mondragón, Reguillo observes, "that destruction of the face opens a new dimension of horror. It is no longer about annihilating you, but dispossessing you, stripping you of what is most important, the specific features of your face."[20] In chapter 1, I discuss the relation between the face and humanism in the context of the close-up. I contrast the face—as an exclusive expression of the human—with the head and its viscera. To deface is to dehumanize, as is undoubtedly the intent behind the literal defacement of Mondragón. The response to this horrific crime, as Reguillo suggests, was to reassert his face, and the faces of all the forty-three disappeared students, by carrying their photographic portraits in marches. Printed on white placards, these faces dominated protests around Mexico and the world, demanding accountability from then president Enrique Peña Nieto.[21] The response to the *necromáquina*'s dehumanization, therefore, is to reassert the humanity of the victims through faciality.

The *necromáquina* has adapted such horrifying tactics in order to foreclose attempts to undermine its power. The authors of these expressive crimes destroy the face so that it cannot be reasserted in a humanist political discourse. By defacing the corpse, the criminal authors seek to render these lives ungrievable. The restoration of the face will only be met with further defacement by the *necromáquina*. In *La libertad del diablo* (*Devil's Freedom*, 2017), documentary filmmaker Everardo González addresses this contemporary crisis of humanism by imagining new, posthuman forms of relation and grief that do not pass through the face. The film documents the process of defacement within gore capitalism and explores cinematic relations through affect.

The convention of the talking head, which relies on the face-to-face encounter, is complicated by the *necromáquina*'s processes of defacement. González turns the format on its head by structuring *La libertad* around a series of talking-head-style interviews with faceless subjects. These witnesses, which include victims, relatives of the disappeared, and perpetrators of violence ranging from assassins to corrupt military and police, give their testimony with their faces obscured by identical skin-toned masks.[22] While they erase the face, these masks are not entirely opaque. Throughout the interviews the masks mutate as the witnesses' tears bleed through the surface of the mask. This documentary strategy is also due to the practical need to obscure the faces of the witnesses to protect their anonymity and guarantee their safety. Through this intervention, González documents both the limits of the talking head and the process of defacement occurring in the *necromáquina.* However, the choice of mask is also an aesthetic and ethical strategy, as it opens the possibility of an embodied and posthuman relation that circumvents faciality. The masks featured in the film are designed to treat burn victims. These prostheses are unadorned and skin-toned, with openings for eyes, ears, and the mouth. Their color and fit—they cling tightly to the head and are a neutral beige tone meant to mimic skin—simulate a sort of nudity while also erasing the image of subjectivity present in the face. Crucially, the fabric of the mask is porous to allow the burn victim's skin to breathe as it heals. Given this materiality, tears filter through and stain the surface of the mask as witnesses cry during their testimony. The image illustrates the parallel between the screen and the mask as a site of mediation and projection. Rather than pass through the apparatus of the face, ethical relations are grounded in the body, its fluids, and the images of affects projected onto the tear-stained mask.[23]

A major referent for González's experimentation with documentary convention is Claude Lanzmann's *Shoah* (1985), famous for its rejection of archival footage and embrace of the talking-head interview. The filmmaker also travels with some of his interlocutors to the sites of the atrocities they describe. González finds inspiration in this dialectic between face and place in an effort to make the crimes present. Interspersed are brief performances featuring masked actors, filmed at locations that have been the site of the crimes described in the film: ruined buildings on the outskirts of Ciudad Juárez, a *maquiladora,* dusty back roads. This is another tactic borrowed from Lanzmann, who takes victims of the Holocaust back to the camp. In his critique of *Shoah,* Didi-Huberman suggests that this return to the site offsets the potential oversaturation of faces in the film for the spectator, "who leaves the screening overwhelmed by . . . so many faces."[24] González's decision to introduce the mask further implies a critique of the overabundance of faces in the traditional documentary form of the talking head.

By masking his documentary subjects with these medical prostheses, González highlights the *necromáquina*'s production of synthetic and posthuman bodies: the conversion of the face into a severed head in the act of decapitation and defacement. In one example, a man with a patch over one eye faces the camera while in the middle ground of the shot a woman standing in profile stares straight ahead. Both are shirtless; scars and burn marks are visible on the man's torso, and the camera lingers long enough for us to read this record of violence recorded on the body. The lighting is stark and the two figures stand in front of an ominous backlit screen. It is not immediately clear where they are, whether this is a set or the site of a previous crime. Nor does the spectator know who these figures are, whether they are the victims or perpetrators of violence. The man takes the position of a talking head: seated, facing the camera, with a screen behind him. González presents us with an abstraction of the familiar documentary trope. With this second skin covering the man's face, the spectator is unable to read his emotional expressions. Nonetheless, images begin to appear on the surface of the mask. Dark, amorphous forms slowly grow as tears dampen the material from underneath and filter through. While the mask frustrates the humanist identification of the face-to-face encounter, González replaces this with a posthuman ethics that relies on the communication of affect through the surface of the mask.

The spectator becomes frustrated by their inability to anchor the gaze in a face and similarly projects affect onto the mask. Discussing the importance of a subjective observer when interpreting images of suffering, Susan Sontag revisits the work of Kuleshov. In perhaps his most famous experiment with montage, the filmmaker juxtaposes long takes of an expressionless face with unremarkable images of food, a child, a dead woman, and others. The image of the man's face is the same; regardless of the subsequent shot, Kuleshov recycles the same facial close-up. Yet when questioned by the filmmaker and his assistants, the audience identified in the man's face different emotions corresponding to the shot that followed. When paired with a bowl of soup, the face communicated hunger; when followed by an image of a child, happiness; when juxtaposed with the dead woman, sadness. Viewers praised the actor's range of emotional expression when, in fact, each face was exactly the same. Kuleshov thus concluded that montage, not the contents of the individual image, evoked meaning for the spectator. The face was not a vehicle for communicating emotion; it was a syntagma that elicited meaning only in relation to other images. In her account, Sontag highlights the consequences that such subjective readings have on the truth value of violent images, their ability to communicate the pain of others. González makes this condition explicit. Eliminating the face, the mask converts the head into a surface that mediates the affects of the victim and the spectator. Citing Kuleshov, Sontag suggests a relativism regarding the expression of pain in the face. In her account, the face is not a window of the soul. The faces loses its expressive power; the viewer projects what she wishes to see or is conditioned to see by the photographer's framing.[25] Writing at the beginning of the twenty-first century, Sontag captures the crisis of humanism that is also apparent in González's decision to mask his social actors. The filmmaker responds to the degradation of the face both in cinema, as discussed in chapter 1, and in the contemporary violence he documents. These masks betray the face's condition as a screen, a site for the projection of affect by victim and spectator alike.

Faced with such debates surrounding the representation of pain and violence, González develops a strategy that reveals by obscuring. The mask allows the victim to speak without fear of retribution or shame. By eliminating the face, the filmmaker not only documents the destruction of faciality produced by decapitation and defacement in the *necromáquina,* but also opens a space of possibility. In one scene, a man describes his beating, torture, and rape at the hands of municipal police officers in Ciudad Juárez. Speaking slowly, pausing every so often, he admits at the end of the interview that he has never shared this experience. The anonymity of the mask makes the testimony of both victims and perpetrators possible. Furthermore, this prosthesis critiques the traditional documentary tactic of the talking head: the expert who lends authority to the film, or the victim who expresses her grief to the spectator. González implies that this convention is bankrupt and cannot adequately document the current conflict. Following González, we must be careful not to demand too much of faces. As Didi-Huberman reminds us in his critique of *Shoah,* an overreliance on the face through the talking head oversaturates the spectator with this image. *La libertad del diablo* suggests that in conventional documentaries the talking head likewise destroys the face. Its composition is static, compulsively repeated. The talking head typifies and industrializes the face in contemporary media.

By figuratively defacing the witnesses, the masks document the function of the *necromáquina,* which compulsively (re)produces severed heads. González captures this in one of the performances included in the documentary. In this scene, a group of masked men and women work silently in a *maquiladora*. Seated at sewing machines, they manufacture clothing. Though we do not see the products of their labor, there is an immediate connection between the fabric of the mask worn by each worker and the spinning cloth of the sewing machines. The image implies that these workers are manufacturing more masks, more faceless heads. Giuliana Bruno's theory of materiality and affect is especially relevant to understanding González's use of the mask. Addressing the material and haptic qualities of the surface as opposed to the visuality of the image, Bruno reminds us that film theory begins with the recognition, by Balázs, that the face is a surface. Yet Bruno wishes to go beyond this well-trodden theory of faciality in media. As a surface, the face pertains to the body. It is haptic. Its expressions are, thus, not always visual: they may be material as well. Such a theory allows us to look for expressions of affect that precede the subjective face and initiate an ethical

Figure 30. The filtering of affect through the mask. *La libertad del diablo,* dir. Everardo González, 2017.

encounter grounded in the body. This is an important strategy for González's context of contemporary Mexico. I therefore understand his adoption of the mask in the interviews as a strategy to subvert the *necromáquina*'s deliberate eradication of the face, its conversion into a severed head, by means of (synthetic) materiality. For Bruno, affective mediation is material; it is composed of haptic fibers and fabrics.[26] If we understand affect in this manner, then the image of the *maquiladora* uses one of the most potent symbols of global capital in Mexico today—the borderland factories that multiplied after the introduction of NAFTA—to capture how the *necromáquina* (an extension of these same economic forces) manufactures affect, manufactures masks, manufactures severed heads. Bruno urges us to think of the image materially by means of the "textures, traces, and even stains" that accompany the visual text.[27] We see this in *La libertad del diablo* when the witnesses cry and stain their masks with tears. If the face is the site of subjective emotion, then the mask expresses pure affect (Figure 30). Beneath the mask, the neck tightens and twitches. The voice trembles. The speaker bites her lip. She begins to cry: we do not see tears streaming down her face, but the mask dampens around her eyes, changing color and texture. The masks themselves are not static; they morph throughout the interview as they mediate affect. They are themselves moving images.

From the Visual Guillotine to the Cinematic *Tzompantli*

Founded in 2011, five years after violence erupted with Felipe Calderón's declaration of a deceptively named war on drugs, the audiovisual collective Los Ingrávidos responds to the *necromáquina* by disrupting the expressive logic that structures it. The disappearance of forty-three students near Iguala in 2014 further galvanized the group, which continues to operate anonymously both to reprise the avant-garde tradition of collective authorship and to protect its members against retaliation. To facilitate this anonymity and maintain the collective's independence, Los Ingrávidos self-distributes their short films and videos through online platforms even while they exhibit through traditional channels. Influenced by the radical counter-cinemas of the 1970s, Los Ingrávidos reactivates the revolutionary legacy of montage to disrupt the sensationalist representations of violence that incapacitate the critical gaze. Ranging from 16 mm film to electronic video and digital formats, their work resuscitates cinematic strategies including found footage, the cameraless film, and structural film in a postcinematic landscape. The collective combines these analog methods with the processual experimentation seen in digital art and video by manipulating scan lines, glitches, pixelation, and algorithmic abstractions.

Los Ingrávidos responds to the audiovisual ideology that facilitates the *necromáquina* and challenges its performative barbarity by reclaiming the radical political potential of the cut and resuscitating practices of avant-garde primitivism. By manipulating the violence of the cut, the collective engages this audiovisual war machine on its own terms. Los Ingrávidos adopts a media archaeological approach to the audiovisual violence of the narco-conflict. Reviving the concerns that lie at the heart of classic theories of cinematic politics, the collective addresses the latest stage of the genealogy that I have traced throughout this book: from the guillotine to cinema, and later television and new media. In the postcinematic present, their *contramáquina* engages the afterlives of the visual guillotine as it pushes cinematic politics in new directions. While they acknowledge that the violence against the cinematic body that takes place in the editing room—the splicer that inherits the guillotine—has largely been displaced, Los Ingrávidos highlights the relation between cutting images and cutting bodies that survives in the *necromáquina*. Interpellated by the decapitation video, the collective writes, "These are bad times for cinema / when a *sicario* / grabs a camera and films / executions."[28]

Nevertheless, the videos produced by criminal organizations represent only one vector of this conflict. The horrorist apparatus that produces acephalous subjects is aided by the security state and corporate media channels that sustain it. In Reguillo's formulation, the *necromáquina* occupies a sphere parallel to the state, challenging the sovereign control of its territory as well as its monopoly on violence. Crucially, this apparatus does not nullify or replace the state's war machine. A short circuit emerges between these two forces as the security state begins to mimic the symbolic grammar of the *necromáquina*'s horrorism.[29] Consequently, Los Ingrávidos denounces the *necromáquina*'s audiovisual grammar as well as its reproduction by the state and corporate media. In the early years of the conflict, corporate television broadcast these crimes in grisly detail, reproducing the sensationalist tone of the criminals' own audiovisual productions. Whether it is produced by the *necromáquina* or the security state, this horrorism ultimately serves the interests of both parties. As I have argued, the weaponization of the visual guillotine serves necropolitical sovereignty and enables extreme forms of capitalism. The security state, meanwhile, justifies its continued existence by remediating this symbolic grammar. Los Ingrávidos set out to interrupt this feedback loop. By displacing the tactics of counter-cinema to the politics of television, electronic video, and digital media, the collective takes up the unfinished project of political modernism to disrupt the ideologies of the moving image in the *necromáquina*.

Echoing theorists and filmmakers of the 1970s, Los Ingrávidos calls for semiotic counterstrategies that would disrupt the smooth and transparent operation of moving images in the service of the *necromáquina* and the security state. One of their targets is online video, on which criminal organizations have relied to exhibit their horrific crimes. Streaming platforms similarly permit the collective to self-distribute their work. At the time of writing, Los Ingrávidos has uploaded nearly six hundred videos to their official Vimeo account. Such an overabundance of material reflects the total saturation of visual culture under neoliberalism, to which the *necromáquina* contributes. However, Los Ingrávidos's filmography interrupts the accelerationist logic of the digital media economy and introduces a critical gaze by treating the collective's audiovisual production as a mutable assemblage. Self-citation and the remixing of their own work offer a point of departure for a counter-cinema that operates through a poetics of the cut. For example, many of the collective's early titles are constructed by separating two lexical units with a forward slash, such as *2 de octubre/Lejos de Tlatelolco* (*October 2/Far from Tlatelolco,* 2013). Miguel Errazu has compiled an extensive list of the syntagms that make up the building blocks of these titles, though he concludes that their construction does not obey a typology. Rather than produce meaning through an established semiotic system, the competing terms "slash" one another and allow the spectator to deduce meaning through the force of the cut.[30] Far from being a closed body of work, this corpus depends on a logic of montage and de-montage.

The *necromáquina*'s horrorism reaches a wider audience when television broadcasts the cinematic crimes that originally circulate through online video. Los Ingrávidos singles out Televisa—the transnational behemoth of the Spanish-language corporate mediascape—for representing both the *necromáquina*'s symbolic violence and the Mexican government's manipulation of such imagery. Representing narco-violence as exceptional and primitive, the government seizes on such imagery to frame the conflict in terms of a political melodrama that would justify the maintenance of a security state.[31] The culture industry that exploits the excessive violence, heightened affect, and underlying political narrative of good and evil through narco-telenovelas and films justifies the ceaseless expansion of the war machine. By foregrounding melodramatic tropes, the iconography and affect of horrorism obscures underlying networks of power and capital that sustain violence. Televisa has maintained close ties to the state since the network's consolidation in the 1970s, and its political alliances, such as its favoritism of Calderón's successor Enrique Peña Nieto in the 2012 election, have provoked widespread protests. By reproducing images of extreme violence under the pretense of journalistic immediacy and objectivity, the network sustained the atmosphere of horrorism that benefited both the state and the *necromáquina*. Its uncritical representation of violence has made a gruesome spectacle of the conflict.

Los Ingrávidos denounces Televisa's claims of transparency in the audiovisual coverage of violence. As the largest producer of telenovelas in the Spanish-speaking world, Televisa grafted its conservative melodrama onto representations of the conflict. The collective's first manifesto calls for a countervisuality that might disrupt the horrorism this network enables. Denouncing Televisa's role as an agent of propaganda and mouthpiece of conservative politics, Los Ingrávidos issues a semiotic call to arms:

> Destitute the sense of its discourse by intervening in the grammar of its language, inoculate de-comprehension, stutter, and echolalia. Make the preferable content that its tirade would communicate illegible. A generalized aesthetics to unhinge. . . . We have to submit the audiovisual grammar of Televisa traditions to continuous destruction. We have to demolish the neutralized immediacy that the frivolous romanticism of its images invoke.[32]

Drawing on the language of apparatus theory, Los Ingrávidos announces a *contramáquina* that would disrupt Televisa's spectacle of violence by cultivating a critical gaze. These efforts reclaim the radical potential of the cut to introduce a countervisuality that deconstructs the symbolic grammar of horrorism and redirects cinematic affect away from the production of acephalous subjects. Refusing to represent violence directly, the collective renders it unwatchable by pushing violence outside the frame and meditating instead on the role of the apparatus in its reproduction.[33] Rather than directly denounce and thereby center hegemonic images of violence, Los Ingrávidos intervenes in the televisual and cinematic forms that mediate them. The collective draws attention to the formal violence implicit in the moving-image apparatus, which the narcoconflict has appropriated in its aestheticization of politics.

Los Ingrávidos returns to the remains of film stock and the ruins of the cinematic apparatus to reclaim the radical politics of the visual guillotine today. By highlighting the disintegration of the apparatus and filmstrip, *Impresiones para una máquina de luz y sonido* (*Impressions for a Light and Sound Machine,* 2017) resuscitates the metaphor of the cinematic body. Los Ingrávidos reactivates the relation between cutting bodies and cutting images to mount an ideological critique of horrorism. They trace a genealogy of audiovisual affect from the *necromáquina* to the political melodrama of the Golden Age of Mexican cinema.[34] As its title suggests, this film meditates on the material conditions of the apparatus by pointing to the violence of the cut that structures the moving image. The soundtrack opens with the voice of Mexican poet María Rivera as she recites her poem "Los muertos" at a protest in the capital. Through this intertext, *Impresiones* similarly positions itself as a form of protest that denounces both the spectacular violence of the *necromáquina* and the government corruption that abets it. Rivera begins with descriptions of decapitated and dismembered bodies. Speaking into a megaphone, her voice booms, "Here they come / The decapitated, / The amputees, / The torn into pieces, / The women with their coccyx split apart, / Those with their heads smashed in." Coinciding with Rivera's poetic figuration of the *necromáquina*'s horrorism, a damaged print of Emilio Fernández's film *La perla* (1954) flickers onto the screen. As "Los muertos" continues over the soundtrack, the image registers the projection of this wounded body for over six and a half minutes.

Los Ingrávidos arranges a montage of fragments from this source material. Their intervention disarticulates the original narrative and centers the audience's attention on the form and materiality of the cinematic image. The images appear shredded, with vertical gashes across the frame.

The projector struggles to hold onto this precarious filmstrip, which slides off track at times. The cuts appear systematically, frame by frame, and the continued advancement of the filmstrip through the projector animates them (Figure 31). The movement present in *La perla* thus competes with the rhythmic movement of the cuts on the image. In this example, the visual guillotine takes on a life of its own. Like Walter Murch's account of montage discussed in the introduction to this book, the animated slashes visible on the screen remind the spectator that cinematic movement depends on the cutting of an image into frames and the subsequent displacement of these fragments through the projector. The film alienates the spectator, who pauses to reflect on the material violence of cinema that hides in plain sight. These cuts persist throughout the film, momentarily ceasing in the middle of the short and returning to a relatively transparent image to remind the audience of the illusion of fluid movement created by the cut. The violence returns after this pause and continues until the filmstrip finally disintegrates at the end. In *Impresiones,* Los Ingrávidos takes the logic of the visual guillotine to an extreme: excess cutting ultimately disfigures the film, abstracting it beyond recognition. The spectator is left to relate the violence present in the source material, the structural violence of the moving image, and the contemporary horrorism described by Rivera.

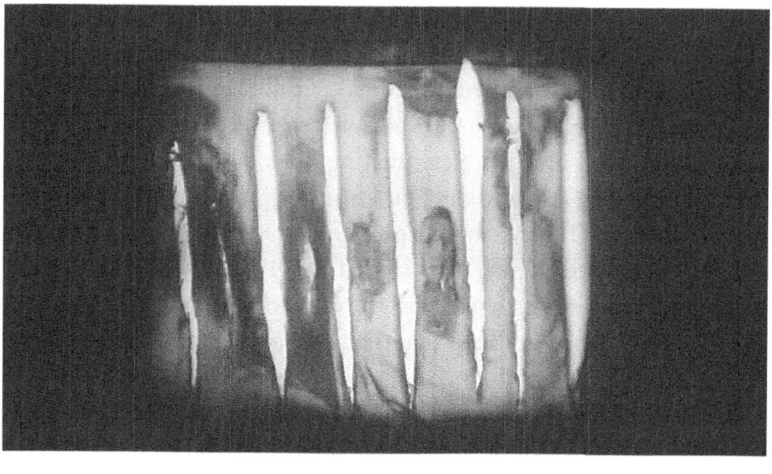

Figure 31. The damaged image of national cinema, cut by a malfunction in the apparatus. *Impresiones para una máquina de luz y sonido,* dir. Colectivo Los Ingrávidos, 2017.

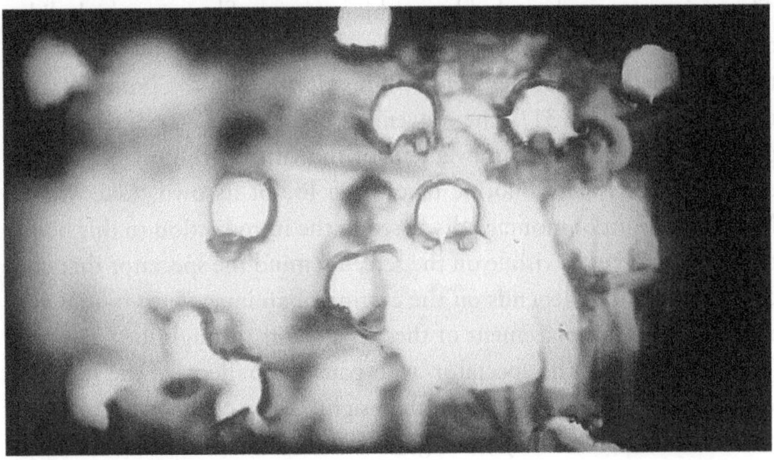

Figure 32. An image perforated by the apparatus, reminiscent of bullet holes. *Abecedario/B*, dir. Colectivo Los Ingrávidos, 2014.

The disfiguration of the cinematic body through the cut offers a potent metaphor of the operation of the *necromáquina*, which continues to disfigure bodies. The destroyed filmstrip, either deliberately damaged by the filmmaker or recovered from the decay of time, has become a common trope in experimental moving-image practices today. The fragile materiality of such works often serves as a point of departure for lyrical meditations on memory and loss, perhaps most prominently in the work of American experimental filmmaker Bill Morrison. Los Ingrávidos imbues such reflections on the obsolescence of cinema with a political resonance and urgency. Resuscitating the legacy of the NLAC, the collective joins the aesthetic and political avant-gardes. This is evident in the juxtaposition of sound and image in *Impresiones*, as well as the similar strategies employed in an earlier short film, *Abecedario/B* (*Alphabet/B*, 2014). This work similarly registers the degeneration of found footage, set to the sounds of a gunfight that the filmmakers extract from a *narco* video. Part of the collective's *Abecedario* series, the film centers on the symbolic language of violence invented by the *necromáquina*. As in the case of *Impresiones*, the image of horrorism is withheld. In its place, Los Ingrávidos again films the projection of a destroyed filmstrip. This unknown reel is perforated by burn holes throughout, which abstract the image almost completely (Figure 32). Again, the juxtaposition of sound and image relates the audible violence with the defacement of the cinematic body. Just as Rivera's descriptions of decapitation and dismemberment in *Impresiones* associate the cutting of the filmstrip with the cutting of the victim's body, in this example the bullets heard in the original recording appear to wound the image. In response to *Abecedario/B*, Errazu argues that the film establishes a mimetic relationship between the victims of narco-violence and the wounded cinematic body: "This figurative annihilation, which addresses the image as remain, as corpse, would thus be the condition of possibility for the image to gain critical consistency and for the image of the disappeared to be recuperated."[35] However, in the case of *Impresiones* a consideration of the ideological frame of the source material allows for a more nuanced interpretation that ties the initially puzzling juxtaposition of a Golden Age melodrama with a denunciation of the *necromáquina*'s crimes.

Without negating the possibility of such a reading, I resist framing the damaged filmstrip as a double of the violated body of the *necromáquina*'s victim. While *Abecedario/B* employs similar aesthetic strategies of destruction, the source of the found footage remains undefined. This allows Errazu to assume the innocence of the appropriated document and interpret it as a substitute for the violated body of the disappeared victim. However, in *Impresiones* the selection of the intertext is politically charged. The destruction of Fernández's *La perla* through the cut drives Los Ingrávidos's critique of the cultural logic of the narco-conflict and signals historical continuities between the conservative ideology of the Golden Age melodrama and the reactionary spectacle of narco-violence today. Though the copy is deteriorated, the historical context of the source material is clear. For example, the visibility of the film's star, Pedro Armendáriz, identifies these images with the cultural nationalism of Mexican cinema's Golden Age. The spectator can similarly distinguish the iconic style cultivated by Fernández and his frequent collaborator, cinematographer Gabriel Figueroa, which became the hegemonic form of Mexican cinema in its classical period.[36] The Golden Age of melodrama defined by Fernández, Figueroa, and the pantheon of stars such as Armendáriz created a national mythology in the service of the state. By invoking Fernández in their denunciation of the narco-conflict, Los Ingrávidos traces a genealogy of audiovisual politics from the present to the cultural nationalism of the postrevolutionary government. The mutilated copy of *La perla* represents the ongoing ties between melodrama and power. Mexico's political landscape has changed irreversibly, yet the necropolitical sovereignty of the *necromáquina* similarly draws on its political affect. Consequently, the images in the source material are far from innocent. Rather, they invoke a political history of cinematic affect that Los Ingrávidos understands as oppressive. In other words, the cinematic body that is destroyed through the cut does not in this case represent the victim of violence that is dismembered by the *necromáquina*. Instead, the collective turns the violence of these cultural forms against themselves. Los Ingrávidos responds to the security state's melodramatization of horrorism by defacing the iconography associated with this affective politics. However, this rejection of melodrama does not repeat apparatus theory's denunciation of emotion in favor of semiotic analysis. As the juxtaposition of Rivera's performance and the excessive visualization of the cut make clear, the relation between affect and film form organizes the political intervention of Los Ingrávidos's counter-cinema.

The audiovisual critique present in *Impresiones* proceeds negatively by destabilizing the melodramatic horrorism of the narco-conflict through the cut. Los Ingrávidos later grafts these formalist interventions onto an affective cinema that embraces the political potential of trance and ritual. Apparatus theory and the discourse of political modernism sought to agitate the spectator by breaking the illusionism of narrative cinema and destroying visual pleasure. As I discuss in my survey of the NLAC in chapters 1 and 2, the visual guillotine released this political affect. In "Theses on the Audiovisual," Los Ingrávidos reframes such concerns in relation to ritual and trance. In Thesis 1 the collective affirms, "In this cinema, agitation no longer emerges from new awareness nor calls for mass mobilization, but rather consists of putting everything in a trance, including the camera itself, relating the different instances of violence to each other."[37] Here, Los Ingrávidos abandons the modernist strategy of mobilizing the spectator and the *pueblo*, which, as we have seen, has disappeared with the mutations to sovereignty represented by the *necromáquina*. The affective politics achieved through the formal violence of the cut counteract the apparatus that produces acephalous subjects, channeling these intensities into modes of resistance. In Thesis 77, Los Ingrávidos specifies that they elaborate this framework "so that through trance, violence, myth, ancestry, precariousness, and extinction a new cosmological and cosmopolitical perception of the Missing People is formed."[38] Through what they refer to as a shamanic materialism, the collective invokes the spirit of the *pueblo* that haunts contemporary politics. Following the eclipse of popular sovereignty, this revenant returns in the form of a communal intensity released through postcinematic ritual.

By invoking rituals of dismemberment and decapitation in their responses to contemporary violence, Los Ingrávidos seeks to reclaim the affective force of the cut that has been weaponized in the decapitation video. The collective's revival of avant-garde primitivism nullifies the *necromáquina*'s dissimulation of horrorism through a performative savagery by revealing this violence for what it is: an apparatus of necropolitical governmentality that structures contemporary forms of sovereignty and capital. In this vein, the collective's short film *Coyolxauhqui* (2017) meditates on the gendered violence of the *necromáquina* by invoking the mythic origins of patriarchal violence. The film's title refers to the decapitation and dismemberment of Coyolxauhqui, Aztec goddess of the moon, at the hands of her brother Huitzilopochtli, god of sun, war, and sacrifice.[39] *Coyolxauhqui* is itself structured like a ritual that entrances the audience through its modernist formalism and startling manipulation of the cut.

Shot on expired film stock, the images feature washed-out colors and other imperfections, such as scratches and lens flares. The lack of narrative, jarring handheld camera movement, and rapid montage further agitate the spectator and encourage a meditation on questions of form and materiality. The film proceeds through a series of shaky extreme close-ups that lose their focus as they are swiftly displaced. The first few minutes feature images of fruiting cacti and mango trees, which the camera abstracts through framing and camera movement before zooming out and orienting the spectator in a vast landscape. A disorienting soundtrack dominated by syncopated percussion enhances these chaotic jump cuts. Shot in the high desert of La Mixteca, Oaxaca, an area infamous for its *maquiladoras* and high rates of *feminicidio*, the surroundings initially appear lush and bountiful. However, night falls in the film's second act, and the bright fruits seen earlier are lost in the darkness. A haunting chorus emerges from the soundtrack as we see the moon, the embodiment of Coyolxauhqui, shining through the clouds. Having established a ghostly atmosphere, the camera then profiles a series of abandoned objects found in the desert. These include women's shoes, underwear, clothes, and bones (Figure 33). The camera initially navigates these remains by centering them in the frame, shooting them from above, and then circling them before splicing these images together in a series of jump cuts. This fragments the movement and creates the illusion that the bones themselves are animated.

Feminicidio is another example of the systemic horrorism that sustains the *necromáquina*. Like other examples of expressive violence in contemporary Mexico, it is often dismissed as an aberrancy—a case of exceptional and savage violence that occurs outside the law. Activists and theorists have resisted the conflation of this gendered violence with the wider narco-conflict because the association overlooks *feminicidio*'s roots in systems of patriarchal power. I agree, and do not wish to reduce the specificities of gendered violence to the activities of criminal organizations. Nevertheless, the horrorism *feminicidio* evokes similarly sustains an apparatus that produces acephalous subjects in the service of capital.

Figure 33. A bone animated in the desert through jump cuts. *Coyolxauhqui,* dir. Colectivo Los Ingrávidos, 2017.

In Mexico, the rapid increase in rates of *feminicidio* since the 1990s speaks to the correlation between this expressive violence and the economic transformations that accelerated neoliberalism.[40] The murder of women on an industrial scale first came to public consciousness in the industrial border town of Ciudad Juárez in the wake of NAFTA. Hundreds of *maquiladoras* exploited the vulnerability of young women who migrated to fill low-paying manufacturing jobs. As women disappeared in greater numbers and human remains began to be discovered in the surrounding desert with increasing frequency, politicians and journalists began to account for the phenomenon of *feminicidio* by correlating economic and gendered violence. Though Juárez served as the laboratory, *maquiladoras* dispersed throughout Mexico. Today, La Mixteca is a hub of such precarious labor with high rates of *feminicidio.*

Through their cinematic ritual, Los Ingrávidos recovers the remains of the female body that have been cast off as a by-product of contemporary capital. *Coyolxauhqui* creates a jarring effect through the jump cut. These cuts coincide with the bones that remain from the crimes, animating the remains of the victims of *feminicidio.* The relation between cutting images and cutting bodies prominently returns, reframed in terms of a mythic beheading. By creating a montage of bones, the collective avoids making a spectacle of necropolitical violence.[41] The visceral response to these images is not channeled to the creation of acephalous subjects, but the invocation of the disappeared victims. The barrage of cuts releases the intensities inscribed within cinematic form, entrancing the spectator and creating an affective community outside the scope of the *necromáquina.*

In relating the decapitation and dismemberment of the female body to ancestral ritual, Los Ingrávidos invokes a longer history of violence. In their essay "The Language of Bones in the New Tenochtitlán," Los Ingrávidos relates *feminicidio*, and contemporary horrorism broadly conceived, to the nexus of capital, colonialism, and extreme violence that emerged with the conquest of the Americas.[42] The collective thus ties the overwhelming presence of violated and dismembered female bodies to a history of colonial violence that continues in the *maquiladora.* They refer to this contemporary landscape as the New Tenochtitlán, arguing that the destruction of the Aztec capital by Hernán Cortés inscribed criminality in the political and economic structures that emerged at the dawn of Latin American modernity. The iconography of decapitation and dismemberment that facilitated the conquest survives in the *necromáquina*'s horrorism. In tracing this genealogy, Los Ingrávidos juxtaposes the instrumental violence of the conquest, antecedent of contemporary horrorism, with the sacred violence present in Indigenous cultures. Through the cinematic cut, the collective reclaims the nonproductive expenditure that, following Bataille, organized Aztec ritual as a subversion of the violent capitalist order imposed by the Spanish empire.[43] In other words, Los Ingrávidos elaborates a mythic cinema that contests the audiovisual logic of the *necromáquina,* which in turn serves the interests of contemporary capital.

Los Ingrávidos observes that the audiovisual production of the *necromáquina* continues the political genealogy of spectacular violence initiated during the conquest and sustained throughout the history of Latin American cinema. In the opening of the essay the collective declares, "It is possible to trace the history of an authentic politics of extermination in the bones and flesh of cinema."[44] In opposition to this genealogy of the visual guillotine, Los Ingrávidos invokes the legacy of the *tzompantli,* an Aztec altar that displayed the severed heads of sacrificial victims for religious and political ends.[45] Employed in ritual sacrifice, the *tzompantli* was also used to intimidate the Spanish conquerors during the siege of Tenochtitlán by displaying the severed heads of the invaders. Los Ingrávidos reappropriates this device as a symbol of resistance and inverts established accounts of the narco-conflict that trace the performative violence of the decapitation video to Aztec ritual.[46] Instead, the collective associates the *necromáquina*'s violence with the European barbarity that launched capitalist modernity in Latin America and laid the foundation for the brutal violence the *necromáquina* currently employs in the service of capital. In this revisionist account, the mythic violence represented by the *tzompantli* resists the utilitarian cruelty of the *necromáquina.* Inverting the performative barbarism and instrumental violence realized by criminal organizations, Los Ingrávidos inscribes their cinematic radicalism within Mexico's mythic heritage. Drawing on Indigenous cosmography, they reimagine cinema as shamanic ritual capable of healing a country torn by conflict. The concept of the cinematic *tzompantli* thus reclaims the subversive potential of the cinematic cut from the *necromáquina*'s appropriation by refracting the visual guillotine through an avant-garde primitivism. The collective describes the cinematic *tzompantli* in the following terms:

> The radiographic skulls emerge from the darkness, nothing surrounds them. They appear from a river of flesh, though it is not flesh but celluloid, another boiling flesh. Bubbling emulsions give way to flashes of hardened oil, thrown against the dark walls of the oneiric *tzompantli*. Cellulose layers trickle down the radiographically severed heads. . . . Gleaming opacity through clusters of extreme close-ups of ocular cavities. Pulmonary silicosis. Hips and coccyx embodied on screens of cruelty: cinematic *tzompantli*.[47]

By embracing the cinematic *tzompantli*, Los Ingrávidos turns the performative primitivism of the decapitation video on its head. The *necromáquina* dissimulates its apparatus of horrorism through a performance of savagery. However, rather than an exceptional barbarism, this cruelty defines the structures of politics, capital, and cinema that characterized Latin American modernity. By reverting to the *tzompantli*, Los Ingrávidos sees through the *necromáquina*'s strategy and recovers the subversive power of ritual through cinema.

Tzompantli (2016) visualizes Los Ingrávidos's theory of cinematic beheading by juxtaposing radiographic images of skulls with firsthand

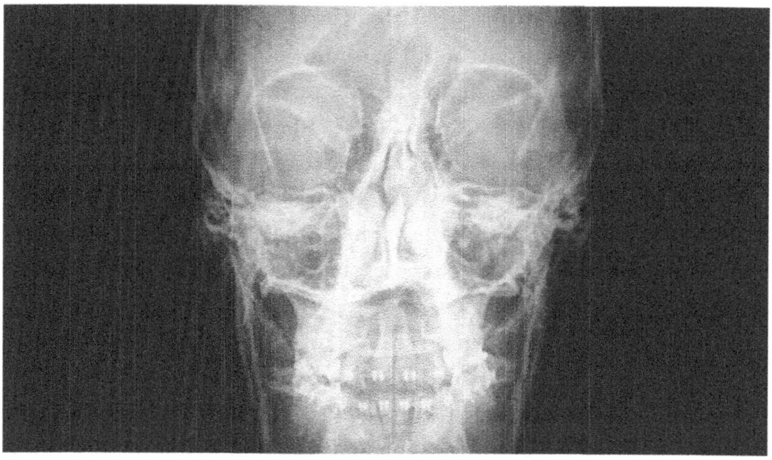

Figure 34. The cinematic *tzompantli* displays a severed head. *Tzompantli,* dir. Colectivo Los Ingrávidos, 2016.

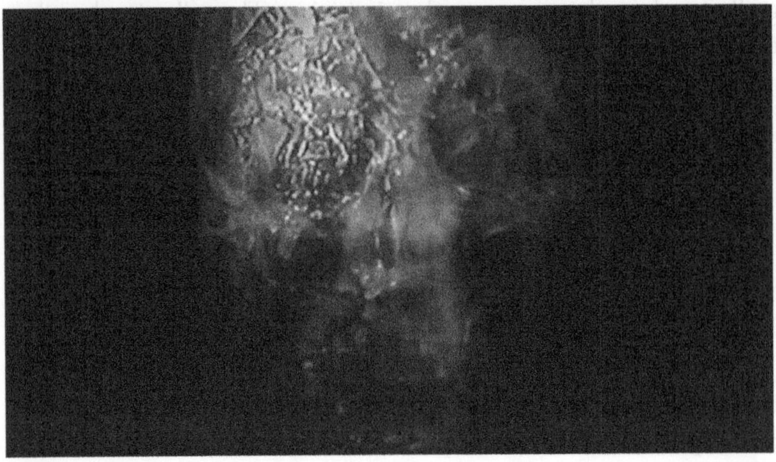

Figure 35. The cinematic *tzompantli* displays a severed head. *Tzompantli,* dir. Colectivo Los Ingrávidos, 2016.

accounts of the *necromáquina*'s violence. The video revives the legacy of political modernism by engaging the strategies of structural film, especially the flicker and loop, to reflect on the apparatus of horrorism. Abandoning narrative, it creates an affective assemblage from the traces of expressive violence. The first image we can distinguish in the film is an X-ray of a skull that briefly flashes across the screen. This visually severed head mutates throughout the film. Moments later, the skull reappears transformed through double exposure and animated through a flicker effect. The familiar blue glow of the radiographic image is replaced with a saturated red that at once evokes decaying flesh, blood, and fire as it flickers against the black screen (Figure 34 and Figure 35). These sinister skulls continue to mutate as they return throughout the short. Meanwhile, the soundtrack juxtaposes the sinister visual effect by weaving together dreadful testimonies of violence. The first comes from a survivor of the 2014 Iguala massacre and mass kidnapping. The witness describes how in the early hours of September 27 a convoy of soldiers in unmarked uniforms opened fire on the buses carrying the students from Ayotzinapa. Rather than offer a coherent reconstruction of the event, the film advances through a disjointed montage of testimony. The voice abruptly shifts to the perspective of a woman who had been kidnapped and tortured by authorities, before returning to the fateful night in Iguala. The soundtrack then enters a loop and begins to repeat fragments of testimony. The experience of viewing *Tzompantli* is unsettling. As in the example of *Coyolxauhqui,* the intensities released by the formally jarring representation of bodily remains agitate the spectator. Through their invocation of Aztec ritual, the collective embraces a subversive primitivism that challenges the *necromáquina*'s weaponization of the moving image.

Like the other filmmakers analyzed in this chapter, Los Ingrávidos revives a political commitment to form in order to critique the weaponization of the cinematic cut in the present and reevaluate the radical legacy of the visual guillotine. These works are politically urgent because they demystify the culture industry's imagination of the *necromáquina* as a savage force that justifies the declaration of a state of exception. By exhibiting the violence of audiovisual form in relation to the narco-conflict, the *contramáquinas* I have examined here dispute the exceptionality of the decapitation video. Rather, the authors of these cinematic crimes appropriate the violence of audiovisual form, which previously served the radicalism of militant cinema, to advance contemporary necropolitics. Both the decapitation videos studied in the previous chapters and the responses to this imagery in this chapter reflect the transformation of audiovisual politics following the eclipse of cinema's pact with the *pueblo*. Nevertheless, these films reactivate the concern with the politics of form that defined the discourse of political modernism in the 1970s and 1980s in our postcinematic era. While politics and the audiovisual apparatus have mutated in the twenty-first century, theoretical concerns with the politics of form continue to be urgent. The indeterminacy that characterizes postcinema, which departs from cinematic modes of subject formation without replacing them with a wholly new apparatus, reflects the general state of interregnum that scholars of contemporary Latin American cultural studies have identified with other cultural forms. While the modernist framework of classical film theory faces significant challenges in contesting the audiovisual production of the *necromáquina*, Reygadas, Escalante, González, and Los Ingrávidos seek to fill the gaps in our conceptual vocabulary through their revision of the visual guillotine.

5

CAPITAL VISIONS
SPECTATORSHIP IN THE VISUAL GUILLOTINE

This chapter concludes my account of the politics of the cinematic cut by examining the spectator's position within the visual guillotine. Through their experimentations with the close-up and montage, the filmmakers, videographers, and moving-image artists I have studied throughout this book manipulate the formal properties of cinema—the many cuts required to compose and assemble moving images—to give form to politics. These examples associate the formal and material violence of the cut with the violence that structured political modernity. This force required of politics is not limited to the monopoly on violence. At its core, popular sovereignty originates in the decapitation of the sovereign body. The symbolic transfer of power from the king to the people occurs with the public spectacle of beheading. The scene of beheading gives rise to the people as a political category. Put differently, the act of viewing the severed head of the sovereign positions the spectator as a political subject. The rise and fall of the guillotine's blade and the series of severed heads it produces reaffirm the transference of power to the people. This cut gives form to politics. The affective intensity the spectacle produces in the masses binds the crowd of spectators into a political community. Politics is inscribed within the cut that mechanically reproduces this disarticulated body. The image of the severed head—whether literal or figurative—has accompanied the transformation of sovereignty since the inauguration of modernity.

Throughout this book, I have traced the politics of the cinematic cut back to the guillotine. Given these structural associations between the cut and politics, moving images have been integral to the representation of revolution and popular sovereignty. More recently, the crisis of the nation-state in the neoliberal model has weakened the political agency of the *pueblo* and accelerated the mutation of sovereignty. In this period of interregnum, modern conceptualizations of politics have given way, leaving scholars to speculate as to what remains of the political. For filmmakers and contemporary artists, the moving image remains a site for staging politics through the cut. Interpellated by this visual guillotine, the community of spectators is constituted and bound by the violence that underlies audiovisual form.

In reflecting on how the cinematic cut forms subjects, I revive classical studies of spectatorship. Film theorists in the 1970s and 1980s understood the audience's identification with the moving image through the concept of suture, taken from Lacanian psychoanalysis. In film studies, suture theory holds that subject formation occurs through the spectator's insertion into the film's narrative. Film form encouraged the spectator to abandon the reality outside the cinema, immerse themselves within the diegetic world of the film, and identify with its protagonist. Continuity editing was especially important to this process because it created the illusion of spatial and temporal cohesion from a fragmented succession of shots. Spectators learned to navigate these cuts and suture themselves into the narrative by identifying with its characters.

In the first half of this chapter, I study a series of films that imagine suture as a scene of literal and figurative beheading. Staging the violence implicit in suture, these films represent cinematic identification as the transposition of heads. In other words, filmmakers recast the desire for identification as a desire for the severed head. Searching to fulfill this psychic lack, the spectator becomes a headhunter. As we will see, this is not an innocent affair; to satisfy psychic lack, the spectator sublimates a latent sadism. Through such examples, I reconsider the behaviors that Laura Mulvey refers to as fetishistic spectatorship. The ephemeral image of the star in the projected film, which cannot be fixed or touched, awakens a desire to possess the star and her likeness.[1] Driven by a desire for material contact with the star, the spectator fetishizes her body to a point of excess and seeks to control it, even mutilate it. For example, the devoted fan collects the heads of his favorite stars by cutting them out of magazines, posters, or other traditional vehicles for the distribution of the star image. These materials trace the contour of a violent spectatorship that is motivated by a desire to resolve lack by possessing the severed head.

If in psychoanalysis suture refers to the process by which the subject emerges in discourse, film theorists in the 1970s and 1980s argued that cinema's materiality and aesthetics produced ideological subjects. Daniel Dayan and Stephen Heath concluded that suture—especially as it manifested in the form of the shot/countershot—positioned the spectator politically.[2] As a fundamental operation in the process of suture, the cinematic cut represents the structuring lack that allows the spectator to emerge in discourse. Theorists such as Mulvey, Kaja Silverman, and Teresa de Lauretis, among others, further politicized suture to critique the fetishistic representation of woman in classical narrative cinema. Feminist film theory critiqued the logic of identification, which relied on the close-up and montage to suture the spectator into the narrative, for reproducing hegemonic gender subjectivities. Similarly, filmmakers experimented with cinematic form to disrupt the inscription of gendered violence within film form. As I will discuss in more detail, these efforts identified the cinematic cut with the patriarchal desire to dominate the female form. In other words, the violence of the visual guillotine contributes to the ideological reproduction of gender through suture.

The obsolescence of film and rise of new, transmedial forms has provoked a resurgence of interest in the politics of spectatorship. If anything, the expansion of audiovisual exhibition has revived critical interest in questions of materiality and form. For example, the transformation of the audiovisual apparatus in recent decades has not halted the commitment of film theorists and filmmakers to critiquing the role of gender within formal and material violence of the moving image. After revisiting classical modes of reception in light of the visual guillotine, I conclude this chapter by turning to a series of postcinematic works that intervene in the politics of spectatorship by expanding the conceptualization of the cinematic cut. By experimenting with new modes of exhibition, specifically digital video and film installation, these works intervene in the process of suture and disrupt normative viewing positions. Their authors subvert the fetishizing logic of classical spectatorship and embrace affective and embodied modes of reception over identification. Revisiting debates on fetishization and the gendered politics of the moving image, these works reorient the politics of the visual guillotine in our postcinematic age. In their formal and material experiments, they interrogate how the cut continues to create political subjects. Even after the mutation of the apparatus, these filmmakers reimagine the cut as a force with which to construct communities of spectators.

The Transposed Heads

Alejandro Jodorowsky's debut short, *La cravate* (*The Severed Heads,* 1957), centers on a game of transposed heads in a playful fantasy of love and transformation. The young protagonist, played by Jodorowsky himself, pursues an ill-fated courtship. When the woman he desires rebuffs his advances, he visits a store that offers a variety of severed heads for sale. Clients are seated while the shopkeeper twists off their heads and replaces them with one from the display, after which they leave their original heads behind. Each head in the shop corresponds to a different social type, which is embodied through a performance in pantomime. When he assumes the head of a clown, the protagonist adopts an upbeat gait and a wide smile; when he chooses the head of a mustachioed poet, he frowns and elaborates his gestures elegantly; finally, as a strong man with a square jaw, he lumbers about stiffly. The projectionist tries on a series of heads that he believes might capture the woman's fancy, but his advances are routinely spurned. The woman rejects each of these types. When at last he loses hope and returns to buy back his original head, the young man finds that the shop has closed and the head is nowhere to be found. The shopkeeper, a young woman, has come to admire the head and has taken it home, where she displays it on the mantle like a trophy. She plays with the head, pets it, and gazes at it with desire. In the meantime, however, the man's body wanders the city in search of its lost head. The film concludes when the protagonist is finally reunited with his head and enamored with the young shopkeeper.

La cravate loosely adapts Thomas Mann's novella *The Transposed Heads* (1940), which is itself an interpretation of an Indian legend.[3] The original narrative ponders whether subjectivity resides in the head or the body. After a man decapitates himself at a shrine, his brother discovers the body and beheads himself as an expression of his grief. The first man's wife discovers the bodies of her husband and brother-in-law. When she is about to sever her own head in despair, the deity of the shrine intervenes and allows the wife to revive the men. Overjoyed, the woman mistakenly attaches the heads to the wrong bodies. This leads to a conflict, as both claim to be the woman's husband. The legend concludes by posing this riddle to the king, who rules that subjectivity resides in the head and that therefore the brother's body with the husband's head is rightfully the wife's partner.[4] *La cravate* maintains this concern with the definition of subjectivity by way of the severed and transposed head. Throughout this whimsical adaptation, Jodorowsky exhibits a preoccupation with beheading and subject formation, which I relate to the process of suture.

Jodorowsky's playful fascination with the severed head pays homage both to the surrealist tradition and cinema's roots in stage magic. Recalling the films of Georges Méliès, *La cravate* relies on theatricality and cinematic trickery for its fantastic effects. Méliès's influence is further reinforced by the fact that the film does not contain dialogue. The actors perform in pantomime, relying entirely on the body as a medium of communication. The fusion of mime and the oneiric fantasy of beheading in *La cravate* gives insight into an early stage in Jodorwsky's trajectory as a filmmaker, before he became a countercultural phenomenon. After abandoning his aspirations to become a poet in his native Chile, Jodorowsky relocated to Paris in 1953 to study under Marcel Marceau and to seek an audience with André Breton. *La cravate* is the product of this dual influence of mime and surrealism on the young Jodorowsky. While he continued to explore dialogues between surrealism and cinema in his feature films, in *La cravate* the filmmaker embraces Méliès's playful displacement of violence onto film form. Self-financing the production and working out of his apartment in Paris, Jodorowsky initially turned to cinema as a medium for representing the surrealist pantomimes he had created.[5] While Jodorowsky's interest in surrealism and embodiment continued in his feature films, his treatment of mime in *La cravate* explores the body's role in signification. The severed head lies at the heart of Jodorowsky's corporeal grammar. With the playful decapitations driving the film's narrative, we are taken back to the primordial treatment of the severed head as sign.[6] Cinema continues this genealogy in which signification and figuration occur by means of the severed head.

I read *La cravate* as an allegorical account of suture that meditates on the role of the body and the cut in the act of signification. In its original formulation in psychoanalysis, Jacques-Alain Miller, a disciple of Lacan, proposes this concept to explain the subject's emergence in discourse through their relation to the signifier. Suture designates the subject's resolution of lack by their insertion in the chain of signification by taking on the form of the signifier.[7] Film theorists subsequently embraced suture in their elaboration of an account of cinematic signification. In its adaptation of Lacanian psychoanalysis, suture theory took the individual shot as equivalent to the signifier and the film's sequence of shots as the chain of signification that constructs its discourse. Analogously, the spectator takes on a subject position by inserting themselves into the film's chain of shots. As in Miller's original formulation, the spectator's desire to satisfy a sense of lack drives their identification with the diegesis and the narrative's protagonist through suture.[8] The cinematic cut enables this process. Both editing—particularly the shot/countershot—and framing heighten this lack and the spectator's desire to resolve it. As Silverman concludes in her overview of suture theory, the cut makes cinematic signification possible by providing this structuring lack.[9] The spectator is captivated by the lack created by the cut, whether through editing or framing. In other words, the cut is the source of desire, and it is through this symbolic violence that the spectator emerges as a subject. Jodorowsky explores these concerns in relation to the body, visualizing the cut's role in subject formation through the trope of the severed head.

In psychoanalysis, the severed head symbolizes psychic lack. In his interpretation of the Medusa, Freud initially associated beheading with castration.[10] Julia Kristeva similarly equates the cut that decapitates with the lack that gives rise to desire.[11] She identifies the first signs of human subjectivity with the veneration of severed heads in prehistoric rites. In the decoration and display of human heads, early humans expressed their desire to identify with the other. Severed from the sacrificial body, the head was converted into a sign within a new symbolic system. Following Kristeva, this moment marks the origin of figuration. In other words, the aesthetic processes of visual signification and symbolic communication arise from decapitation. Although religion and art later displaced the ritual violence of decapitation, the severed head has resurfaced in symbolic form throughout cultural history.[12] Modern aesthetics revived the power of the cut, which organized new technologies of representation.

The cut became structurally necessary within the mechanical reproduction of the image. In *La cravate*, Jodorowsky expresses the persistence of the fascination with decapitation in modernity. Through the game of decapitation and transposition, the film correlates the structural cut that makes possible the spectator's identification with the image with the psychological lack that grounds their desire. Echoing Kristeva, Jodorowsky theorizes the psychic and cinematic processes of suture through the figure of the severed head.

Jodorowsky's spectator is sutured into the narrative during the scene of beheading. When the protagonist approaches the shop, the camera triangulates three severed heads: the young man is beheaded by the frame, in front of a sign on the shop that advertises the transposition of two heads (Figure 36). On the right, the image of an ugly head, freckled and featuring an exaggerated nose and teeth, gazes toward another that is more attractive. The protagonist stands under this ugly head and identifies with it. After he is spurned, the young man later enters the shop to purchase a head. In one shot, he sits in a corner as the shopkeeper prepares the head he has selected (Figure 37). Jodorowsky then cuts to a

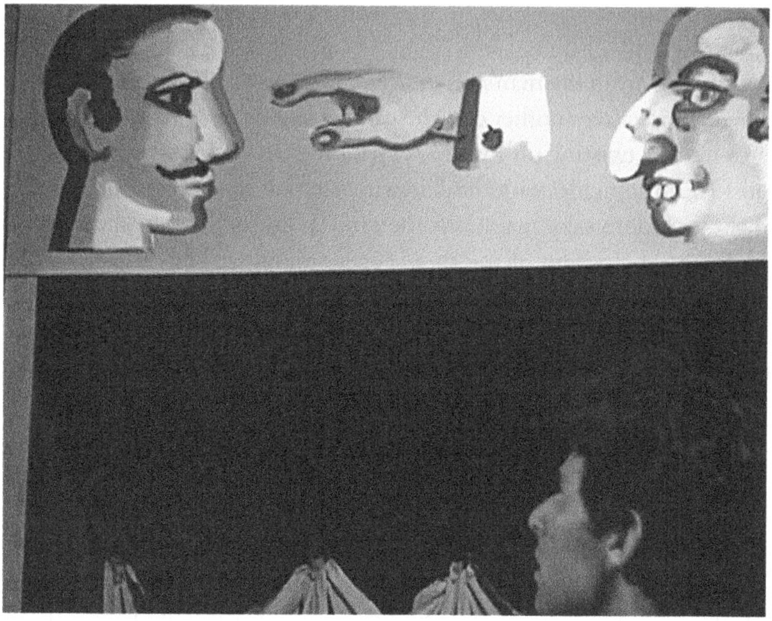

Figure 36. The transposition of heads. *La cravate*, dir. Alejandro Jodorowsky, 1957.

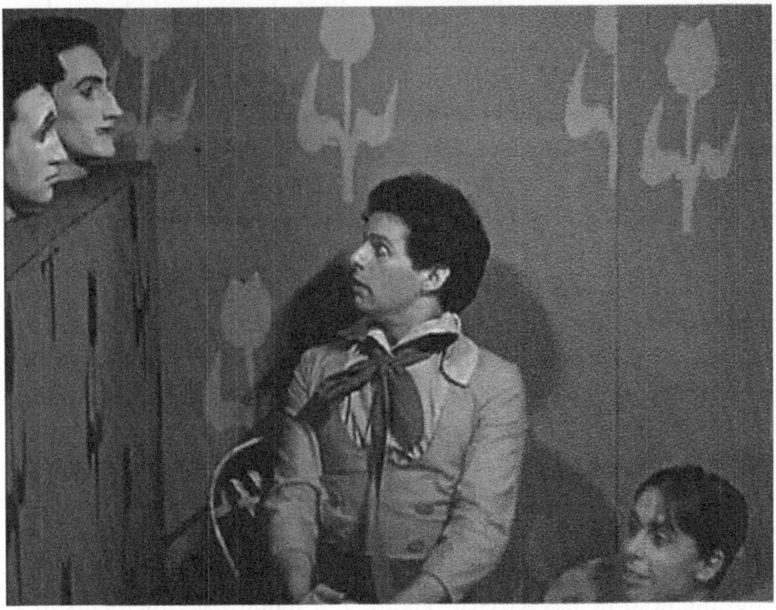

Figure 37. Inside the head shop. *La cravate,* dir. Alejandro Jodorowsky, 1957.

countershot from the man's perspective. The shopkeeper approaches the camera, and, after another cut, the camera begins to spin as she decapitates him by twisting off his head. Here, the cut that severs the protagonist's head coincides with the cinematic cut that structures the sequence of shots. Jodorowsky maintains the same point of view in the following image, a close-up of the shopkeeper smiling at her customer after the successful transposition of heads. The camera finally abandons the man's perspective and cuts to a medium shot to register his new appearance. While the rest of his body remains the same, his behavior and gestural communication have transformed. With this new head, the man has become a different person. The protagonist repeats this process throughout the film, and with each iteration he tries to win the favors of the woman by adopting a series of identities. Each severed head corresponds to a new position in this lover's discourse. However, by constantly shifting his position, the protagonist takes on a serious risk: when he returns for his original head, he cannot find it. *La cravate* cautions against these identifications; ultimately, the man longs for his original position but can no longer retrieve it. His head is lost in the series of transpositions. In the darkness of the movie theater, their head suspended above their seat, the spectator substitutes themself for Jodorowsky's protagonist. Gradually losing consciousness of their body, they are sutured into the narrative. The spectator symbolically loses their head and assumes the position of the character, identifying with the protagonist's gaze and metaphorically possessing their head. Like the protagonist in Jodorowsky's film, they take on new subject positions through such identifications. In other words, a transposition of heads occurs in the scene of projection. Through suture, the spectator transposes their head with that of the character. Jodorowsky renders spectatorship and suture through the metaphorical tête-a-tête that occurs when the floating heads of the character and the spectator encounter one another. Like the protagonist, audiences take on a series of subject positions in the cinema, since they identify with the protagonists of each film. The spectator similarly risks losing themself in this shuffle of heads.

Venezuelan filmmaker Mariana Rondón likewise captures the importance of the severed head to spectatorship in her debut short *Cáscaras* (*Eggshells,* 1992). Set in a cinema, *Cáscaras* underscores the dark side of suture as the film's denouement hinges on the inevitable disenchantment experienced by the spectator when the ugliness of reality overtakes cinematic fantasy and the spell of identification is broken. The disembodied head structures Rondón's perverse revision of the magic of classical spectatorship. Rondón's narrative follows two cinema employees as they engage in a romantic pursuit. We are first introduced to a young woman who sells tickets. Isolated in the box office, only her head is visible from behind the glass. The camera briefly enters the woman's world and reveals her to be a devoted spectator. Inside, the walls of the booth are covered with the severed heads of movie stars, which she has cut out from fan magazines, lobby cards, and other ephemera (Figure 38). The woman catches the eye of one of the theater's projectionists, a little person who never approaches his love interest directly because he fears she will reject him. Instead, he flirts with her through an object in the theater's lobby that serves to promote the fictional film being screened at the theater: *Almas gemelas* (*Soulmates*). This is a poster for a classical melodrama, featuring the leading couple in an amorous embrace. However, the head of the male lead has been cut out and the poster attached to a mirror so that spectators can project their own heads onto the body of the character (Figure 39). Angling himself so that the ticket seller cannot see his figure, the projectionist assumes the head of the star and meets the woman's gaze through the mirror. Rondón represents the process of suture through the man's visual beheading; his identification with the protagonist of *Almas gemelas*, and the ticket-taker's desire, occurs through a transposition of heads made possible by the mirrored cutout.

During the projection, the woman sits in the box office stacking coins out of boredom and watching the mirror in hopes that the projectionist will return. When he finally appears, the couples' desire for one another is presented in a shot/countershot without dialogue. After a close-up of the woman's gaze from the window, Rondón cuts to a countershot of the projectionist's head in close-up, as reflected in the mirror. Rondón cuts between these two disembodied heads as they smile at one another. Over these images, the dialogue between the couple in *Almas gemelas* filters into the lobby. Even when they are not active spectators,

Figure 38. The cutout onto which the spectator projects their head. *Cáscaras*, dir. Mariana Rondón, 1991.

the couple continues to identify with the stars of the film. Through the trope of the cutout, *Cáscaras* captures how cinema positions spectators as subjects in romantic discourse. In other words, Rondón represents how cinema mediates social relations through suture. However, once the fantasy is dispelled, this identification ends in tragedy. After the final showing of *Almas gemelas,* the movie theater removes the cutout and leaves the mirror behind. Yet the couple is so immersed in their flirtation that they fail to notice this change. The woman returns to the box office and eagerly tidies up her appearance as she anticipates the projectionist's return. Without the promotional cutout to obscure the rest of his body, the man's stature is betrayed by his reflection. Humiliated, he shatters the mirror with the metal case of a film reel. The symbolic order has been ruptured, and the subject position into which the projectionist had been sutured dismantled. The woman searches for him after he flees, and when she is unable to find him she throws herself from the roof of the cinema. Rondón then cuts to a grisly scene following the

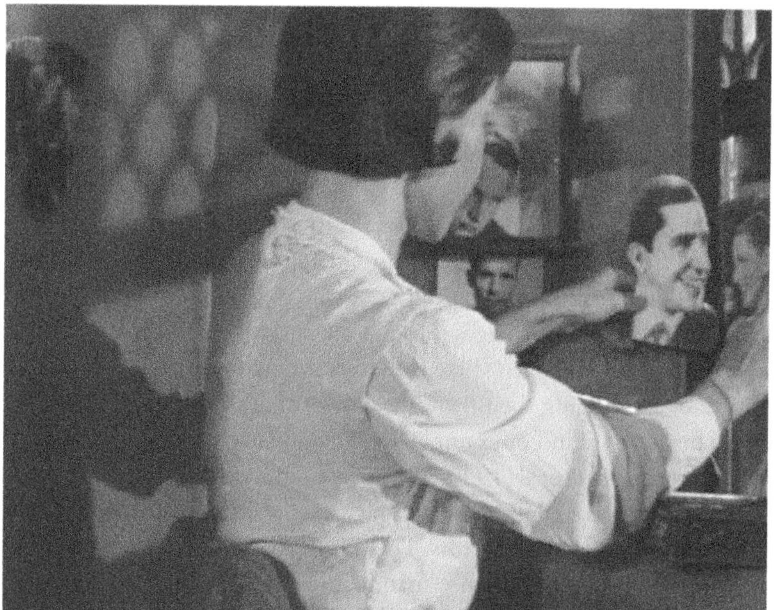

Figure 39. The fetishistic spectator and her collection of severed heads. *Cáscaras,* dir. Mariana Rondón, 1991.

woman's death, in which the remains of her body are being scrubbed off the street. Through this melodramatic narrative, *Cáscaras* signals the symbolic violence that structures romantic discourse. The couple's fetishistic desire to possess the severed head of the other is sublimated through the game of the cutout. As in the example of *La cravate,* both the romantic desire that drives the film's narrative and the form of the cinematic cut that structures suture derive from a lack that is represented through the severed head. Cinema channels this discursive violence through the cut that interpellates the spectator. Through the image of the severed head, *Cáscaras* gives form to the cut, which represents the structuring lack that suture attempts to resolve through romantic intimacy.

While Rondón provides an account of suture that relates lack and desire to the projectionist's visual beheading in the cutout, the protagonist's altar of severed heads reminds us that cinematic identification is not limited to the scene of projection. The moment of suture, which is represented here through the mirrored cutout, is fleeting. Outside of her evasive encounters with the projectionist, the woman prolongs her identification with this cinematic fantasy through the star images that she cuts out from magazines. Through these severed heads, the ticket seller establishes the intimacy Kristeva associates with the ancient rites of decapitation. Mulvey herself defines these extra-cinematic practices in terms of religious fervor, comparing the star images that graced magazines and pinups in Hollywood's classical era to Christian icons.[13] Given the ephemerality of the moving image, spectators turned to material practices that stemmed from the studio systems' publicity apparatus. Film stills and portraits of the stars supplemented the spectator's identification via suture. By intervening in such images through the cut, the spectator could possess the iconic star image.[14] Like Rondón's protagonist, devout fans seek this head, exchanging their own likeness for that of the star in order to derive power from it. For example, in her study of the popular Brazilian film magazine *Cinearte* (1926–42), Maite Conde highlights how fans utilized the material culture of the star system to transform themselves and embody their favorite actors. The stars featured in the magazine and admired by spectators became "mannequins of modernity."[15] Performers embodied a commodified modernity that was peddled via the shop window of the movie screen. Fan magazines played an influential role in the construction of spectators as consumers. Conde demonstrates that this was especially true in Latin America, which sought to achieve the image of modernity exported by Hollywood. Spectators collected film stills and photographs of their favorite stars that they cut out from magazines. Through these obsessions, they sought to embody the image of modernity by "creating a personal investment in Hollywood's film industry."[16] Rondón stages this fetishistic spectatorship in her short. In another example, the protagonist drops a box as she rushes to leave her booth. Its contents spill out onto the floor, revealing dozens of headshots. Locked away, this collection of heads represents her symbolic capital.

The Pedagogy of the Cut

In my reflection on the violence of the close-up in chapter 1, I recalled Béla Balázs's anecdote regarding the Siberian peasant girl who, on a visit to the city, sees a film for the first time. By the time of Balázs's writing, the fragmentation characteristic of film form was no longer shocking to audiences. The film theorist references the naive spectator to advance an argument on the pedagogical function of cinema in the scopic regime of modernity. Though the cut had become a structural element of classical narrative with which Balázs's readers would have been familiar, it was nonetheless violent for the sensibilities of those uninitiated in the fragmentation and speed that characterized modern visuality. As a trope of film theory, the naive spectator underscores the effects of film form, and in particular the cinematic cut, on perception. Balázs recounts the girl's stunned reaction to the force of the cinematic cut. She recoils at a typical sequence of close-ups that dismembers the body, and the montage that disrupts the duration of the shot and joins these fragments. While this account is likely apocryphal, imagined for rhetorical effect, film historians have highlighted the negative reactions of film producers and the public when filmmakers such as D. W. Griffith began experimenting with the close-up. Yuri Tsivian corroborates Balázs's anecdotal evidence, citing early Russian film critics who were repulsed by the image of these gigantic severed heads.[17] To audiences accustomed to perceiving the bodily unity of the stage actor, the disarticulation of the cinematic body proved violent.[18] We witness the formation of a spectator who must learn to navigate the cinematic cut. The girl's reaction likely would have seemed as preposterous to Balázs's readers as it does today. While the shock of modernity certainly remained a constant, the spectator had become gradually desensitized to the onslaught of fragmented images, texts, and experiences. In other words, cinema's formation of the modern subject relied on the cut as a form of perceptual shock therapy.

Octavio Cortázar theorizes the political dimensions of this pedagogy of the cut when documenting cinema's role within the Cuban Revolution's modernization efforts. In 1967, Cortázar embarked on a search for a naive spectator, one whom he could expose to cinema for the first time. The desire to document this encounter and expose rural Cubans to cinema for the first time begets the title of Cortázar's film, *Por primera vez* (*For the First Time,* 1967). In this documentary short, the filmmaker follows the mobile cinema campaign promoted by the Instituto Cubano del Arte e Industria Cinematográfica (ICAIC) to bring the moving image to the most remote and underdeveloped regions of the island. Cortázar interviews the men who for twenty-six days at a time travel the country in a truck loaded with a 16 mm projector, a generator, a cot, and a handful of films. The filmmaker inquires if they had ever encountered communities that have never seen cinema and learns that the truck has been unable to enter the mountainous villages in the eastern municipality of Baracoa. *Por primera vez* follows the mobile cinema as it makes its way to the remote village of Los Mulos in hopes of discovering a naive spectator. Taking on the role of an ethnographer, Cortázar interviews the villagers and asks them to imagine what a film screening must be like.[19] After we hear Cortázar's questions from off-screen, a woman balancing a child on her lap answers, "It must be something important if you are so interested in it."[20] Following these hypotheses, the villagers gather at night for a screening of Charlie Chaplin's *Modern Times* (1936) in an improvised movie theater. As the projectionist rolls the film, Cortázar fixes the camera on the spectators. Framed in a series of close-ups, the villagers gaze up at the screen. Laughing and smiling, children point at the screen. Others appear unfazed. Cortázar closes with an intertitle that reads, "Thus, on April 12, 1967, in the village of Los Mulos, in the mountains of Baracoa, more than one hundred people saw cinema for the first time."

Couched in a documentary on ICAIC's mobile cinema program and an ethnographic portrait of an isolated Cuban village, *Por primera vez* likewise constitutes a metacinematic film on the pedagogy of spectatorship. Like the revolutionary government's literacy campaign, ICAIC's mobile cinema program sought to bring rural communities into the fold of modernity.[21] The ICAIC sought not only to train spectators in order to create a receptive audience for its productions, but to prepare the public to forge a modern Cuba outside the cinema as well. Following Nicholas Balaisis, the mobile cinema campaign strove to address the problem of technological illiteracy in rural Cuba and prepare the population to participate in the industrialization of the island. In other words, the revolutionary government saw cinema as an initiation into the shocks of modernity.[22] The selection of the film-within-the-film is significant and belies Cortázar's comment on cinematic spectatorship. Cortázar implies that the rural audience identifies with Chaplin's Tramp, who humorously struggles to adjust to the harsh realities of industrial labor. The film thus fulfills a pedagogical function by orienting the technologically illiterate audience in the travails of modernity. And yet, unlike Balázs's anecdote, Cortázar dispels the myth of the horrified audience that recoils at the sight of the dismembered body. The inhabitants of Los Mulos delight in Chaplin's slapstick. While the camera registers the audience's faces smiling and pointing at the screen, the juxtaposition of these close-ups with the Tramp struggling in the factory imagines a smooth transition to modernity, one facilitated by the revolution.

Por primera vez and its intertext highlight the violent effects of industrialization and cinema on the body, both on-screen and in the audience. Cortázar intercuts close-ups of the spectators' faces with the famous scene of the feeding machine in *Modern Times*. The Tramp struggles against this device, which is designed to automatically feed the worker while still on the assembly line, thereby eliminating the need for a lunch hour and extracting more labor from the worker. The body is inserted into the machine, which sits just below his shoulders, severing the head as it brings food up to his mouth (Figure 40). The device predictably goes haywire, to comedic effect. For example, a piece of corn spins too fast for the Tramp to keep up, and his head strains at the mercy of the machine. Cortázar utilizes the film-within-the-film as a form of nested commentary on the spectator's interpellation within the visual guillotine. The children of Los Mulos look on, laughing, before Cortázar cuts to an uncharacteristically serious boy gazing directly into the camera (Figure 41). The shot positions him in the center of the frame and decapitates him. The film represents the mechanical fragmentation of

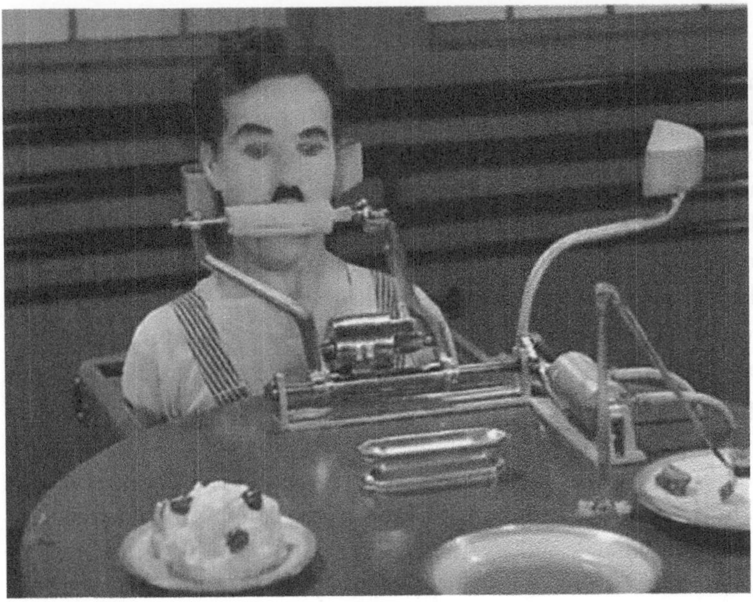

Figure 40. Chaplin struggling with the feeding machine while working the assembly line. *Por primera vez,* dir. Octavio Cortázar, 1967.

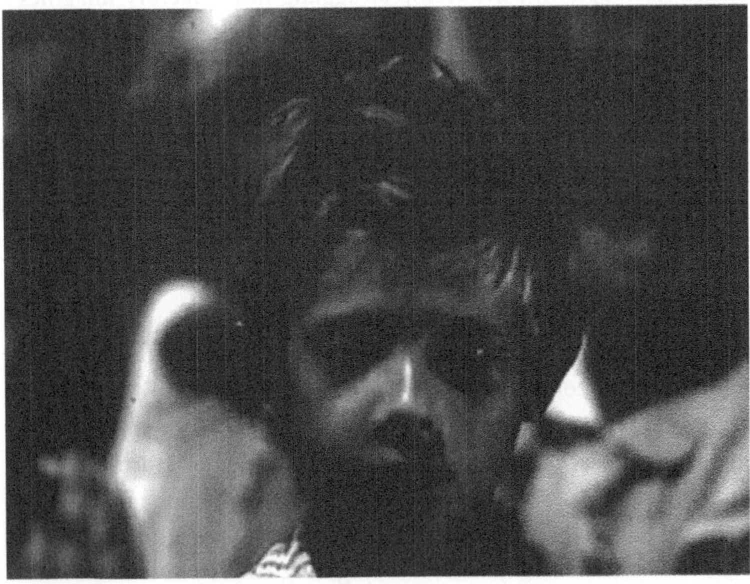

Figure 41. A young spectator pays attention to *Modern Times* in Los Mulos. *Por primera vez,* dir. Octavio Cortázar, 1967.

the body through the conventional form of the shot/countershot. Two severed heads encounter each other in the darkness: that of Chaplin and the Cuban boy. In this juxtaposition, Cortázar implies an identification between the factory worker and the young spectator who will assume his place.

Cortázar visualizes the violent integration of body and machine that characterized industrial capitalism. The assembly line fragments the worker's body, cutting his gestures into the minimal units required of labor. In proposing his concept of the cinematic mode of production, film theorist Jonathan Beller links the assembly line to cinema when he observes that classical cinema primes the spectator to suture fragments of moving images like the worker in the factory. Beller concludes that cinema binds perception to industrial production, reorganizing subjectivity and social relation according to a political economy of visuality.[23] The image of the boy's severed head captures the management of the body that is implicit in cinema and the factory. It acclimates this future worker to the shocks of modernity and prepares him for a productive life in the factory. This process depends on the cinematic cut. We might extend this comparison to the close-up, as both rely on the fundamental operation of the cut. Like the steel and bolts of an automobile, bodies are constructed piecemeal by severing their parts, which are then sutured back together by the spectator. To navigate the factory, the boy will need to adjust to the fragmentation of time and bodies by means of machinery.

In *Por primera vez,* the pedagogy of the body in pieces takes on a decidedly political connotation. The spectator is interpellated by the visual guillotine: he too is symbolically beheaded here as he is being initiated into modernity. Like Beller, Cortázar imagines how cinema primes the audience for the factory, though in *Por primera vez* industrialization serves revolution rather than the forces of capital. The naive spectator is initiated as a political subject through decapitation. If the cut gives form to revolutionary politics, then to be a revolutionary subject requires the spectator to navigate the cut through cinema. The film implies that to be a revolutionary subject is to be a cinematic spectator, and to be a spectator is to negotiate the visual guillotine. Cortázar registers this through the juxtaposition of visually severed heads, that of the

Tramp and the naive spectator. Like other modern technologies, cinema became a symbol of the modernity to which Latin American nations aspired. While each country experienced modernization differently, spectatorship took on a political function early on because it allowed the public to participate in these processes.[24] Yet unlike Cortázar's optimistic account of a smooth transition from underdevelopment in *Por primera vez*, Latin America's entrance into modernity was uneven and turbulent. Consequently, cinema's creation of modern national subjects channeled the broader violence of modernity toward practices of spectatorship.[25]

Decapitation and the Gendered Politics of Suture

Feminist film theorists embraced the intersection of Althusserian Marxism and psychoanalysis in suture theory, arguing that the ways in which the cinematic cut structured the spectator's gaze in narrative film reproduced gendered subject positions. Consequently, such theorists argued that the fragmentation of the female body for the pleasure of the male-coded spectator served patriarchal ideology. Mulvey's "Visual Pleasure and Narrative Cinema" is perhaps the most influential example of such a politicization of suture. Mulvey famously concludes that cinema converts the woman's body into a spectacle to satisfy the male spectator's desire to resolve the anxieties provoked by the image of sexual difference. The representation of woman is reduced to the expression of lack that structures cinematic signification and subject formation through the cut.[26] Narrative cinema resolves this castration anxiety through suture. The spectator identifies with the male gaze of the protagonist and converts the image of woman into a fetish object that is less threatening and more easily controlled.

Through the structure of the apparatus, the male subject satisfies his desire to look at the erotic object while shielding his psyche from the threat of lack posed by the image of sexual difference. The decapitation of the female body through the frame enables its fetishization. The close-up of the female star is thus an ideologically charged image: the apparatus displaces the threat of castration onto the image of this severed head. In a separate essay, published the same year she wrote "Visual Pleasure and Narrative Cinema," Mulvey prefaces her discussion of castration anxiety, fetishism, and the image of woman with a reference to Freud's text on the Medusa.[27] Freud interpreted the threat posed by the

Gorgon as equivalent to castration anxiety: the sight of Medusa's head paralyzed the male gaze because of the threat posed by her lack. In cinema, the close-up of the female star similarly represents castration; however, whereas Freud observes that the image of the Medusa serves to repel the male gaze, in film this threat is contained by fetishizing the severed head of the female star. Stripped of difference, the fragmented female form becomes safe for the male spectator. Through this process, suture resolves the threat of castration through symbolic violence, by decapitating the female form and fetishizing the image of this severed head as the object of visual pleasure. Mulvey thus identifies a latent sadism within the system of suture. The cinematic cut sublimates gendered violence by visually and symbolically decapitating, dismembering, and disfiguring the female body.[28]

Women's cinema in Latin America began to gain momentum in the same years that feminist film theory took hold. With notable exceptions, such as Margot Benacerraf, Sara Gómez, and Marta Rodríguez, film historians have framed the audiovisual politics of New Latin American Cinema as an overwhelmingly masculine affair that erased issues of difference in favor of representing a cohesive, anticolonial, and revolutionary image of the people. By conventional accounts, the rise of authoritarian governments in the 1970s led to the suppression of cinematic militancy associated with the NLAC. This was followed by what Paulo Antonio Paranaguá refers to as the "feminization of the profession," or the late arrival of women's cinema throughout Latin America.[29] From the mid-1960s and throughout the 1970s, the rise of film schools throughout the region gradually democratized access to filmmaking. The 1980s saw the first generation of Latin American women directors achieve international success, including figures such as Suzana Amaral, María Novaro, Fina Torres, Valeria Sarmiento, and Marilú Mallet.[30] One of the most successful filmmakers of this generation, the Argentine director María Luisa Bemberg, bridged the radical filmmaking of the NLAC and the rise of the woman cineaste within the festival and arthouse circuits of world cinema in the 1980s. While her narrative features have drawn the most critical attention, Bemberg debuted with the experimental short *El mundo de la mujer* (*Woman's World,* 1972). She disavowed the film after achieving success, even re-editing it to distance herself from its militant aesthetic, yet recent efforts to provide a fuller account of women's cinema in Latin American film history have led to renewed interest in the avant-garde period that preceded Bemberg's self-styling as an auteur.[31] *El mundo de la mujer* emerged from the filmmaker's militancy in the Unión Feminista Argentina (UFA), of which she was a founding member. The film formed part of the UFA's response to Femimundo, a 1972 consumer trade show in Buenos Aires that showcased the latest trends and products in women's fashion, cosmetics, health, and home goods. In the postwar spectacle of consumerism, Femimundo testifies to capital's role in the reproduction of female subjectivities grounded in traditional concepts of domesticity and beauty. *El mundo de la mujer* critiques consumerism as a mode of oppression that intervenes in the woman's body by manufacturing the desire to be the object of the male gaze. Bemberg documents how the ideological reproduction of heteropatriarchal order becomes an engine of capital, in which women are exploited for their economic potential as they are objectified and coerced into a restrictive life of bourgeois domesticity.

Released shortly before the publication of Mulvey's seminal essay, *El mundo de la mujer* anticipates many of its observations on the image of the fragmented female body as fetish object. Cinema is only one example of Mulvey's broader reflections on the fetishistic representation of women in phallocentric discourse. For example, the discursive mechanisms that structure the male gaze similarly determine female representation in popular spectacles and art. Before turning to film theory, Mulvey was active in the women's liberation movement and was detained for disrupting the 1970 Miss World pageant at Royal Albert Hall in London. Similarly, Mulvey first critiques the fetishization of the female form in the sculptures of British artist Allen Jones before turning her attention to Hitchcock, von Sternberg, and the cinematic apparatus in "Visual Pleasure."[32]

El mundo de la mujer, which similarly arises from an activist intervention, combines feminist and Marxist lenses to critique this fetishization of female form in the spectacle of postwar consumerism. The film realizes this feminist critique of consumption through an ironic montage.[33] Bemberg juxtaposes images of Femimundo with nondiegetic soundtracks appropriated from a variety of sources. These include a male voice-over reading the Femimundo catalog, fragments of the narrator taken from Disney's *Cinderella* (1950), and a female voice reading from the women's magazine *Para Ti.* In combining the political and aesthetic avant-gardes, Bemberg follows the tenets outlined by Mulvey in "Visual Pleasure." *El mundo de la mujer* destroys visual pleasure and represents the fetishization of the female form through the severed head. Bemberg frames the ideological operation that shields the male gaze from the threat of sexual difference in terms of a symbolic decapitation. The cinematic cut gives form to the gendered politics of the apparatus. Bemberg's reflection on the visual guillotine displaces the violence of patriarchal discourse onto audiovisual form to render it visible.

Through the symbolic decapitation of the female form, *El mundo de la mujer* represents the fetishization of woman as a response to castration anxiety and critiques the phallocentric discourse that reduces woman to the image of sexual difference. In the film's opening sequence, which associates the staging of the convention with the construction of the royal palace in *Cinderella*, Bemberg pans over a series of decapitated mannequins as a female voice sings on the soundtrack: "To dream is to leave life behind." As Bemberg documents the workers' transformation of the convention center into Femimundo, she makes clear that the spectator is entering the realm of male fantasy. These initial images stage the condition of woman in this phallocentric discourse. Like the mannequins, the female form is reduced to a synthetic body that is meant to be looked at and arranged according to the active male gaze. By beginning with the image of these undressed plastic bodies, whose curves are meant to draw the gaze, Bemberg reveals that the mannequin is nonetheless sexless. Devoid of genitalia, the image of woman as fetish object that Femimundo promotes does not threaten the male observer (Figure 42). In a subsequent image, Bemberg cuts to a collection of severed mannequin heads that model wigs and makeup. These synthetic bodies cast their eyes downward (Figure 43). Bemberg juxtaposes this image with close-ups of the male spectator at Femimundo. As the spectacle begins, she includes clips of men as they observe models off-camera. The decapitation of the female form represents woman's castrated state. As a result, the severed head and headless body are fetishized for the male gaze. Bemberg represents this symbolic violence visually, relying on the cinematic cut that beheads the female form through the close-up. The headless mannequin, with its exaggerated makeup and coiffure, here satirizes the synthetic materiality of the star's body in the glamour aesthetic of classical Hollywood.

Figure 42. The headless and sexless form of the fetish object. *El mundo de la mujer,* dir. María Luisa Bemberg, 1972.

Figure 43. The female severed head as fetish object. *El mundo de la mujer,* dir. María Luisa Bemberg, 1972.

While *El mundo de la mujer* opens with the image of the decapitated mannequin, the symbolic violence of the male gaze is later displaced onto the bodies of human models. In the spectacle of Femimundo, these women embody the conversion of the female form into a fetish object. Reading from a popular women's magazine, one of the voice-overs describes the archetype of the domesticated woman that these models perform: "The ideal woman for a Cancer should be romantic, generous, and undemanding. That's why you must ask for things very sweetly if you want to bring him to the altar. You should believe in him above all else." Bemberg combines this passage with images of a fashion show at Femimundo, cutting between a close-up of a model walking down the runway and a series of (male and female) heads gazing up from their seats. With this shot/countershot, Bemberg captures how the spectacle sutures the audience into gendered subject positions. In its reliance on the close-up, *El mundo de la mujer* reimagines this scene as a transposition of heads. Commodified in the capitalist spectacle of Femimundo, the female form is reduced to a fetish object, represented by the severed head that is offered up for the spectator's consumption. Bemberg emphasizes the passivity of these synthetic bodies in her critique. When the female voice-over returns, the film cuts to a model reclined on a rotating bed. The woman is so still that she could be confused for a mannequin. The simulation is dispelled only when Bemberg zooms in on the woman's head and registers her blinking. Meanwhile, the voice-over continues: "Take great care of the house, because he loves order. You must be sensual, but not too much. Make him feel sure you'll be an extraordinary spouse." Reframing the image in a wider shot, Bemberg reveals a group of spectators gazing at the lifeless model. *El mundo de la mujer* displaces the violence that underlies the decapitation of the mannequins in the film's opening sequence onto the camera's frame when she represents this same process by visually and symbolically decapitating women in close-up.

Bemberg's denunciation of patriarchal power cannot be divorced from her critique of capital. Men profit from the fetishization of woman in the consumerist spectacle of Femimundo. In a later scene, Bemberg includes images of a hair-styling competition, in which male stylists, under the scrutiny of male judges, showcase their vision of feminine beauty using live models. Bemberg rapidly cuts between close-ups of the models sitting still and male stylists who swarm around them, rushing to finish their showpieces (Figure 44). Bemberg imbues the scene with a sarcastic tone by setting the images to the epic finale of Rossini's *William Tell Overture.* Given the music's cultural association with horses (it was famously used as the theme to *The Lone Ranger*), the juxtaposition suggests that the passive models are treated like show animals to be exhibited for the visual pleasure of the male spectator. After the hair-styling scene, Bemberg cuts to an image of a model's severed head protruding from a machine (Figure 45). The image appears in a sequence that centers on body-modification technologies of questionable efficacy. Subjecting themselves to machines that bear similarity to torture devices, the women tolerate pain and physical discomfort to sculpt their bodies for the male gaze. To be clear, the product marketed in this image is not the body-modification device; it is the ideal image of woman that attracts the male gaze. Bemberg perversely renders this commodification of the female body through a symbolic decapitation. In Femimundo, the female severed head is a form of currency in this libidinal economy. Bemberg represents this commodification of the fetish object—and the spectator's desire—through the image of the severed head.

In these two images—the decapitating close-up of the hair model and the disembodied head of the model protruding from the machine—Bemberg aligns the woman's severed head with the form of capital. This association invokes the etymological relation between *capital* and *decapitation* traced by Judith Butler in her 2014 plenary address to the American Comparative Literature Association, titled "Capital/Punishment." Butler highlights the etymology of *capital* and its relation to decapitation, underscoring the historical relation between capital and the head as an entity that may be severed, counted, and accumulated. To capture the archaeology implicit in Butler's argument, I reproduce a fragment at length:

> The term *capital* derived from the Latin *caput* and *capitalis,* pertaining to the head, and is even linked to the German *kaput* which seems to link the head with something broken, not working, or finished. Apparently, that usage is traced to medieval Germanic burial squads who counted the heads of corpses, that is, those who were done in or finished. So, consider that from the start, capital implied something about a severable and exchangeable head. The

Figure 44. The model's synthetic body is constructed in a hair-styling competition. *El mundo de la mujer,* dir. María Luisa Bemberg, 1972.

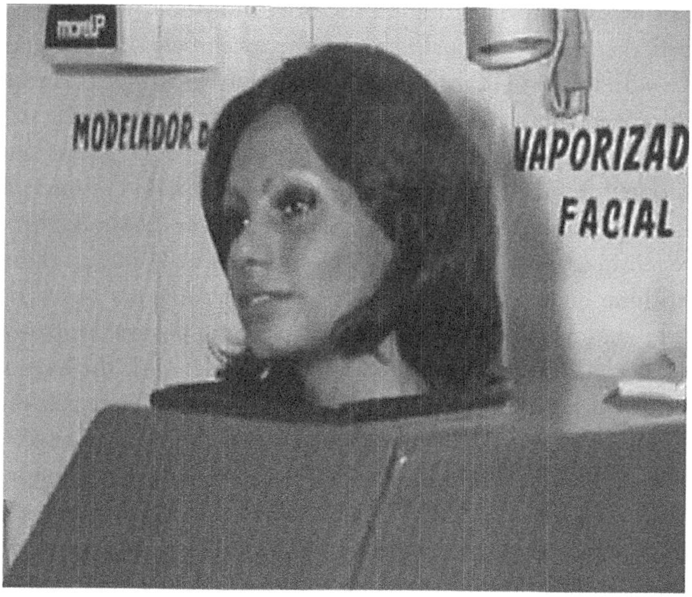

Figure 45. The head of a model protruding from a body-modification device. *El mundo de la mujer,* dir. María Luisa Bemberg, 1972.

> term *capital* emerged in the thirteenth century as a way of measuring wealth by counting the number of cattle heads a person had—his moveable stock. It seems that cattle and chattel both have etymological links with capital, and that all of them seem to be related to countable heads, heads that stand for larger bodies and to some extent separable from them. . . . A certain functional synecdoche has already taken hold, since we are talking about a head that can be moved, sold, and traded. The head is a figure for what is countable and can be consolidated as wealth. One's capital would be then the unified effect of all the heads that one can count as belonging to one's own domain; the head is figured here as a discrete and countable mass, a figure that will become a monetary unit that establishes forms of equivalence among human, animal, and object dimensions of wealth.[34]

The severed heads that appear throughout *El mundo de la mujer* represent the intersection of patriarchal and capitalist violence that has been directed at women throughout history. This association shapes the history of the close-up and its fetishization of female beauty. While film historians have struggled to identify the precise origins of the close-up, Mulvey observes that its institutionalization in the style of classical cinema coincides with the birth of the female star; in Mulvey's words, "Consumer seduction and the seductive powers of the female image on the screen grew side by side."[35] Put differently, the close-up of the female star cannot be separated from the commodification and fetishization of the female form. Mulvey's argument bridges psychoanalytic and Marxist theories of the fetish, arguing that cinema's resolution of male anxiety through the fetishization of woman through the close-up could not be separated from the commodity spectacle.[36] In the context of postwar Hollywood, the glamorous image of the female star coincides with the height of consumerism; while advertising created a spectacle of the female form, the film industry sold this image of woman to the world. As a result, the close-up conflated the spectacular image of woman with commodity fetishism.[37] The domesticated woman idealized by Femimundo is treated as her husband's property; in other words, she is part of his capital. Bemberg's ironic close-ups of the mannequins and perverse decapitation of the models visualizes the gendered association of capital and the severed head in Femimundo.

Fetishization and the Afterlives of the Cut

Following Bemberg's international success in the 1980s and early 1990s, Lucrecia Martel has emerged as the central figure of a second generation of internationally acclaimed women filmmakers in Latin America.[38] In the context of my reflection on spectatorship, the severed head, and the cinematic cut, I turn to Martel's critique of fetishization in her narrative feature *La mujer sin cabeza* (*The Headless Woman,* 2008) and online videos *Muta* (2011) and *AI* (2019). Like Bemberg, Martel critiques the disciplining of the female body within the audiovisual apparatus by displacing patriarchal violence onto the cinematic cut. By decapitating and disfiguring the body, her films unsettle the spectator by signaling the symbolic violence of audiovisual form.[39] I focus especially on Martel's correlation of the cut with decapitation and defacement. Martel continues the tradition of defacement that Jacques Aumont first identified in postwar modernist cinema; however, she employs the cut to critique fetishization in narrative cinema and signal the survival of this visual guillotine in the digital apparatus. The theme of decapitation is made explicit in Martel's third feature. *La mujer sin cabeza* marks the final entry in what critics have come to recognize as Martel's Salta trilogy. Forming the core of her oeuvre, these films share a concern with the position of women within the patriarchal order of Argentina's provincial bourgeoisie. A growing body of criticism has highlighted Martel's interrogation of the stagnant effects of the patriarchy and the subversive potential of female desire throughout the trilogy.[40] I read *La mujer sin cabeza* in light of my reflections on the visual guillotine and the feminist politics of form. Martel engages a long history of theorizing the cinematic woman as symbolically castrated. Here, again, we may interpret the severed head—and specifically the headless woman—along psychoanalytic lines; she is reduced to an expression of sexual difference. Through the close-up, Martel represents the inscription of male dominance over the female body that is characteristic of the audiovisual apparatus. At the heart of this critique is the head, severed in the frame of the close-up.

La mujer sin cabeza opens with a group of boys, accompanied by their dog, playing along a remote stretch of highway. The camera then cuts to a suburban party with raucous children, establishing a juxtaposition with the previous scene that highlights the contrast in race and class between the darker features of the boys and their white, middle-class counterparts. After leaving, the camera accompanies Vero as she drives along the road seen previously. When Vero turns away to answer her phone, she strikes something on the highway. In the immediate aftermath of the collision, the camera remains focused on Vero and leaves the audience to speculate as to what has just happened. After readjusting her sunglasses, she drives off. The camera cuts to an image of the road as the car leaves the scene, shot through the back windshield. An ambiguous form lies in the road; the spectator is unable to determine whether it is human or animal. Vero is visibly shaken by the event. Pulling over, she exits the vehicle and begins pacing. The camera remains motionless inside the car, looking out through the windshield. As it begins to rain, a blurry Vero stands still in the frame with only her torso and arms visible. This is the first image we have of the headless woman that gives Martel's film its title. Throughout the work, Martel repeatedly decapitates Vero. This violence against the body on-screen is also a form of disappearance; Vero's head constantly vanishes from and reappears in the frame.

Visibly disturbed, Vero later shares her experience with her husband and brother-in-law. Though the men insist that she must have killed an animal, they call the local police to inquire of any deaths in the area and cover any potential tracks. Vero later learns from a shopkeeper that a local boy has failed to come to work for several days after the accident. At once a reference to the protagonist's mental unease as she is wracked with guilt following the hit-and-run, Vero's headlessness also represents the lack of female subjectivity in a patriarchal society that erases her voice and actions. While obliquely addressing the violence suffered by Indigenous communities in Argentina, as well as the impunity of the upper class under dictatorship, *La mujer sin cabeza* is simultaneously a study of Vero's fetishization and lack of agency. Following the accident, the protagonist is characterized by what Valeria de los Ríos refers to as a radical fracture in her subjectivity.[41] Vero is not only disoriented; she begins to lose control of her actions. The men in her life repeatedly gaslight her by insisting that she hit a dog, though they nevertheless erase any evidence of her having checked into a nearby hospital and hotel on the day of the accident. Meanwhile, Vero wanders around in a daze, unable to function. Underlying Vero's subjection is the assumption that she is mad. Vero's headlessness may thus also be read along traditional psychoanalytic lines, as an allegory for both her neurosis and lack of subjectivity. This is expressed formally through the frame, which visually decapitates Vero.

Martel reinforces her reflection on the politics of form and the fetishization of the female body through her citation of Alfred Hitchcock's *Vertigo.* In her reading of *La mujer sin cabeza,* Patricia White compares Vero to Madeleine, Hitchcock's female protagonist played by Kim Novak. White cites the repeated framing of Vero's blond hair in profile, an image that re-creates Hitchcock's presentation of Madeleine (Figures 46 and 47).[42] Martel's reference to *Vertigo* in her examination of the agency and cinematic treatment of the female form is not fortuitous. The film plays a central role in Mulvey's theory of spectatorship, and indeed much of the criticism of Hitchcock's film has revolved around the male gaze and the fetishization of the female form.[43] The image of Madeleine that Martel cites captures this point. In the original scene, the audience is introduced to Novak's character. We begin with a glimpse of Scottie, played by James Stewart, who is seated at the bar of a restaurant. A private detective, Scottie has been hired to follow Madeleine, whose husband believes she has gone mad. Madeleine's entrance highlights her passivity. In a classic shot/countershot, Hitchcock begins with an image of Scottie as he looks over his shoulder from the bar to the table where Madeleine is seated. The camera then zooms out and pans over the dining room to follow his gaze, finally landing on Madeleine. As she stands to leave and walks toward him, the camera periodically cuts back to Scottie to reinforce that she is the object of his gaze until finally she enters the frame with her profile in close-up: this is the severed head, object of the male gaze. The reference to Hitchcock recalls Mulvey's theory of fetishization in narrative cinema. Revisiting "Visual Pleasure and Narrative Cinema" on the fortieth anniversary of its publication, Mulvey underscores the centrality of *Vertigo* in her argument but admits that Hitchcock's treatment of Madeleine is more nuanced than she had initially realized. Mulvey concludes that the film is a self-reflexive meditation on the fetishization of the female star, rather than simply another example of this process.[44] Through his close-up of Novak, Hitchcock aligns the symbolic violence of this formal device—the decapitation of Madeleine—with cinema's fetishization of the female figure. In her citation of *Vertigo,* Martel inscribes *La mujer sin cabeza* within this theoretical and cinematic tradition, which associates the close-up and fetishization. The visual guillotine gives form to the fetish object. In the spectator's consumption of the woman's severed head, the patriarchal structure of the apparatus is displaced onto the violence of the cut.

Martel continues to reflect on the relation between gender and form in her more recent experiments with digital video. Following the success of the Salta trilogy, which Martel shot on 35 mm film, the acceleration of digital and streaming technologies forced the filmmaker to abandon analog formats.[45] Yet far from lamenting the pressure to adapt to new

Figure 46. A decapitated Vero following the accident. *La mujer sin cabeza,* dir. Lucrecia Martel, 2012.

Figure 47. A decapitated Madeleine. *Vertigo,* dir. Alfred Hitchcock, 1958.

technologies, Martel embraces the potential of electronic and digital media to disrupt the conventions of cinematic spectatorship. Indeed, the unsettling potential of technology represents a subtle current that runs throughout her work. Martel's style privileges ambiguity, and her films often employ technology to introduce uncertainty or reinforce an ominous mood.[46] While her Salta trilogy subverts narrative clarity through the disruptive potential of electronic images and sound, in recent years Martel has embraced the imperfections of digital aesthetics. She has openly expressed her fascination with YouTube in particular, and Gerd Gemünden has observed that the platform plays an important role in her recent productions.[47] For example, Martel cites YouTube's algorithm, along with its immense archive of content, as a source of inspiration: "The YouTube autoplay system combined with the word you use to start the search is my favorite psychopharmaceutical."[48] Here, Martel underscores the creative potential of digital montage. The algorithm's juxtapositions of moving images provoke unexpected insights, reminiscent of the epistemological flashes Walter Benjamin associated with photography and montage. The comment highlights the survival of cinematic forms—especially the cut that fragments the stream of videos—in the digital apparatus.[49] This extends to the cinematic cut that severs the head in the close-up. However, while *Muta* and *AI* continue the tradition of cinematic defacement identified by Aumont, they associate this process with a form that is proper to the digital apparatus: the pixel. In her exploration of the pixel's potential to deface, Martel reflects on the potential of digital form to unsettle perception and disrupt the ideological structure of the gaze. In his encounter with the pixelated face, the spectator must navigate the moving image through a new form of the cut.

Even after the transition to the digital apparatus, the visual guillotine continues to ground spectatorship. The digital image is the result of an algorithmic process that converts patterns of light into information, which is then encoded digitally by cutting its plane into a grid of pixels. The numerical array of this grid allows the image to be communicated electronically over a network. The higher the resolution, the larger the grid and the less visible the pixel on the screen. An image appears pixelated when the resolution is lowered and the grid enlarged so that it contains less information and may be more easily stored and transferred. For this reason, pixelation occurs most commonly in processes of compression that economize the transfer of audiovisual information in streaming. Streaming platforms such as YouTube depend on compression algorithms to adjust the resolution of a video to match the speed with which information can be transferred given the limits of the spectator's connection. At a certain resolution, the spectator becomes aware that, unlike the analog image, in which spatial and tonal qualities are continuous, the digital image is cut up into discrete elements.[50] When enlarged to the point of visibility, this cutting of the image into pixels with clearly demarcated borders becomes apparent.

In 2011, the fashion house Miu Miu commissioned Martel to direct a digital short intended for exhibition over YouTube.[51] Entitled *Muta,* the video takes place on the Río Paraná, on Argentina's northern border with Paraguay. As is typical of Martel, an opening soundscape sets the tone of the film. Martel prefaces the image with the buzzing of insects, followed by a flurry of bugs shot against the undulating dark water. In the video uploaded by Miu Miu to its official YouTube account, limited to a low resolution of 360p, the insects appear fuzzy and pixelated. The spectator is then introduced to the mise-en-scène: an elegant boat floats along the river, with no signs of life on board. Ambient noise combined with shots of empty interiors gives it the air of an abandoned spaceship. Slowly, the vessel comes to life and a humanoid figure emerges from a corner of the screen. Its movement is alternately sped up and slowed down as it gradually unfolds to stand upright, emphasizing a gaunt and angular silhouette reminiscent of a praying mantis. Played by runway models wearing Miu Miu's 2011 spring/summer collection, these figures appear as hybrid insect-women. The models' posthuman appearance is reinforced by Martel's decision to never reveal their faces. The video achieves this opacity through compositional strategies: women angle themselves away from the camera, cover their faces with their hair, or wear a range of prostheses including gas masks and oversized glasses. The defacement of these figures contributes to the video's unsettling atmosphere. Furthermore, it aligns the models with the sexless materiality and absence of facial features in the shop mannequin.[52] As I have argued by way of Mulvey, the image of the face, especially when framed in close-up, converts woman into a fetish object by creating a spectacle of the female body. This is especially true in the context of fashion, and

Martel resists this fetishization by denying the spectator a glimpse of the models' faces.

Rather than structure *Muta* along a narrative, Martel follows a string of oneiric associations. In one scene, we hear two forms breathing heavily through gas masks that give them a bug-eyed appearance, as they spray a third with a chemical (Figure 48). Again, the low resolution of the official video causes the pixelation of the image to reinforce their facelessness. Though the film revels in its strangeness and indeterminacy, the ambiguity of these bodies forms part of Martel's critique of fashion, specifically the fetishization of the female form by means of dress. In the following scene, a group of models lounges on a couch and drinks a viscous insecticide from martini glasses while a telephone tone drones in the background. One wraps another in a strand of white thread, as if she were a spider trapping her prey in a web. By the end of the film, the insect-models retreat to separate corners of this elegant hive and dematerialize, leaving behind only their fashionable adornments. Dresses lay crumpled and cast aside, without a body to give them form. Martel returns to the image of her establishing shot, closing the circular logic of the film: as the screen fades to black, a swarm of insects flies around the frame. Liberated from the fetishization of the fashion industry, these forms mutate into insects. As the credits begin to roll, Martel leaves the viewer with the sound of their buzzing.

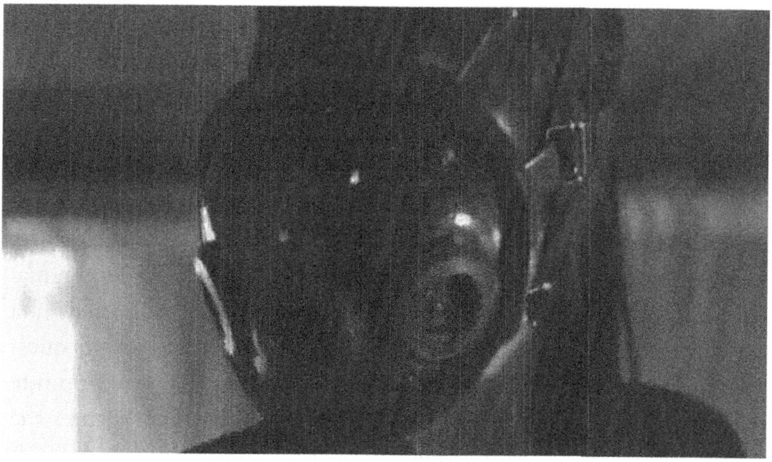

Figure 48. Martel's faceless model. *Muta,* dir. Lucrecia Martel, 2010.

As one of Martel's first digital productions, the video establishes a metaphorical relation between the insect and the pixel. Insects have long served as models and metaphors for theorizing new media.[53] Indeed, like the insect, the pixel flickers, swarms, and mutates.[54] In *Muta,* the relation between the pixel and the insect stems from the correlation between the cutting of the image and the cutting of the body, which defines the visual guillotine. Central to an insect poetics in natural and cultural history is the observation that the insect's body is naturally fragmented. The insect is conceived as an assemblage, and this logic of corporeal fragmentation underlies Martel's representation of the insect-models in *Muta.*[55] Their forms frequently appear dismembered in the frame or assume contorted positions. Like the pixel, these bodies are cut into discrete elements from which they are assembled. Martel's defaced and symbolically decapitated insect-human hybrids critique the discursive construction of femininity in which Miu Miu participates by disavowing its fetishization of the female form. Within the context of its production, the short subverts the hegemonic image that the fashion label seeks to construct by estranging its brand of feminine luxury. In its uncanny representation of the consumerist ideal of the feminine form, *Muta* recalls the spirit of *El mundo de la mujer.* However, these bodies are not just decapitated by the frame; they are further defaced through pixelation.

If *Muta* subtly updates Martel's reflection on the cut and the fetish object for the digital apparatus, *AI* experiments with the form of the pixel explicitly. The video was also commissioned for the purposes of publicity, in this case to promote the 2019 Viennale. Less than two minutes long, *AI* abandons narrative structure and embraces experimental aesthetics. Martel appropriates a fragment of an old medical film that has found a viral afterlife on YouTube. Produced for the Psychiatry Department of the UCLA School of Medicine in 1961, the source material features an interview with a young man diagnosed with catatonic schizophrenia. The composition of the original image initially frames the patient in a full body shot. Seated but communicating discomfort, he answers questions from a psychiatrist who is positioned off-camera. The ten-minute interview alternates between this shot and a close-up that captures the patient's expressive facial movements. Martel samples ninety seconds of this image, which she reframes in an even tighter close-up. She then pixelates the man's face so that all but his right eye is illegible (Figure 49). The video consists of the defaced interview subject, which Martel interrupts at moments by splicing in flashes of other popular YouTube videos. As the only unpixelated element of the image, the eye, which darts around as the man speaks, draws the spectator's attention. In their encounter with this abstracted face, spectators cannot anchor themselves in a reciprocated gaze. This assemblage of pixels interpellates the audience, which feels watched by the apparatus.[56] The effect of the pixelation in *AI* is ominous, and the lack of context reinforces this atmosphere. The pixels move while this figure speaks, and although the spectator manages to anchor this voice in a body, the abstraction of the face transforms this uncanny form into an anthropomorphized representation of the opaque digital apparatus.

Despite *AI*'s radical departure from Martel's auteur aesthetic, its themes remain consistent with the filmmaker's oeuvre. The selection of the source material suggests a critique of fetishization. First, the original film reproduces the medical gaze that reduces the mentally ill patient to a specimen.[57] This image is further converted into a spectacle in its digital afterlife; at the time of writing, it has been reproduced more than twenty-four million times. Though the spectator's position is grounded in a voyeuristic curiosity that has marked the tradition of psychiatric photography and cinema, the audience similarly reduces the patient to a

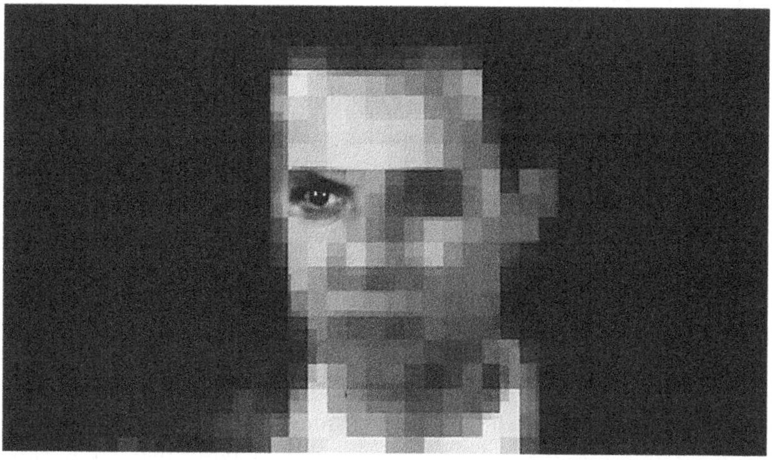

Figure 49. The pixelated face of a schizophrenic. *AI*, dir. Lucrecia Martel, 2019.

one-dimensional model of alterity. Through such fetishization, both the discursive framing of the original image and its digital reception metaphorically deface the patient. From *El mundo de la mujer* to Martel's digital videos, we see that filmmakers resist fetishistic spectatorship by defacing and decapitating the body. However, while the close-up and montage continue to orient the spectator's relation to moving images, the visual guillotine also takes on new forms with the conceptual expansion of the cut in the digital apparatus.

Expanding the Cut After Cinema

The mutation of exhibition practices with the shift from cinema to electronic media and the digital apparatus transformed the spectator's relation to the moving image at the end of the twentieth century. While many have lamented the shift away from traditional modes of production, exhibition, and spectatorship in recent decades, the visual guillotine has stubbornly persisted. The cut continues to organize spectatorship and audiovisual politics. However, as I argued in my account of the decapitation video in chapter 3 and discussed in relation to Martel's treatment of the pixel, the concept of the cut has expanded with the cultural displacement of cinema and the rise of new intermedial forms. With the transition to the digital apparatus, the cinematic cut no longer implies a physical assault on the body of the film. Nonetheless, it has taken on new forms while still preserving the force of the close-up and montage.

In Latin America, the precarization of film production in the final decades of the twentieth century forced filmmakers to adopt postcinematic technologies comparatively early due to their lower production cost. The prohibitive expense of purchasing and developing film stock, the lack of funding for film preservation, and the push toward private financing have meant that for many, Latin American cinema has been mediated through low-quality electronic reproductions. The displacement of spectatorship from the public sphere of the movie theater to the private space of the home in the 1980s and 1990s alarmed scholars in the region, prompting Néstor García Canclini to sound the death knell of Latin American cinema by the end of the century.[58] The precarious state of cinema has also led filmmakers throughout the region to explore its uncertain future through a series of mournful works that Sarah Ann Wells labels "late cinema."[59] In this postcinematic landscape, funding for feature films has become scarce, and opportunities for filmmakers to exhibit theatrically are few. Expanded cinema has emerged from the protracted eclipse of traditional filmmaking and exhibition. This term refers to a heterogeneous set of practices that, beginning in the 1960s, displaces the moving images to nontraditional venues, such as the gallery. In the final decades of the twentieth century, filmmakers and moving-image artists began imagining cinematic spaces beyond the movie theater and questioning the perceptual, spatial, and political limits of their practice.[60] These concerns reached a head with the introduction of home video and digital technologies, to the point that expanded cinema has passed from the fringes to the mainstream of contemporary art. In other words, expanded cinema gradually emerged from the exhaustion of cinema as an independent medium and the mutation of the moving image into an intermedial object. By intervening in the materiality of exhibition, filmmakers critique the ideological charge behind the distribution of light, sound, and bodies in the movie theater. These film installations enact new collective experiences by reimagining spectatorship.

Framed in the white cube of the gallery, the film installation *La Passion de Jeanne d'Arc (Rozelle Hospital)* (2004), by Venezuelan artist Javier Téllez, invites the viewer to engage a defamiliarized object. A red velvet curtain, reminiscent of a movie theater, demarcates the black box of the viewing area. Before crossing this threshold, the audience first passes a blackboard that announces the installation's title and lists the signatures of twelve women who collaborated with the artist on this work. Once inside, the spectator encounters a two-channel projection. On one screen, Téllez displays an altered copy of Carl Theodor Dreyer's *La Passion de Jeanne d'Arc* (1928). The intervention in this classic avant-garde film is the result of the artist's collaboration with twelve patients from Rozelle Hospital, a psychiatric facility in Sydney, Australia. *Rozelle Hospital* is the first in a series of cinematic collaborations between Téllez and psychiatric patients from around the world. For these projects, the artist typically receives a commission from an art institution and collaborates with patients in a local psychiatric hospital.[61] In the production of *Rozelle Hospital*, the artist screened *Jeanne d'Arc* for the patients, who then rewrote the film's intertitles over the course of a monthlong workshop. The original film departs from the archival record of Joan of Arc's trial. Testifying before a clerical tribunal, Joan stands accused of heresy after claiming to have experienced divine visions and voices. Dreyer's adaptation of this document famously experiments with cinematic style to represent Joan's transcendental experience, which the priests attempt to rationalize. *Rozelle Hospital*, in turn, preserves Dreyer's images but imagines a new narrative that is similarly grounded in the persecution of unreason. In Téllez's collaboration, a woman is admitted to Rozelle Hospital and diagnosed with delusions of grandeur. She believes herself to be Joan of Arc and suffers at the hands of the cruel hospital staff. Dreyer's priests become doctors, and Joan's trial a psychiatric evaluation.

As the altered copy of Dreyer's film plays on one screen, Téllez projects a 16 mm film opposite it. Titled *Twelve and a Marionette,* these images were shot and edited by the artist himself. The film contains a series of monologues by the patients at Rozelle Hospital, each of which begins with a series of headshots taken from the front, side, and back of the head. Following these images, each woman appears in a close-up with her head filling the frame. One after another, they face the camera and recall their time in the psychiatric system. Some recount the abuse they suffered as girls, leading up to their institutionalization. Others tell how patronizing staff in the hospital have belittled their knowledge. While recalling their negative experiences, the film avoids reducing them to a spectacle. For example, Téllez foregrounds the patients' ability to subvert clinical discourse through mimicry. Throughout the interviews, the women imitate the psychiatrists and hospital staff. One goes further and role-plays an interaction with a psychiatrist, who is played by a marionette under her control. Téllez explains that he was drawn to these representational strategies when creating the film because they allow the patients to construct their personal narratives from a position of agency.[62] By disturbing the divisions between (male) psychiatrist and (female) patient, the women are able to challenge the gendered construction of mental illness. The visual form of the interviews also contributes to the installation's critique of gender in cinema and psychiatry. On one hand, the headshots that open each interview invoke the tradition of psychiatric photography that invented hysteria by making a spectacle of the female body.[63] On the other, Téllez's extensive reliance on the close-up recalls the disciplining of the female body that structures cinematic form and materiality. Visually invoking this tradition, *Twelve and a Marionette* then disrupts it by blurring the distinction between patient and psychiatrist through mimicry.

Téllez positions the spectator between *Twelve and a Marionette* and the altered copy of *Jeanne d'Arc*. By forcing the audience to navigate these images, the materiality of the installation produces an embodied spectatorship that becomes crucial to *Rozelle Hospital*'s intervention in the genealogy Téllez invokes. The installation abandons the conventions of theatrical spectatorship that cinema inherited. Rather than sit in rows, spectators must position themselves in one of twelve chairs corresponding to the twelve patients. With the two screens opposite one another, the spectator can only immerse themselves in one moving image at any given moment and must constantly rotate their head if they wish to alternate between them. The result of this spatial distribution can be maddening. If they are following the projection of Dreyer's film with the new intertitles written by the Rozelle patients, the spectator hears the testimonies from *Twelve and a Marionette* nondiegetically. These disembodied voices simulate an auditory hallucination. In forcing the spectator to repeatedly move their head from screen to screen, the installation activates the spectator's body. If facing the opposite direction, watching Téllez's 16 mm film, the spectator is conscious of Dreyer's film playing behind them. Though unable to see it, they inevitably imagine the scenes being projected outside their field of vision, thus mimicking a visual hallucination. There is also a third option: the spectator faces the wall, as if they too were a patient in the asylum, with either screen in her peripheral vision. To draw them even closer to the experiences of his collaborators, Téllez lines the interior of the installation with linens taken from Rozelle Hospital. Like the adaptation of Dreyer and Téllez's 16 mm film, this exhibitionary apparatus operates through a subversive mimesis. *Rozelle Hospital* seeks to shorten the gap between patient and audience by nullifying the disembodied clinical gaze and staging an ethical encounter through an embodied spectatorship.

Through the intermedial practices of expanded cinema, *Rozelle Hospital* encourages an embodied reception by destabilizing a mode of viewing that underlies the history of unreason. Elaine Showalter argues that the construction of madness as a female malady has long depended on a binary cultural paradigm that associates disembodied reason with masculinity and an embodied irrationality with femininity.[64] In his study on the invention of hysteria, Georges Didi-Huberman advances a similar argument from the perspective of visual culture, proposing that psychiatric photography pursued an ideal (male) clinical gaze—one that was disembodied and objective, capable of decoding pathology.[65] The purpose of Téllez's simulation of unreason is not to romanticize mental illness by abandoning reason. Rather, the installation reconfigures the codes of cinematic exhibition to encourage a momentary suspension or even weakening of disembodied cognition in order to bridge the representational gap between spectator and patient.[66] Through its mimetic strategies, both the patients' imitations of psychiatrists in *Twelve and a Marionette* and the spectator's embodied encounter through the installation's materiality, *Rozelle Hospital* realizes such an aesthetics by deconstructing the binary opposition between disembodied rationality and embodied spectacle that has structured definitions of madness.[67]

A canonical example of modernist cinema, *La Passion de Jeanne d'Arc* famously represents Joan's trial, execution, and torture at the hands of the church almost exclusively through a disjointed series of close-ups. Dreyer's use of the close-up frustrates the perceptual-cognitive processes that drive the narrative system of classical cinema and the conventional form of spectatorship to which audiences are accustomed. This classical style employs the cinematic cut to reinforce temporal and spatial cohesion and facilitate the spectator's rational comprehension of the narrative.[68] In classical cinema, emotion, affect, and other embodied responses are secondary to the cognitive act of narrative comprehension.[69] Consequently, classical narration privileges a disembodied gaze. Dreyer's experimentation with the close-up breaks with the narrative and spatial unity on which this disembodied spectatorship relies, leading David Bordwell to regard *Jeanne d'Arc* as "one of the most bizarre, perceptually difficult films ever made."[70] The frame's visual mutilation of Joan coincides with the torture represented in the film. Severed by the shot, Joan's contorted face expresses both agony and transcendence. The camera's symbolic violence converges with this diegetic violence. These close-ups become the primary vehicle in Dreyer's elaboration of a transcendental style. The filmmaker did not intend for these images to represent pain, but to express Joan's mysticism and evoke a similarly sublime experience in the spectator. Gazing up at these enormous heads, the spectator experiences an affective state intended to provoke an experience analogous to Joan's sublime visions.

I tie the affective power of Dreyer's close-ups—and Téllez's citation of these images—to the iconography of the severed head. As I have explained, Julia Kristeva argues that this image marks the origins of figuration, of our first attempts to express the ineffable experience of inner life and spirit through images: "Inner experience is a transubstantiation that necessitates a beheading, a traversal of consciousness so that the inferno of the void can be revealed."[71] Like Bataille's figure of the *acéphale,* the image of the severed head—or the decapitated body—represents the irrational forces that guide us. Kristeva echoes Bataille when she identifies the image of the severed head with the negation of disembodied knowledge. Throughout her cultural history of beheading, Kristeva traces the severed head's relation to transcendental experience back to Byzantine icons, the iconography of decapitated saints in the Catholic tradition, and primordial skull rites. Following Kristeva, a strong bond exists between the severed head and an embodied unreason. As *Jeanne d'Arc* demonstrates, cinema holds a special place in this genealogy that links beheading with the transcendence of reason. Gazing up at a head severed by the close-up, the audience is transfixed. This icon induces a state that cannot easily be psychologized.

To go mad, the popular refrain tells us, is to lose one's head. Psychoanalysis viewed the severed head as a root of pathology, but French cultural historian Laure Murat offers a compelling account of this relation between beheading and madness that will allow me to return to Dreyer's close-ups and their interpretation by Téllez. Murat argues that a political history of madness must begin with the guillotine. This symbol of the Terror inspired more than just political reflections on violence and the state; it was also at the heart of medical debates at the end of the eighteenth century. Of these, the burgeoning field of psychiatry expressed keen interest in the guillotine and the severed heads it manufactured. Among the physicians present at public beheadings was Philippe Pinel, the founder of this discipline. Murat argues:

> The perfect coincidence of the birth of psychiatry with the invention of the guillotine stems not so much from chance as from historical correlations—including a semantic one, as suggested by the

> literal and figurative connection between "losing your head" and "losing your mind." As far removed as treating the mentally ill may seem from beheading enemies of the Revolution—as distant as the development of a medical field is from the making of a death-dealing machine—psychiatry and the guillotine share an attachment to the link between head and body (whether joined or separated), to the integrity of self and consciousness.[72]

Pinel explored the connection between madness and beheading in his journals. Many of his patients at the time suffered from delusions that they had been decapitated by the guillotine and had had their heads replaced with another's. They wandered around Pinel's asylum at Bicêtre in search of their true heads. Pinel studied these cases in order to elaborate the connection between politics and mental illness. In these historical phenomena, Murat argues, the semantic connection between losing one's head and losing one's mind was established. Dreyer understood cinema's position in the historical relation between decapitation and transcendental experience. By relating the close-up and unreason, he brought together genealogies of the severed head in cinema and psychiatry.

Citing *Jeanne d'Arc*'s signature aesthetic, Téllez's film *Twelve and a Marionette* is also shot exclusively using close-ups. Facing the camera, the artist's collaborators recall their experiences in psychiatric hospitals. Prior to their testimony, the film introduces each patient with a series of headshots that invoke the tradition of psychiatric photography. The artist admits that "the use of close-ups and physiognomy make reference to one of the foundational tools of psychiatry."[73] Psychiatry repurposed portraiture in its attempt to objectively represent madness as an object of study. It cut up the patient's body in the pursuit of clinical knowledge.[74] Inheriting the tradition of physiognomy, psychiatric photography registered the patient's contorted expressions as the outward projection of inner pathology. While creating a spectacle of the patient's body, the psychiatrist maintained his distance. The embodiment of madness was performed for the disembodied gaze of the clinician. These visually severed heads were the image of madness. Cinema and psychiatry intersect in this shared origin in the guillotine. In both cases, the severed head provides an image of unreason: its place at the origins of figural representation historically ties it to the expression of the irrational forces of inner experience, which Bataille defines as "*mystical experience:* the states of ecstasy, of rapture, at least of meditated emotion."[75] Seeking to reproduce the embodied character of inner experience, Dreyer and Téllez repurpose the close-up to subvert this tradition. By frustrating cognitivist modes of reception—Dreyer through his fragmentation of narrative space, Téllez through his intervention in the exhibitionary apparatus—they strive to neutralize the clinical gaze. Their close-ups do not place the spectator in the position of the psychiatrist. Rather, they function as affection images that transmit intensities to the audience.[76] In other words, these images have the opposite effect of psychiatric photography by altering the spectator's position. Eliminating the critical distance that separates the psychiatrist from the patient, these close-ups embrace cinema's ability to bring the spectator closer to the patient's embodiment of unreason.

Unlike the psychiatrist, who carefully studies the photographic image of the hysteric in a clinical environment, Téllez's audience encounters these close-ups while navigating expanded cinema's aesthetics of unreason. Téllez positions the spectator between two screens. With the altered version of *Jeanne d'Arc* and *Twelve and a Marionette* opposite one another, the type of passive spectatorship that permits a disembodied gaze becomes impossible. Furthermore, the possible viewing positions imposed by the installation imitate experiences of embodied unreason. As I have mentioned, spectators have three options. They might view the screen projecting the repurposed copy of Dreyer and hear the testimonies from *Twelve and a Marionette,* or observe Téllez's film while nevertheless imagining Dreyer's images that play behind them. In either case, the installation encourages the simulation of auditory or visual hallucinations. Finally, the spectator might sit between the two screens and face forward so as to rotate her head between the two projections. In this case, Téllez ensures an active spectator whose body is drawn into the installation. *Rozelle Hospital* thus blurs the line between spectator and performer by physically interpellating the audience. Through the spatial distribution of the installation, *Rozelle Hospital* encourages the spectator to suspend a passive and disembodied gaze that would adopt the position of the psychiatrist. Instead, the spectator mimics the patient that is confined to a room in the psychiatric hospital. Through this installation, the spectator symbolically loses his head.

CONCLUSION
INVITATION TO A BEHEADING

I glance around nervously as I take my seat in Princeton University's Firestone Library. On a Friday night in October 2014, only a few bleary-eyed students are scattered among the long tables. My movement draws the attention of another patron, and I carefully angle my screen so it is out of her line of sight. I double-check the volume of my laptop and ensure that it is silenced. From Google, I pull up a collection of videos to begin my research. My finger hovers over the touchpad. After a pause, I click play. My muscles tighten in anticipation of the images I am about to view. A pit deepens in my stomach.

Even the most disciplined scholar is unprepared to witness a beheading. Critical distance collapses at the sight of a body cut into pieces. The initial reaction is of sublime horror from which I cannot look away. My screen doubles as Perseus's shield, reflecting the image of the Gorgon. The authors of these images have created a macabre spectacle that for years has circulated on social media, sensationalist blogs, and seedy internet forums. In August 2014, Daesh militants constructed a soundstage in the Iraqi desert and beheaded the American journalist James Foley on-camera. A wave of decapitation videos overtook the international news cycle, reminiscent of recordings produced in Afghanistan and Pakistan at the start of the war on terror. A month after Foley's decapitation, forty-three *normalistas* disappeared in Iguala, Mexico. Within days of the mass disappearance, images of torture victims, alleged to be among the missing students, began circulating on social media. The narco-conflict had gone viral, and not for the first time, drawing attention to the audiovisual production of what Rossana Reguillo dubs the *necromáquina*. Through this systematic reproduction of expressive violence and death, criminal forces have erected a parallel state in Mexico.[1] Echoing the tactics of religious extremists, criminal organizations in Mexico have proven adept at manipulating digital media for ideological ends. These amateur videographers have produced dozens of decapitation videos since former Mexican president Felipe Calderón's declaration of a deceptively named "war on drugs" accelerated violence in 2006. The authors of the videos seized the potential of Web 2.0. The first decapitation video to go viral in Mexico, titled *Haz patria, mata un Zeta*, was uploaded to YouTube in 2006—months after the platform had launched. Echoing Walter Benjamin's conclusion in his seminal essay on the technological reproducibility of the image, these forces wielded digital media to aestheticize politics.[2] After all, decapitation lies at the origin of both figuration and the political.[3]

The decapitation video is a product of the transformation of cinema and politics in the present. The growing accessibility of digital technology accelerated the representation of political violence. Every militant, soldier, and *narco* carried with them a digital camera with which to register their cruelty. Changes to image distribution and spectatorship precipitated by digital media further enabled the consumption of violent imagery at an unprecedented scale. A tide of unwatchable imagery—decapitated, dismembered, and mutilated bodies—saturated the internet. These images frequently went viral on social media and drew millions of monthly viewers to sensationalist outlets.

The elegant reading room of a prestigious research library is an odd place to view a snuff film. I watch video after video, taking notes on composition, camera movement, mise-en-scène, and editing. To understand these images, I aim to elaborate a critical viewing position that evades both moralism and sensationalism. I decide not to shield my eyes so that I may subject this object to aesthetic judgment and political critique. To emphasize their deliberate manipulation of audiovisual form, I extract screenshots and juxtapose these compositions with images taken from film history. However, my response to these videos is not part of any specific political project or emancipatory narrative. In creating this montage of images, I invite viewers to reflect on these brutal images and their place in the history of audiovisual politics by creating their own associations. Ultimately, I ask: What does the decapitation video reveal about audiovisual politics in the present, and what cinematic genealogies can we trace to better understand this unconventional object?

Just as the materiality of the audiovisual apparatus mutated at the turn of the twenty-first century, so too did political institutions emerge transformed by the neoliberal model. The influence of the nation-state, which had positioned itself as the agent of Latin American modernity, receded as power became concentrated in transnational institutions. Furthermore, within the nation's territorial borders, nonstate actors such as criminal and paramilitary organizations challenged the state's sovereignty and monopoly on violence. The social contract frayed, and the *pueblo* no longer legitimated the state through hegemony. Cinema, one of the most politically influential technologies of the twentieth century, ceased to mediate the relation between the masses and state power. The crisis of Latin American cinema coincided with the demise of popular sovereignty. These developments have forced scholars of Latin American cultural studies to reckon with the remains of cinematic politics today.

In *Haz patria, mata un Zeta,* the act of beheading is itself suppressed by audiovisual form. A nude torso is positioned with its head severed by the framing of the shot. After a brief interrogation, in which the victim confesses to his membership in the criminal organization Los Zetas, two disembodied hands enter the frame and place a razor wire around the man's neck. As the victim's body stiffens, the authors of the video cut to an image of the decapitated corpse. The act of beheading is not represented; rather, it is displaced onto the cut that juxtaposes these images.

Mexican filmmakers quickly responded to the appropriation of the cinematic cut in these videos. The audiovisual production of the *necromáquina* flooded the news cycle and culture industry. As Oswaldo Zavala has argued, the Mexican government and the media have crafted an image of the *narco* to justify the state's security strategies. Furthermore, the boom in the Colombian drug trade at the end of the 1980s, combined with the deceleration of the Cold War, caused drug trafficking to replace communism as a top national security threat; as a result, Hollywood has reinforced the mythologization of the *narco* in films such as Denis Villeneuve's *Sicario* (2015) and the Netflix series *Narcos* (2015–17) and *Narcos: Mexico* (2018–21).[4] Filmmakers such as Carlos Reygadas, Amat Escalante, Everardo González, and Colectivo Los Ingrávidos have responded to the brutal imagery produced by criminal organizations, drawing attention to their weaponization of audiovisual form.

In substituting montage for decapitation, the authors of the video repeat a strategy that gave rise to film editing at the end of the nineteenth century. The proto-cinema of Thomas Edison startled early audiences by simulating the act of beheading through the substitution splice. As the pro-filmic body is about to lose its head in *The Execution of Mary, Queen of Scots* (1895), Edison cuts, substitutes the actor for a mannequin, and beheads this synthetic body instead. When the edited film is played back, this cut goes unnoticed and the splice simulates a decapitation. The technique was soon adopted by Georges Méliès, the pioneer of special effects, who delighted in beheading himself on-screen through a combination of the substitution splice and double exposure. Furthermore, Ferdinand Zecca explicitly associates this trick of early cinema with the guillotine in *Histoire d'un crime* (1901). At the time of filming, this revolutionary apparatus had become an instrument of capital punishment in France. Zecca's film concludes with the execution of a criminal. After the actor is inserted into the guillotine, the filmmaker cuts and replaces him with a mannequin. The blade falls and this synthetic body is beheaded. Like Edison, Zecca splices the two clips together to simulate a decapitation through film editing. These examples associate the cinematic cut, a structural element of audiovisual form, with the severed head. The decapitation video's aestheticization of violence continues a tradition that has accompanied cinema since its infancy. Like the short films of Edison, Méliès, and Zecca, these images overwhelm their audiences.

The decapitation video weaponizes the affect that these early filmmakers had commercialized as a form of entertainment. Film historian Tom Gunning famously refers to this period of early film history as the cinema of attractions. Borrowing the term from Sergei Eisenstein, Gunning defines the attraction as a spectacle intended to solicit the spectator's attention by disrupting the codes of visuality and generating sensation through the novelty of cinematic technology.[5] The authors of these contemporary snuff films appropriate an aesthetic strategy that defined cinema, reconceptualizing its politics. The avant-garde first politicized the perceptual effects of the cinematic cut pioneered by early filmmakers. Eisenstein experimented with the shock of montage, drawing on the cut to stage the delirium of revolution and mobilize the spectator. Mexico was a point of inflection in Eisenstein's film theory. In his intellectual, artistic, and cinematic work from this period, the filmmaker drifted from his previous conceptualization of intellectual montage to explore the cinematic cut as a sensuous and "prelogical" form of thought. The relation between the severed head and the cinematic cut shaped Eisenstein's account of Mexican history in his unfinished film, *¡Qué viva México!* In a sequence on the roots of the Mexican Revolution, a group of peasants on a Porfirian hacienda revolts after an episode of unjust violence. The young men are soon captured and buried up to their necks in the maguey fields. With only their heads protruding from the earth, their overseers trample them on horseback. Eisenstein captures the intensity of this violence in a rapid montage. At its climax, the filmmaker inserts a close-up of a peasant screaming in pain. This severed head, decapitated by the frame, fills the screen and charges the image with pathos.

Cuts of Eisenstein's unfinished film circulated throughout Latin American cineclubs in the years following the filmmaker's abrupt return to Moscow. *¡Qué viva México!* proved influential among the generation of filmmakers that collectively defined the New Latin American Cinema. In the wake of the Cuban Revolution, the NLAC experimented with cinematic form to mobilize spectators and create the conditions for further revolutionary movements throughout the region. Film historians have long framed the NLAC as a regional project that advanced a didactic and cerebral cinema. Filmmakers such as Santiago Álvarez, Tomás Gutiérrez Alea, Sara Gómez, and Fernando Solanas and Octavio Getino, among others, developed an intellectual montage that represented capitalist and neocolonial exploitation and mobilized the spectator through political lessons. Laura Podalsky offers a necessary corrective to this historiography, arguing that this account overlooks the politics of affect in the NLAC.[6] Following Podalsky, through the association of the cinematic cut and the severed head it is possible to trace an alternative current of montage within the NLAC that privileges affect over intellect. For example, Glauber Rocha's *Cabezas cortadas* (1972) and Fernando Birri's *Org* (1978), long overlooked in the history of the NLAC, both associate decapitation and the cinematic cut through loose political narratives and an experimental montage meant to heighten the spectator's sensation. In conflating the severed head with an affective montage, Rocha and Birri advance a politics of cinema that exceeds representation.

In framing political struggle as an intellectual and didactic affair, conventional accounts of the NLAC overlooked the role of catharsis in revolution. There is no better example of revolutionary affect than the guillotine. Of course, one of the great ironies of the French Revolution lies in the fact that this device was championed as a symbol of rationalism and scientific progress. Designed by a physician, the guillotine promised to reduce human suffering by mechanizing political execution and capital punishment. Nevertheless, it staged a Dionysian spectacle of cruelty and mediated a torrent of bloody passion among the masses.[7] The legacy of the guillotine's affective force leads film theorist Raymond Bellour to trace the origins of cinematic affect to this apparatus.[8] Both guillotine and cinema hypnotized the urban crowd through the cut. Not unlike the rise and fall of the guillotine's blade, the razor of the film splicer, which editors use to execute a cut, unleashes intensities in the audience. I coin the concept of the visual guillotine to refer to this conflation of decapitation and cinema, which filmmakers such as Rocha and Birri thematized in the service of revolution.

The visual guillotine and its politics are not limited to montage. Film and media theorists have long associated the edges of the frame with dangerous blades. Cutting the field of vision, the camera severs the actor's head in the frame. While the close-up became indispensable to the classical style of cinematic narration, it initially shocked spectators who were unaccustomed to the fragmentation of the actor and the magnification of this body in pieces. Critics chastised early filmmakers for filling the screen with monstruous severed heads. Yet by the 1920s film theorists such as Béla Balázs praised the power of this device to access the depths of the soul, thus initiating a humanist tradition of the close-up that lasted until the rise of postwar cinematic modernism. Humanist reflections on the close-up have provoked rich theories of cinema's ethical potential, though they have often overlooked cinematic politics. In Latin America the close-up became politicized in the national cinemas of the 1930s and 1940s. For example, Mexican filmmakers working in the state-sponsored studio system advanced a hegemonic politics through the close-up. The glamorous close-ups of the stars, carefully stylized to reflect the racial ideology of *mestizaje*, imposed a face on the postrevolutionary nation.

Yet by the 1950s, the global spread of neorealism and the decline of the studio system contributed to a shift in the politics of the close-up. Filmmakers associated with the NLAC continued the humanistic tradition of the close-up but shifted toward a counterhegemonic politics. Rejecting the glamorous close-ups of the film studios, these independent filmmakers traveled to the rural and urban margins to capture the authentic face of the people. Filmmakers such as Margot Benacerraf, Fernando Birri, Sara Gómez, and Marta Rodríguez, among many others, sought to advance a revolutionary politics by staging a scene of identification between the facial close-up and the audience. However, the violent repression of radical movements provoked a crisis of humanism. Filmmakers abandoned the tradition of the close-up initiated by Balázs and displaced this violence onto the close-up. Filmmakers such as Fernando Solanas, Octavio Getino, Luis Ospina, Carlos Mayolo, and Ugo Ulive defaced the pro-filmic body and reduced the facial close-up to the image of a severed head.

As a concept, the visual guillotine allows me to trace a through line in audiovisual politics across the divide of the 1980s and 1990s, a period in which the political allegedly receded from Latin American cinema. By the 1980s, the political project of the NLAC had lost its momentum. The adoption of the neoliberal model throughout the region led to a shift in politics and audiovisual aesthetics throughout the 1990s. The liberalization of trade and acceleration of globalization provoked a crisis of the nation-state and the *pueblo* as the locus of cinematic politics. The politicization of aesthetics, such as the utilization of montage toward revolutionary affect in the NLAC, had been eclipsed by a politics of representation organized around new identity forms. While the *pueblo* is no longer the collective subject of cinema, the decapitation video offers a counterexample to this broader shift away from a politics of form. The cinematic cut, which continues to be associated with the severed head as political sign, grounds the politics of the audiovisual apparatus in this conflict. The most concerning consequence of this development, of course, is that the register of a political aesthetics has shifted from the emancipatory movements of the 1960s and 1970s to a reactionary politics intended to paralyze the public sphere through horrorism.

An apparatus (*dispositif*) is a material and discursive formation that functions as an instrument of governmentality. The apparatus establishes relations between heterogeneous elements—practices and objects—that displace power from (state) institutions to the practice of everyday life.[9] The concept of the apparatus was central to the theories of cinematic politics that emerged in the 1970s, which combined the thought of Althusser and Lacan to critique the formation of ideological subjects through cinema. Film theorists appropriated the concept of suture to conceptualize how the cinematic apparatus reproduces subject positions. Through the material arrangement of the movie theater and aesthetics of the classical style, cinema encouraged spectators to immerse themselves in the film's narrative and identify with its protagonist. The cinematic cut enables this identification by creating a structuring lack. For example, the conventional style of the shot/countershot allows the spectator to immerse themselves in the narrative. Alejandro Jodorowsky and Mariana Rondón underscore the symbolic violence that structures this process when they reimagine the scene of identification as a figurative decapitation and transposition of severed heads. Echoing Kristeva, these films insist that decapitation gives rise to subjectivity.

Feminist film theorists politicized this critique of the apparatus by arguing that the subjectivities reproduced through suture reinforced patriarchal ideology. In other words, the apparatus enforced gendered visualities that depended on the fragmented and decapitated image of the female form. This severed head became a fetish object, resolving the threat posed by woman's symbolic lack. María Luisa Bemberg represents this process, tying the symbolic beheading of the female form, and its effect on the spectator, to the machinations of capital. Lucrecia Martel extends this critique of fetishization to the digital apparatus that has displaced the cinema. Though digital video has enacted new modes of spectatorship, the logic of fetishization persists. In her recent experiments with online media, Martel expands the concept of the cut to include digital forms such as pixelation. She draws the spectator's attention to the fact that the digital apparatus cuts the image into minimal units and frustrates the spectator's fetishization of the image by exaggerating this logic. However, these more recent interventions in the cinematic cut are not political in the traditional sense. For example, Bemberg bridges the militancy of the 1970s and the identity-based politics that would succeed the *pueblo* in the 1990s. In her eerie experiments with the digital apparatus, Martel reimagines the cut on the other side of the popular.

By the early 1990s, theorists interested in conceptualizing cinematic affect reacted against this tradition, which they accused of privileging a heady formalism over sensation. The audiovisual apparatus faded from their concerns as the spectator's body came to the forefront of film theory. Decades later, Eugenie Brinkema critiqued these theories of cinematic affect for their overzealous rejection of cinematic form.[10] Instead, Brinkema proposes a radical formalism that locates affect not in filmmakers' representation of affective states, nor even in the ways that moving images affect the audience, but in form itself.[11] Brinkema's defense of formalism is a significant development for efforts to conceptualize the role of affect in the audiovisual apparatus, which is also one objective of my concept of the visual guillotine. However, I distance myself from Brinkema's similarly overzealous rejection of the concerns with the spectator's body that affect theory prioritized. Furthermore, Brinkema's radical formalism is not radical in the political sense, and in fact sidesteps the questions of politics that guided the formalism of apparatus theory. As we see in the example of *Haz patria, mata un Zeta*, the cut that substitutes for decapitation gives form to affect, but the video's authors politicize this affect through horrorism.

More than a macabre oddity in the history of early internet culture, the decapitation video exhibits the transformation of audiovisual politics in the twenty-first century. Its weaponization of form and affect exemplifies a posthegemonic politics. In advancing political affect, which it inscribes in the form of the cut, and which consequently can only be sensed and not seen, the visual guillotine offers an example of an audiovisual politics beyond representation, from the avant-garde to the present. Yet this return of political aesthetics is alarming because it radically reorients audiovisual politics from emancipatory radicalism to reactionary horrorism.

ACKNOWLEDGMENTS

I began writing this book in the fall of 2019, soon after defending my dissertation in the Department of Spanish and Portuguese at Princeton University and taking up a Mellon Postdoctoral Fellowship in the Leslie Center for the Humanities at Dartmouth College. I could not have predicted the journey ahead, as institutions of higher education have reeled from one crisis to the next. I am deeply grateful to the transnational network of mentors, colleagues, friends, and family that has supported me over the years.

The Visual Guillotine would not exist without the keen eye and unwavering support of Javier Guerrero. Gabriela Nouzeilles has also been a steadfast mentor since I began my academic career, and feedback from Rachel Price and Rubén Gallo was invaluable as I quickly pivoted and reimagined this project as a book. Finally, I am grateful to Arcadio Díaz Quiñones and Pedro Meira Monteiro, who shaped my development as a Latin Americanist early on. Princeton's Program in Latin American Studies and Institute for International and Regional Studies generously funded fieldwork.

I owe an immense debt to Silvia Spitta, who offered mentorship and support at a vulnerable stage in my career. The staff at Dartmouth's Baker-Berry Library facilitated access to research materials under extraordinary circumstances. Thanks to them, the development of this book did not stall during the onset of the pandemic. My time at SWPS University in Warsaw allowed me to ride out the turbulence that continued to affect higher education in the United States after the initial shock of Covid-19. The writing of this book would have been impossible otherwise. I am especially grateful to Mirosław Filiciak and Agnieszka Pantuchowicz, and I acknowledge the financial support of the Institute of Humanities and grant-writing assistance from the Office for Research at SWPS. I finished writing the manuscript at Columbia University, where I spent February 2023 as a Visiting Scholar in the Hispanic Institute. This would not have been possible without the support of Graciela Montaldo and a grant from Poland's National Science Center. Finally, I am especially grateful to Leah Pennywark at the University of Minnesota Press for believing in this project over the years, and to the anonymous reviewers for their invaluable feedback.

For taking the time to discuss my work and offer a sounding board, I am grateful to Mario Bellatin, Nathalie Bouzaglo, Paola Cortés Rocca, Florencia Garramuño, Erin Graff-Zivin, Camilo Hernández Castellanos, the late Ana López, Alejandro Martínez, Rossana Reguillo, Alicia Ríos, the late Rafael Sánchez, Ignacio Sánchez Prado, Paul Schroeder Rodríguez, Juana Suárez, Juan Felipe Ureña, María Victoria Uribe, Alejandra Uslenghi, and Sayak Valencia. The references and ideas that I took away from these conversations enriched this book. I owe a special mention to the late Sylvia Molloy, who encouraged me to pursue this project long before I had realized its scope.

I am also indebted to Madera Allan, Gustavo Fares, and Rosa Tapia, who supported my budding interest in Latin American cinema and cultural studies as an undergraduate at Lawrence University. I thank them for their support over the years. I am grateful to friends who offered support and a curious ear, especially Adam, Alex, and Marty.

After a circuitous journey, I began revising this book shortly after joining the Michele Bowman Underwood Department of Modern Languages and Literatures at the University of Miami. I thank my colleagues for welcoming me warmly to Miami, especially Susanna Allés Torrent, Chrissy Arce, Steven Butterman, Christina Civantos, Logan Connors, Tracy Devine Guzmán, Viviana Díaz Balsera, Rebecca Doran, Ager Gondra, Elena Grau-Lleveria, Andrew Lynch, Lilian Manzor, Yolanda

Martínez San Miguel, Ludovic Mompelat, Patoimbasba Nikiema, Gema Pérez-Sánchez, Suja Sawafta, Allison Schifani, Maria Stampino, and Ómar Vargas.

Finally, my career has been possible thanks to the unconditional love and support of my family in the United States and Poland. Thank you, Krystyna, Brian, Alex, Anna, Barbara, and Jarosław.

NOTES

Introduction

1. Of course, political cinema has not vanished. Community-based and Indigenous filmmaking and media carry on the legacy of the NLAC by privileging popular representation and identity, but these practices are marginalized in the contemporary production and exhibition landscape. In contrast, the turn to transnationalism has reterritorialized the category of identity. Marvin D'Lugo observes that, prompted by these globalizing forces, Latin American filmmakers found themselves guided by questions of cultural hybridity that challenged the formerly stable division between the cultural center and periphery. Marvin D'Lugo, "Authorship, Globalization, and the New Identity of Latin American Cinema: From the Mexican 'Ranchera' to Argentinian 'Exile,'" in *Rethinking Third Cinema,* ed. Wimal Dissanayake and Anthony Guneratne (New York: Routledge, 2003), 104.

2. Laura Podalsky has recently critiqued the logic of periodization that underlies teleological models in the historiography of Latin American cinema. By segmenting national and regional histories into stages, Podalsky argues, scholars ignore continuities and privilege certain objects and methodologies over others. These conventions have led to an abundance of scholarship on the role of narrative cinema in shaping twentieth-century cultural nationalisms, for example, while marginalizing experimental cinema, intermedial practices, and theoretical questions. Laura Podalsky, "Unpacking Periodization," in *The Routledge Companion to Latin American Cinema,* ed. Marvin D'Lugo, Ana M. López, and Laura Podalsky (London: Routledge, 2018), 63–64.

3. Podalsky, 72.

4. Regina Janes echoes this observation in her cultural history of beheading when she writes, "a severed head is the first time that hominids are thinking in symbols." Regina Janes, *Losing Our Heads: Beheadings in Literature and Culture* (New York: NYU Press, 2005), x.

5. Julia Kristeva, *The Severed Head: Capital Visions,* trans. Jody Gladding (New York: Columbia University Press, 2012), 23.

6. Kristeva, 12–13.

7. Kristeva, 117.

8. Linda Nochlin, *The Body in Pieces: The Fragment as Metaphor of Modernity* (London: Thames & Hudson, 2001), 23.

9. Scott Combs, *Deathwatch: American Film, Technology, and the End of Life* (New York: Columbia University Press, 2014), 34.

10. Combs, 32.

11. Béla Balázs, *Theory of the Film: Character and Growth of a New Art,* trans. Edith Bone (New York: Dover, 1970), 35.

12. Yuri Tsivian, *Early Russian Cinema and Its Cultural Reception* (London: Routledge, 1994), 196.

13. Mary Ann Doane, *Bigger Than Life: The Close-up and Scale in the Cinema* (Durham: Duke University Press, 2021), 34.

14. Karla Oeler, *A Grammar of Murder: Violent Scenes and Film Form* (Chicago: University of Chicago Press, 2009), 4.

15. Patrick Wald Lasowski, *Guillotinez-mois! Précis de décapitation* (Paris: Gallimard, 2007), 9. Unless otherwise indicated, all translations are my own.

16. Lasowski, 64. This conclusion echoes the observations of Daniel Arasse, who compares the visual logic of the guillotine to portraiture. Daniel Arasse, *The Guillotine and the Terror*, trans. Christopher Miller (London: Penguin, 1989), 134. However, Lasowski proposes an analogy between the guillotine and the photographic apparatus to emphasize the scaffold's mechanization of the spectacle of decapitation. In his words, "The scaffold will always inspire the pure photographer's dream: pressing the trigger at the moment of the cut. Anonymity of the camera, immobilization of the subject, effect of speed and immediacy: the guillotine secretly controls the camera" (63). The close-up in cinema carries on this legacy by severing the head from the body.

17. Raymond Bellour, *El cuerpo del cine: Hipnosis, emociones, animalidades,* trans. Julián Mateo Ballorca (Santander: Shangrila, 2013), 31–32.

18. Walter Murch, *In the Blink of an Eye: A Perspective on Film Editing* (Los Angeles: Silman-James, 2001), 6.

19. This conjures the image of a small sun within the apparatus, as its light filters into the camera obscura of the movie theater through the projector's lens. I associate this metaphor with an interpretation of the solar body by

Georges Bataille, who writes, "One might add that the sun has also been mythologically expressed by a man slashing his own throat, as well as by an anthropomorphic being *deprived of a head.*" Georges Bataille, "Rotten Sun," in *Visions of Excess: Selected Writings, 1927–1939,* ed. Allan Stoekl, trans. Stoekl et al. (Minneapolis: University of Minnesota Press, 1985), 57–58.

20. Murch, *In the Blink of an Eye,* 7.

21. Murch, 57.

22. Industrial Moviolas, the standard editing device in Hollywood for decades, were typically large and cumbersome machines that required the operator to stand. Murch explains that editing on a Moviola became a full-body experience. The editor would use his feet to navigate the film strip by pressing pedals to move forward or backward, while using his hands to mark the splice or operate a handbrake. Murch, 105.

23. Enzo Traverso, *Revolution: An Intellectual History* (London: Verso, 2021), 96.

24. Nico Baumbach, *Cinema/Politics/Philosophy* (New York: Columbia University Press, 2019), 2.

25. Baumbach, 2.

26. Gareth Williams, *The Other Side of the Popular: Neoliberalism and Subalternity in Latin America* (Durham: Duke University Press, 2002), 7–9.

27. Jon Beasley-Murray, *Posthegemony: Political Theory and Latin America* (Minneapolis: University of Minnesota Press, 2010), x.

28. Jean Franco, *Cruel Modernity* (Durham: Duke University Press, 2013), 8.

29. Ileana Rodríguez describes examples of systematic violence from different cultural and historical contexts, from the Colombian civil conflict of the 1950s known as La Violencia to the extermination of Indigenous communities in the Guatemalan Civil War and the rampant femicide in post-NAFTA Mexico, as structural consequences of the development of modern sovereignty. Ileana Rodríguez, *Liberalism at Its Limits: Crime and Terror in the Latin American Cultural Text* (Pittsburgh: University of Pittsburgh Press, 2009), 3. Furthermore, Franco traces the development of the sovereign state, its pact with the national popular and its commitment to modernization, to the spectacular displays of cruelty, and traces this process to the Spanish conquest. For example, Franco notes that the descriptions of the atrocities committed by the *kaibiles,* the elite forces of the Guatemalan military whose name derives from a sixteenth-century Indigenous leader, echo the accounts of the spectacular violence of the conquest in the work of Bartolomé de Las Casas. Franco, 6.

30. Sergio Villalobos-Ruminott, *Soberanías en suspenso: Neoliberalismo, violencia e imaginación* (Buenos Aires: La Cebra, 2013), 69.

31. Villalobos-Ruminott, 27–28.

32. Achille Mbembe, "Necropolitics," *Public Culture* 15, no. 1 (2003): 21.

33. Mbembe, 24.

34. Rossana Reguillo, *Necromáquina: Cuando morir no es suficiente* (Barcelona: Ned, 2021), 31.

35. Prominent examples include Charles Ramírez Berg, *Cinema of Solitude: A Critical Study of Mexican Film, 1967–1983* (Austin: University of Texas Press, 1992); Tamara Falicov, *The Cinematic Tango: Contemporary Argentine Film* (London: Wallflower, 2007); Jeffrey Middents, *Writing National Cinema: Film Journals and Film Culture in Peru* (Hanover: Dartmouth College Press, 2009); Sergio de la Mora, *Cinemachismo: Masculinity and Sexuality in Mexican Film* (Austin: University of Texas Press, 2006); Andrea Noble, *Mexican National Cinema* (London: Routledge, 2005); and Lisa Shaw and Stephanie Dennison, *Brazilian National Cinema* (London: Routledge, 2007). This tradition continues today, in the work of Rebecca Janzen, *Unholy Trinity: State, Church, and Film in Mexico* (Albany: SUNY Press, 2021); Matt Losada, *The Projected Nation: Argentine Cinema and the Social Margins* (Albany: SUNY Press, 2018); Cynthia Tompkins, *Affectual Erasure: Representations of Indigenous Peoples in Argentine Cinema* (Albany: SUNY Press, 2018); and others who revise and expand on the national film history to fill in its gaps by emphasizing the representation of subjects previously excluded from cinematic politics, such as racial, religious, and ethnic minorities. The field's turn to national film history in the 1990s was a response to scholarship on the NLAC in previous decades. Scholars such as Julianne Burton-Carvajal, Ana López, Robert Stam, and Michael Chanan introduced Latin American cinema to film studies and foreign language departments in the Anglophone academy through their work on cinema and the politics of the Third World. However, if it was to institutionalize itself as a field, Latin American film studies needed to historicize its object of study through the framework of cultural nationalism. See Thomas Matusiak, "The Limits of National Film History and the Logic of Expansion," *Revista Hispánica Moderna* 74, no. 2 (2021): 227–29.

36. Néstor García Canclini, "Will There Be Latin American Cinema in the Year 2000? Visual Culture in a Post-National Era," in *Framing Latin American Cinema: Contemporary Critical Perspectives,* ed. Ann Marie Stock (Minneapolis: University of Minnesota Press, 1997), 255.

37. D'Lugo, "Authorship," 103.

38. Ignacio Sánchez Prado, *Screening Neoliberalism: Transforming Mexican Cinema, 1988–2012* (Nashville: Vanderbilt University Press, 2014), 4.

39. Paul A. Schroeder Rodríguez, *Latin American Cinema: A Comparative History* (Oakland: University of California Press, 2016), 245–46.

40. Gonzalo Aguilar, *Más allá del pueblo: Imágenes, indicios y políticas del cine* (Buenos Aires: Fondo de Cultura Económica, 2015), 118.

41. Glauber Rocha, "An Aesthetics of Dreams," in *On Cinema,* ed. Ismail Xavier, trans. Stephanie Dennison and Charlotte Smith (London: I.B. Tauris, 2019), 123.

42. Rocha, 124.

43. Aguilar, *Más allá del pueblo,* 14.

44. Rudy Pradenas, *Política del anonimato en el cine de América Latina* (Santiago: Ediciones Macul, 2024), 27.

45. In *The Image Book* (2018), Jean-Luc Godard's final essay film, the filmmaker includes clips of ISIS videos in his reflection on cinema's place in the history of destruction wrought by the twentieth century. Similarly, the spectacular violence in these productions has drawn the attention of Jean-Louis Comolli, one of the leading figures of 1970s political film theory, who reflects on the relation between cinema and death in ISIS's videos. Jean-Louis Comolli, *Daech, le cinéma et la mort* (Lagrasse: Verdier, 2016).

46. Jacques Aumont, *Montage Eisenstein,* trans. Lee Hildreth et al. (Bloomington: Indiana University Press, 1987), 154.

47. Oeler, *A Grammar of Murder,* 13.

48. Aguilar, *Más allá del pueblo,* 189–90.

49. Sánchez Prado, *Screening Neoliberalism,* 4–5.

50. Sigmund Freud, *Writings on Art and Literature* (Stanford: Stanford University Press, 1997), 264–65.

1. Defacement

1. Doane, *Bigger Than Life,* 1.

2. While the classical style codified a typology of the close-up, a broader scope of analysis signals a significant degree of ambiguity in its definition. Just how narrow must the frame be for a shot to qualify as a close-up? The fact that there can be no exact science of the close-up "elicits both panic and delight" in film theorists. Given its inherent instability, Doane defines the close-up not in terms of any specific size or proportion, but as a discourse on the concept of cinematic scale itself. Like Doane, I am less interested in strict definitions of this device and instead center my attention on how the close-up intervenes in the pro-filmic body and the body in the audience. Specifically, I draw attention to the ways in which this treatment of scale resonates with a politics of popular sovereignty in Latin America. Doane, 18.

3. Margo Glantz, *Las genealogías* (Mexico City: Alfaguara, 2013), 59.

4. Doane, *Bigger Than Life,* 34.

5. In *A Grammar of Murder,* Karla Oeler observes that filmmakers and theorists in these decades conceived of cinematic form in relation to murder. For example, Vsevolod Pudovkin thematized the threat posed by the close-up's fragmentation of the body by contrasting the isolated image of the face with that of a gun. Eisenstein goes even further when he compares the guillotine and the frame. Oeler concludes, "The metaphors of film theorists and critics reveals [*sic*] the resonance between violence and framing." Oeler, *A Grammar of Murder,* 36.

6. Daniel Arasse compares the visual logic of the guillotine to portraiture, arguing that "by removing the head from the body to set it before the spectator's eyes, the guillotine springs one last surprise. It becomes a sort of portraitist, a veritable, indeed a terrifying 'portrait machine.'" Arasse, *The Guillotine and the Terror,* 134.

7. Bellour, *El cuerpo del cine,* 31–32.

8. Since my objective here is to theorize cinematic form, I follow a conventional periodization of Latin American cinema. For a discussion that blends formal concerns with historiographic revision, see chapter 2.

9. Balázs, *Theory of the Film,* 35.

10. Nochlin, *The Body in Pieces,* 8.

11. Deborah Poole, *Vision, Race, and Modernity: A Visual Economy of the Andean Image World* (Princeton: Princeton University Press, 1997), 135–38.

12. Jesse Lerner, *The Shock of Modernity: Crime Photography in Mexico City,* (Mexico City: Turner, 2007), 21.

13. Béla Balázs, "The Face of Things," in *Béla Balázs: Early Film Theory. Visible Man and the Spirit of Film,* ed. Erica Carter, trans. Rodney Livingstone (New York: Berghahn, 2010), 46.

14. Jacques Aumont, *El rostro en el cine,* trans. José Ángel Alcalde (Barcelona: Paidós, 1998), 189.

15. Jean Epstein, "Magnification and Other Writings," trans. Stuart Liebman, *October* 3 (Spring 1977): 9.

16. Gilles Deleuze, *Cinema 1: The Movement Image,* trans. Hugh Tomlinson and Barbara Habberjam (Minneapolis: University of Minnesota Press, 1986), 100.

17. Balázs, *Theory of the Film,* 44–45.

18. Balázs, "The Face of Things," 14.

19. Doane, *Bigger Than Life,* 121–22.

20. Schroeder Rodríguez, *Latin American Cinema,* 11.

21. Georges Didi-Huberman, *Pueblos expuestos, pueblos figurantes,* trans. Horacio Pons (Buenos Aires: Manantial, 2014), 22.

22. Zuzana M. Pick, *Constructing the Image of the Mexican Revolution: Cinema and the Archive* (Austin: University of Texas Press, 2010), 84.

23. Carlos Monsiváis, "Mythologies," in *Mexican Cinema,* trans. Ana M. López, ed. Paulo Antonio Paranaguá (London: BFI, 1995), 117–18.

24. Joanna Hershfield, *The Invention of Dolores del Río* (Minneapolis: University of Minnesota Press, 2000), 9–10.

25. Monica García Blizzard, *The White Indians of Mexican Cinema: Racial Masquerade Throughout the Golden Age* (Albany: SUNY Press, 2022), 17.

26. Aumont, *El rostro en el cine,* 66–67.

27. Dolores Tierney, *Emilio Fernández: Pictures in the Margins* (Manchester: Manchester University Press, 2007), 89.

28. Carlos Monsiváis, "Dolores del Río," in *Mexican Postcards,* trans. and ed. John Kraniauskas (London: Verso, 1997), 81.

29. Aumont, *Montage Eisenstein,* 52.

30. Aumont, *El rostro en el cine,* 53.

31. Schroeder Rodríguez, *Latin American Cinema,* 92.

32. Gary W. Wynia, *The Politics of Latin American Development* (Cambridge: Cambridge University Press, 1990), 44.

33. In its melodramatic narrative, which centers on the failed aspirations of a child actor and her mother, Luchino Visconti's *Bellisima* (1951) explicitly renounces the synthetic face of the star in favor of neorealist humanism. In this example, beauty lies in the close-up of the nonprofessional actor—the child's face—and not in the star image. Aumont, *El rostro en el cine,* 123.

34. Aumont, *Montage Eisenstein,* 116.

35. Aumont, 116.

36. Margot Benacerraf et al., "An Interview with Margot Benacerraf: *Reverón, Araya,* and the Institutionalization of Cinema in Venezuela," *Journal of Film and Video* 44, nos. 3–4 (Fall 1992/Winter 1993): 69.

37. Javier Campo, "Latin American Ethnographic Cinema: Between Exploration and Denunciation," *Studies in Documentary Cinema* 13, no. 2 (Spring 2019): 181–82.

38. After shooting on location on the Araya Peninsula, Benacerraf completed postproduction in France. Lauded upon its premier at the 1959 Cannes Film Festival, the film successfully toured the European festival circuit. Although it did not screen in Venezuela until 1977, critics have simultaneously inscribed *Araya* in national, regional, and global canons of cinema. Nevertheless, *Araya*'s appeal to universality drew criticism from Venezuelan critics who claimed that the film did not sufficiently engage the material circumstances of the workers' exploitation. Julianne Burton-Carvajal, "*Araya* Across Time and Space: Competing Canons of National (Venezuelan) and International Film Histories," in *Visible Nations: Latin American Cinema and Video,* ed. Chon. A. Noriega (Minneapolis: University of Minnesota Press, 2000), 51.

39. Salomé Aguilera Skvirsky aligns *Araya* with what she terms the process genre, or the sequentially ordered representation of labor, which straddles artisanal and industrial modes of production. Salomé Aguilera Skvirsky, *The Process Genre: Cinema and the Aesthetic of Labor* (Durham: Duke University Press, 2020), 3–4, 150.

40. Benacerraf et al., "An Interview with Margot Benacerraf," 64.

41. André Bazin, "An Aesthetic of Reality: Neorealism," in *What Is Cinema?,* vol. 2, ed. and trans. Hugh Gray (Berkeley: University of California Press, 2005), 21.

42. Didi-Huberman, *Pueblos expuestos, pueblos figurantes,* 54. Aumont hints at a similar logic in neorealism when he describes this movement as "a network of faces." Yet while he frames neorealism as an apparatus of humanist relation, Aumont overlooks politics and confines his argument to the sphere of ethics. Aumont, *El rostro en el cine,* 125.

43. Michael Chanan, "Rediscovering Documentary: Cultural Context and Intentionality," in *The Social Documentary in Latin America,* ed. Julianne Burton (Pittsburgh: University of Pittsburgh Press, 1990), 38. This is true not only of Birri but also of the other examples of the utopian close-up in NLAC cited above. Indeed, Didi-Huberman identifies a similar dialectic in his iconography of populism.

44. Fernando Birri, *Soñar con los ojos abiertos: Las treinta lecciones de Stanford* (Buenos Aires: Aguilar, 2007), 95.

45. Carlos Ossa, *El ojo mecánico: Cine político y comunidad en América Latina* (Santiago: Fondo de Cultura Económica, 2013), 18.

46. Ossa, 11.

47. Both filmmakers developed prolific careers, despite Gómez's untimely death at the age of thirty-one. Nevertheless, Rodríguez has primarily been remembered for her codirected documentary *Chircales* and Gómez for her feature *De cierta manera* (1974). Arsenal Institute for Film and Video Art, located in Berlin, recently restored Marta Rodríguez and Jorge Silva's *Chircales* and *Nuestra voz de tierra, memoria y futuro* (1981), which I analyze in this section. A selection of Gómez's short documentaries, including *Iré a Santiago* (1964), *Guanabacoa: Crónica de mi familia* (1966), *Una isla para Miguel* (1968), and *Mi aporte* (1972), has been restored recently by L'immagine Ritrovata film restoration and conservation lab in Bologna and the Vulnerable Media Lab of Queens University in Ontario. These restorations have screened in festivals, retrospectives, and special engagements in Europe and the Americas, drawing attention to the wider oeuvre of these two filmmakers in the twenty-first century.

48. Franco, *Cruel Modernity,* 7.

49. María Caridad Cumaná, "Racial Identity and Collisions: Gómez and Guillén Landrián," in *The Cinema of Sara Gómez: Reframing Revolution,* ed. Susan Lord and María Caridad Cumaná (Bloomington: Indiana University Press, 2021), 256.

50. Cumaná, 257.

51. Pedro Pablo Gómez, "Marta Rodríguez, descolonizando la representación documental latinoamericana," *Artísticos: Revista de Investigación Creadora,* no. 3 (2017): 126–28.

52. *El chacal de Nahueltoro* was released amid Salvador Allende's presidential campaign and played an important role in the candidate's bid against the incumbent, Jorge Alessandri. John King notes that in this context the film "was an important element of popular mobilization." The events re-created by Littín took place in the early 1960s, during Alessandri's administration. Audiences therefore identified the marginalization of rural populations depicted in the film with Alessandri's policies and saw in Allende's platform an opportunity to liberate the poor and working classes from such oppression. John King, *Magical Reels: A History of Cinema in Latin America* (London: Verso, 2000), 173.

53. Vallejo first conceives of the film in 1961, while studying at Birri's Documentary School of Santa Fe. On a train from Santa Fe he meets El Viejo's son, and the film begins to germinate. Vallejo undertakes research and lives with the Reales family for a period in 1964, commences filming in 1968, and releases the film clandestinely in 1971 due to censorship from the military junta.

54. Deleuze and Guattari's theory of faciality identifies the face with European values that are abstracted and assumed to be universal. The Western tradition of faciality, they argue, originates in the sacred face of Christ: "The face is not a universal. It is not even that of the white man; it is White Man himself, with his broad white cheeks and the black hole of his eyes. The face is Christ. . . . Jesus Christ superstar: he invented the facialization of the entire body and spread it everywhere (the Passion of Joan of Arc, in close-up)." Gilles Deleuze and Félix Guattari, *A Thousand Plateaus,* trans. Brian Massumi (Minneapolis: University of Minnesota Press, 1987), 176.

55. Mariano Mestman, "The Last Sacred Image of the Latin American Revolution," *Journal of Latin American Cultural Studies* 19, no. 1 (2010): 30.

56. Mestman, 38–39.

57. Since this crisis of revolutionary humanism was not as abruptly perceived in revolutionary Cuba, its highly centralized film industry offers an exception to this turn from the face to defacement in the close-up. For example, the same humanist logic of political representation through the facial close-up can be seen in Santiago Álvarez's *Mi hermano Fidel* (1977). This documentary short

stages a conversation between Fidel Castro and Salustiano Leyva, an elderly peasant. At eleven years of age, Leyva witnessed José Martí's return to Cuba in 1895 with the commencement of the Cuban War of Independence. Fidel has come to meet this blind man who once saw Martí's face. Álvarez's short consists primarily of long takes, shot with a handheld camera, that pan back and forth between the interlocutors. Álvarez opens with an extreme close-up of Leyva, as Fidel asks him to lift his hat to reveal his face. When asked if he remembers seeing the national hero, Leyva responds with a description of Martí's features while tracing his hands over his own face. For example, when recalling Martí's facial hair, the man touches his own cheeks and chin. Álvarez thus traces a revolutionary physiognomy from Martí to Castro by way of Leyva. With his trademark beard, Fidel inherits the face and the revolutionary spirit of Martí, while Leyva's features mediate between these historic figures. The camera's back-and-forth movement between Fidel and Leyva establishes an equivalency between the two, encouraging the Cuban audience to also identify with the revolutionary leader by way of the facial close-up.

58. Drawing on the thought of Jean-Paul Sartre and Frantz Fanon, whom Solanas and Getino cite in the first part of *La hora de los hornos,* this discourse decentered the Western tradition and searched for a new definition of the human that would be grounded in the experiences of colonized peoples. Fanon issues a call for this new humanism in his conclusion to *The Wretched of the Earth,* where he writes: "When I search for Man in the technique and the style of Europe, I only see a succession of negations of man, and an avalanche of murders. The human condition, plans for mankind, and collaboration between men in those tasks which increase the sum total of humanity are new problems, which demand true inventions. Let us decide not to imitate Europe; let us combine our muscles and our brains in a new direction. Let us try to create the whole man, whom Europe has been incapable of bringing to triumphant birth." Frantz Fanon, *The Wretched of the Earth,* trans. Constance Farrington (New York: Grove, 1963), 312–13.

59. Robert Stam, "*The Hour of the Furnaces* and the Two Avant-Gardes," in *The Social Documentary in Latin America,* ed. Julianne Burton (Pittsburgh: University of Pittsburgh Press, 1990), 252.

60. Aumont, *Montage Eisenstein,* 154.

61. Mark Polizzotti, *Los olvidados* (London: British Film Institute, 2006), 54.

62. Adam Lowenstein, *Dreaming of Cinema: Spectatorship, Surrealism, and the Age of Digital Media* (New York: Columbia University Press, 2015), 128–30.

63. Ernesto Acevedo-Muñoz, *Buñuel and Mexico: The Crisis of National Cinema* (Berkeley: University of California Press, 2003), 7.

64. Juana Suárez, *Critical Essays on Colombian Cinema and Culture: Cinembargo Colombia,* trans. Laura Chesak (New York: Palgrave Macmillan, 2012).

65. Suárez, *Critical Essays on Colombian Cinema and Culture,* 73–74.

66. Born in Montevideo, Ulive moved to Cuba in 1960 to participate in revolutionary theater. By the end of the decade, he had settled in Caracas and turned his attention to militant cinema.

67. Aguilar, *Más allá del pueblo,* 143.

2. From the Guillotine to the Splicer

1. In an early theoretical essay, Luis Buñuel associates montage with assembly and unity while attributing the disruption of visual segmentation with the process of *découpage.* In other words, Buñuel understands montage in terms of pasting, not cutting. The dissection of the film into minimal units occurs during *découpage,* a process that includes the segmentation of ideas and mental images into individual shots during storyboarding and scriptwriting. Whereas *découpage* is an intellectual and aesthetic process, montage is, to Buñuel, a vulgar manual task. In the filmmaker's words, "The idea of a *découpage*—written or not—is, like the lens, immanent in the notion of the film. Editing, by contrast, is simply putting hand to plow—the materiality of joining one piece after another, coordinating the different shots with each other, removing unwanted images with a scissors. A delicate operation, but extremely manual. However, the guiding idea, the silent procession of images that are concrete, decisive, measured in time and space—in a word, the film—was first projected inside the brain of the filmmaker." Luis Buñuel, "*Découpage,* or Cinematic Segmentation," in *An Unspeakable Betrayal: Selected Writings of Luis Buñuel,* trans. Garrett White (Berkeley: University of California Press, 2000), 134–35.

2. Genevieve Yue refers to this process in terms of *escamontage,* whereby the cut "composes through concealment." Genevieve Yue, *Girl Head: Feminism and Film Materiality* (New York: Fordham University Press, 2021), 74. In this process, the cinematic apparatus suppresses the violence of cutting on which it relies to construct a narrative. Yue introduces this concept to advance a feminist account of film materiality, arguing that the violence of the cut (both the pro-filmic body cut in the narrative and the body of the film cut in the editing room) is gendered. In such films, including the paradigmatic example from Edison, it is a woman's body that is attacked through *escamontage.* In other words, the decapitation of the female form coincides with the cutting of film in these examples. Yue, *Girl Head,* 85.

3. In addition to the two traditions mentioned in this chapter—intellectual and affective—Jorge Sanjinés's theory of the integral sequence shot marks a

third approach to the politics of montage in the NLAC. Sanjinés rejects the symbolic and perceptual violence of montage. The integral sequence shot embraces unity and immersion in editing over disjunction and juxtaposition to more closely align cinematic form with an Indigenous cosmography and thus elaborate a decolonial politics of montage. Jorge Sanjinés, "El plano secuencia integral," *Cine Cubano* 125 (1989): 70. Dennis Hanlon defines the integral sequence shot, and its realization in Sanjinés's *La nación clandestine* (1989), in terms of a "dialectical transculturation to transform and indigenize certain art cinema techniques while, at the same time, [introducing] European audiences to new forms of subjectivity grounded in a specifically Andean cosmovision." Dennis Hanlon, "Traveling Theory, Shots, and Players: Jorge Sanjinés, New Latin American Cinema, and the European Art Film," in *Global Art Cinema: New Theories and Histories,* ed. Rosalind Galt and Karl Schoonover (Oxford: Oxford University Press, 2010), 352–53.

4. Traverso, *Revolution,* 87.

5. Bellour, *El cuerpo del cine,* 31–32

6. In Latin America, Eisenstein's cinema was initially received within the cosmopolitan cineclub culture of the 1930s and 1940s. In this bourgeois sphere, Eisenstein was valued for his contributions to avant-garde aesthetics rather than for his radical politics. His cinema would not be explicitly politicized until the generation of militant filmmakers encountered his writings on montage and cuts of his unfinished film on Mexico. Sarah Ann Wells, "Parallel Modernities? The First Reception of Soviet Cinema in Latin America," in *Cosmopolitan Film Cultures in Latin America, 1896–1960,* ed. Rielle Navitski and Nicolas Poppe (Bloomington: Indiana University Press, 2017), 153–54.

7. Sergei Eisenstein, *Film Form: Essays in Film Theory,* ed. and trans. Jay Leyda (New York: Harvest, 1977), 83.

8. Aumont, *Montage Eisenstein,* 156.

9. Michael Chanan, *Cuban Cinema* (Minneapolis: University of Minnesota Press, 2004), 228.

10. Paul Schroeder Rodríguez, *Tomás Gutiérrez Alea: The Dialectics of a Filmmaker* (London: Routledge, 2003), 57.

11. Tomás Gutiérrez Alea, *Dialéctica del espectador* (Mexico City: Federación Editorial Mexicana, 1983), 83.

12. Stam, "*The Hour of the Furnaces,*" 259.

13. B. Ruby Rich, "An/Other View of New Latin American Cinema," in *New Latin American Cinema,* vol. 1, *Theory, Practices, and Transcontinental Articulations,* ed. Michael T. Martin (Detroit: Wayne State University Press, 1997), 281.

14. Robert Burgoyne, "The Political Topology of Montage: The Conflict of Genres in the Films of Godard," *Enclitic* 7, no. 1 (1983): 14.

15. To paraphrase Jacques Rancière, in the intellectual montage of the early NLAC, the filmmaker occupied the position of schoolmaster and the spectator that of his pupil in a lesson on revolutionary consciousness. The effects of such a montage could be stultifying. The post-1968 montage of the late NLAC emancipated the spectator from this hierarchical logic.

16. Sarah Hamblin, "Exhausted Montage: Radical Cinema Post '68," *Cultural Politics* 15, no. 3 (2019): 360. Peter Bürger would disagree that any discourse of montage would remain politically viable outside the context of the historical avant-garde because its shock eventually loses its perceptual novelty and the political power stemming from it. Peter Bürger, *Theory of the Avant-Garde,* trans. Michael Shaw (Minneapolis: University of Minnesota Press), 80–81. This echoes Adorno's argument that the disturbing power of montage eventually exhausts itself. Thus, neither theorist concedes that a neo-avant-garde politics of montage existed. Hamblin disagrees, arguing that montage did survive in the discourse of political modernism that was active in the 1960s and 1970s. However, the individualistic approach to montage it elaborated, in which the spectator, not the filmmaker, makes sense of the juxtaposed images, would become subsumed within the neoliberal politics to come in subsequent decades. Political modernism, in other words, would be montage's last radical moment in cinema. Theodor W. Adorno, *Aesthetic Theory,* ed. Gretel Adorno and Rilf Tiedemann, trans. Robert Hullot-Kentor (London: Continuum, 2002), 155–56.

17. Laura Podalsky, *The Politics of Affect and Emotion in Contemporary Latin American Cinema: Argentina, Brazil, Cuba, Mexico* (New York: Palgrave Macmillan, 2011), 31–32.

18. Sergei Eisenstein, *Beyond the Stars: The Memoirs of Sergei Eisenstein,* ed. Richard Taylor, trans. William Powell (Calcutta: Seagull, 1995), 62.

19. Anne Nesbet, *Savage Junctures: Sergei Eisenstein and the Shape of Thinking* (London: I.B. Tauris, 2003), 76.

20. Aumont, *Montage Eisenstein,* viii–ix.

21. In his memoirs, Eisenstein repeatedly refers to Lucien Lévy-Bruhl's *La mentalité primitive* (1922) and James Frazer's *The Golden Bough* (1890). From Lévy-Bruhl, Eisenstein appropriated the concept of the "prelogical" to theorize cinema. Georges Bataille, whom the filmmaker met on his visit to Paris, was another influence on this shift in Eisenstein's thought.

22. Comparing *¡Qué viva México!* with Maya Deren's unfinished film on Haitian vodou, *Divine Horsemen,* Annette Michelson also notes that Mexico was a turning point for Eisenstein when she writes, "From Mexico and Haiti,

each returned as well, with the memory of determinant experience, one which was to permeate all subsequent theory and practice, further accentuating their problematic status as filmmakers. This was the memory of their encounters with the *ecstatic.*" Annette Michelson, "On Reading Deren's Notebook," *October* 14 (Fall 1980): 52.

23. Peter Wollen, *Readings and Writings: Semiotic Counter-Strategies* (London: Verso, 1982), 62.

24. Harry M. Geduld and Ronald Gottesman, *Sergei Eisenstein and Upton Sinclair: The Making and Unmaking of "Que viva Mexico!"* (Bloomington: Indiana University Press, 1970), 14.

25. The production history of *¡Qué viva México!* is well documented, and I will give only a brief overview here. Eisenstein's budget of $25,000 stipulated a schedule of four months of shooting. After a month, Eisenstein had yet to film any material at all and claimed that he needed more time for research. Relations between Eisenstein and Sinclair soon began to sour. After weeks of tense communications, the two terminated the contract with approximately fifty hours of rushes but little narrative or structure. By the end, Eisenstein had extended his agreement to thirteen months and spent over twice his original budget. The Soviet government simultaneously became concerned with Eisenstein's prolonged absence. Stalin himself telegraphed Sinclair directly, informing him that the filmmaker must return to Moscow or lose his good standing. Aware that the film was becoming a financial failure, Sinclair ended the venture and retained the rights to the footage. Eisenstein was forced to return to Moscow via New York; he was unable to edit the film. Geduld and Gottesman, 212.

26. Eisenstein's arrival coincides with what the Mexican-American anthropologist and author Anita Brenner dubbed the Mexican Renaissance. Following the Revolution, Mexico experienced a vibrant cultural nationalism thanks in large part to government support for the arts. A central element of this revival was the synthesis of Mexico's pre-Columbian past and the promise of modernity represented by the revolution. While the movement of Mexican muralism famously emerged in this period, the Mexican government's simultaneous investment in tourism also attracted members of the European avant-gardes including André Breton, Antonin Artaud, Leonora Carrington, Remedios Varo, and others.

27. Marie Rebecchi and Elene Vogman, *Sergei Eisenstein and the Anthropology of Rhythm* (Rome: Nero, 2017), 19.

28. In her account of *¡Qué viva México!,* Masha Salazkina summarizes the film as a synthesis of the nation's pre-Columbian mythology and modern revolution. Of importance here is Eisenstein's ethnographic gaze, which was influenced by Franz Boas's thought via two of his students: Mexican anthropologist

Adolfo Best Maugard, who served as Eisenstein's consultant throughout his travels, and Anita Brenner. Masha Salazkina, *In Excess: Sergei Eisenstein's Mexico* (Chicago: University of Chicago Press, 2009), 18.

29. In the same letter cited above, Eisenstein remarks on his drawings and their relation to his other activities, asserting, "Actually, the filming, theory, and drawing are done in 'relays' so as to keep going at all costs." Rebecchi and Vogman, *Sergei Eisenstein,* 56.

30. Eisenstein writes: "To put it more simply, the theoretical work continues without interruption. Analytic methods of great refinement and endless synthetic amplifications present themselves on the most curious occasions (crocodile hunting or at Indian dances involving turkeys, during which each dancer has to strangle a live turkey. . .) . . . My theoretical work has come a long way from its position prior to my departure. Fortunately, its headed in the direction of ever-greater simplification, clarity, and scale." Rebecchi and Vogman, 56.

31. Salazkina, *In Excess,* 43.

32. Eisenstein, *Film Form,* 144.

33. Eisenstein, 238.

34. Salazkina, *In Excess,* 47.

35. Whether the culture depicted here actually practiced violent ritual at one point is irrelevant. In his writings, Eisenstein—a foreigner with little knowledge of Mexico, who performed scant research on specific Indigenous groups—essentialized Mexico's pre-Columbian heritage and associated diverse cultures with the Aztecs and the ritual violence they practiced.

36. Eisenstein drew on and off throughout his lifetime, and his archive includes approximately five thousand drawings. However, the depictions of sexualized violence that he produced during his Mexican period did not receive scholarly attention until the 1990s and were not published until 1999. Joan Neuberger, "Strange Circus: Eisenstein's Sex Drawings," *Studies in Russian and Soviet Cinema* 6, no. 1 (2012): 6–7.

37. Salazkina, *In Excess,* 119. Eisenstein's biographer Marie Seton corroborates this account, claiming that Eisenstein had filmed a Corpus Christi festival at Tletapayac in 1931. The festivities "culminated with one of the Indian peons of the hacienda 'going out of himself' into a state of penitential ecstasy, [and this] was to be intercut with the enacted death of the peon." This montage never found its way into Alexandrov's 1979 cut. Salazkina, 205.

38. The film influenced cinematographer Gabriel Figueroa and filmmaker Emilio "El Indio" Fernández, who together came to define Mexico's cinematic nationalism in the 1930s and 1940s. Furthermore, Eisenstein's epic representations of the Mexican landscape both drew on and influenced the Mexican muralist movement. Charles Ramírez Berg, *The Classical Mexican Cinema: The*

Poetics of the Exceptional Golden Age Films (Austin: University of Texas Press, 2015), 65–66.

39. Birri, *Soñar con los ojos abiertos,* 261.

40. After its debut, *Org* nearly disappeared from film history. The film proved so shocking that upon viewing the rough cut, Birri's producer Terrence Hill—who also performs in the film—tried to have it burned. When he failed to destroy all remaining copies, Hill buried *Org* by withholding public screening rights. It did not resurface until 2016, when an archival copy restored by Arsenal Institute for Film and Video Art circulated widely. Birri, 94.

41. Birri, 93.

42. Birri, 93.

43. Wollen, *Readings and Writings,* 81–82.

44. Birri, *Soñar con los ojos abiertos,* 82–84.

45. Fernando Birri, "Cinema and Underdevelopment," in *New Latin American Cinema,* vol. 1, *Theory, Practices, and Transcontinental Articulations,* ed. Michael T. Martin (Detroit: Wayne State University Press, 1997), 90.

46. Birri, *Soñar con los ojos abiertos,* 84.

47. Birri, 83.

48. Birri, 85.

49. Here Birri illustrates Laura Podalsky's revisionist account of affect in the NLAC. Whereas this radical cinematic movement was thought to have abandoned feeling for militant didacticism, Podalsky argues that the NLAC drew on an affective archive to "promote an embodied, emotional commitment" to anticolonial politics. Podalsky, *The Politics of Affect,* 21.

50. Birri, *Soñar con los ojos abiertos,* 91.

51. Anand Mahadevan, "Switching Heads and Cultures: Transformation of an Indian Myth by Thomas Mann and Girish Karnad," *Comparative Literature* 54, no. 1 (Winter 2002): 24. The story serves as the basis for Thomas Mann's novella *The Transposed Heads,* published in 1940. Birri first encountered the narrative as mediated through this adaptation. He later attained a translation of the source material from Octavio Paz, who was then serving as the Mexican ambassador to India. Birri claims that *Org* synthesizes the legend itself and Mann's interpretation. Also inspired by Mann's retelling, Alejandro Jodorowsky adapted this narrative in his short film *La cravate* (1957), which I discuss in chapter 5. Birri, *Soñar con los ojos abiertos,* 91.

52. D. N. Rodowick, *The Crisis of Political Modernism: Criticism and Ideology in Contemporary Film Theory* (Berkeley: University of California Press, 1994), x.

53. Rodowick, 4–5.

54. Hamblin, "Exhausted Montage," 360.

55. Paul Schroeder Rodríguez, "After New Latin American Cinema," *Cinema Journal* 51, no. 2 (Winter 2012): 105. In framing Birri's montage excess as political, I echo Schroeder Rodríguez when he associates *Org* with the neobaroque aesthetic of the late NLAC. In the 1960s, the Cuban art historian and author Severo Sarduy famously theorizes the revolutionary potential of the neobaroque, defined as an excess of signifiers. Schroeder Rodríguez identifies this tactic at work in the late films of the NLAC, corresponding to the 1970s and early 1980s, after the militant strategies of its first phase were crushed by reactionary forces and dictatorship. Thus, while it broke with the documentary and neorealist aesthetics of militant cinema, the neobaroque NLAC was no less radical in its politics.

56. Birri, *Soñar con los ojos abiertos,* 87.

57. Birri, 89.

58. Tom Gunning, "The Cinema of Attraction[s]: Early Film, Its Spectator, and the Avant-Garde," in *The Cinema of Attractions Reloaded,* ed. Wanda Strauven (Amsterdam: Amsterdam University Press, 2006), 381.

59. I follow Schroeder Rodríguez in considering Cinema Novo a national inflection of the regional project of the NLAC. Schroeder Rodríguez, "After New Latin American Cinema," 105.

60. Glauber Rocha, *On Cinema,* ed. Ismail Xavier, trans. Stephanie Dennison and Charlotte Smith (London: I.B. Tauris, 2019), 43.

61. Rocha first presented "An Aesthetics of Hunger" in January 1965. This marks the end of what conventional historiography considers the first period of Cinema Novo (1960–64), which was symbolically brought to a close with the 1964 coup d'état in Brazil. Early Cinema Novo, which includes films such as Nelson Pereira dos Santos's *Vidas secas* (1959) and Ruy Guerra's *Os fuzis* (1964), was marked by a neorealist meditation on national issues, especially rural poverty. Randal Johnson, *Cinema Novo x 5: Masters of Contemporary Brazilian Film* (Austin: University of Texas Press, 1984), 2.

62. Rocha, *On Cinema,* 44.

63. Rocha makes the decolonial character of his epistemic politics explicit when he writes, "The Indigenous and Black roots of Latin American people should be understood as the only developed force on this continent." Rocha, 124.

64. Rocha, 123–24.

65. P. Adams Sitney, *The Cinema of Poetry* (New York: Oxford University Press, 2015), 17.

66. Pier Paolo Pasolini, "The Cinema of Poetry," in *Movies and Methods,* vol. 1, ed. Bill Nichols (Berkeley: University of California Press, 1976), 545.

67. Pasolini, 552.

68. Ismail Xavier, *Allegories of Underdevelopment: Aesthetics and Politics in Modern Brazilian Cinema* (Minneapolis: University of Minnesota Press, 1997), 66–67.

69. David Bordwell, "Jump Cuts and Blind Spots," *Wide Angle* 6 (1984): 6.

70. Rocha, *On Cinema,* 123.

71. Bellour, *El cuerpo del cine,* 31.

72. Pasolini, "The Cinema of Poetry," 6.

73. Screenwriter Augusto M. Torres, who assisted Rocha with the Spanish script, recalls the strong critical reaction at the film's release. Torres cites one reviewer who claimed, "This film seems like it was directed by the patients of Leganés [psychiatric hospital], though I doubt even they would understand it. . . . We recommend that Señor Rocha change the title from *Severed Heads* to *Crazy Heads.* He could count us among them, since we left the Victoria Eugenia theater in a fit of madness." Augusto M. Torres, *Glauber Rocha y "Cabezas cortadas"* (Barcelona: Anagrama, 1970), 104.

74. Rafael Rojas frames Guillén Landrián's drug use and alleged madness as the return of all that was repressed by the institutional left in order to uphold revolutionary reason, arguing that his films "coincided with a generational tendency to explore the limits of technocratic rationalism that castrated the emancipatory and utopian impulses of the counter-culture." Rafael Rojas, "Documentos en la sombra: Asedios al texto fílmico de Nicolás Guillén Landrián," in *Guillén Landrián o el desconcierto fílmico,* ed. Julio Ramos and Dylon Robbins (Leiden: Almenara, 2019), 63.

75. Manuel Zayas, "Cine, archivo y poder: Entrevista," in Ramos and Robbins, *Guillén Landrián,* 77.

76. Julio Ramos, "Guillén Landrián: Cine, poesía y locura," in Ramos and Robbins, *Guillén Landrián,* 89.

77. Bill Nichols, *Representing Reality: Issues and Concepts in Documentary* (Bloomington: Indiana University Press, 1991), 3–4.

78. Ramos, 99.

79. Guillén Landrián anticipates this gesture in *Los del baile* (1963), a documentary short that fuses images of Afro-Cuban street dance and *santería* possession dances. The film's montage mimics the rhythm of music through montage in order to represent the mental state of the dancer. As Juan Antonio García Borrero argues, the film constructs a phenomenological image rather than a purely representational one. In other words, Guillén Landrián's cinema inserts the spectator into the frenzied state of the dancer rather than register the dance in an observational mode. Juan Antonio García Borrero, "Nicolás Guillén Landrián: El fantasma del café," in Ramos and Robbins, *Guillén Landrián,* 42.

80. Ramos, "Guillén Landrián," 105.

81. I follow Anne Garland Mahler's conclusion that *Coffea arábiga* critiques the racial politics of the revolutionary government from within by "pointing to the continuation of the racial hierarchies of the colonial past under the Revolution's present agricultural model." Anne Garland Mahler, "'Todos los negros y todos los blancos y todos tomamos café': Raza y desigualdad laboral en *Coffea Arábiga* de Nicolás Guillén Landrián," in Ramos and Robbins, *Guillén Landrián,* 67.

82. The educational film also overlaps with what Salomé Aguilera Skvirsky terms the "process genre." Skvirsky, *The Process Genre*, 54–58.

83. Jacques Rancière, *The Emancipated Spectator,* trans. Gregory Elliott (London: Verso, 2014), 9–11.

3. Cinematic Crimes

1. Max Weber, "Politics as Vocation," in *From Max Weber: Essays in Sociology,* ed. and trans. H. H. Gerth and C. Wright Mills (London: Routledge and Kegan Paul, 1948), 115.

2. Aurora Vega, "Maras adiestran a cárteles mexicanos; decapitaciones aprendidas de pandillas: PGR," *Excelsior,* July 22, 2012, https://www.excelsior.com.mx/node/849193.

3. Juan Villoro, "La tierra en préstamo: Una gramática de la violencia en México," *New York Times,* July 30, 2020, https://www.nytimes.com/es/2020/07/30/espanol/opinion/aztecas-violencia-narco-amlo.html.

4. Patrick Dove, *Literature and "Interregnum": Globalization, War, and the Crisis of Sovereignty in Latin America* (Albany: SUNY Press, 2016), 1–2.

5. While it is easy to assume that they are members of rival organizations—*sicarios,* traffickers, informants—this is not universally true. Federico Mastrogiovanni reports that migrants who cross into a cartel's territory are often kidnapped, extorted, tortured, and killed. Often, they are misinterpreted or even falsely presented as *narcos.* In such cases, the torture and decapitation represented in the video operate according to an inquisitional logic that converts poor and marginalized subjects into *narcos* in a performative act of constituting power. Erin Graff-Zivin, *Figurative Inquisitions: Conversion, Torture, and Truth in the Luso-Hispanic Atlantic* (Evanston: Northwestern University Press, 2014), 7–8.

6. Both *norteño* and *narcocorrido* refer to subgenres of Mexican popular music. As the name suggests, *norteño* is a variety of folk music that emerged in Northern Mexico, and the addition of this music to decapitation videos in postproduction reflects the geographic importance of the US–Mexico border in representations of narcotrafficking. *Narcocorridos* are a contemporary example of the folk tradition of the *corrido.* This genre of narrative music evolved from the Spanish romance ballad, though its modern form in Mexico has been

traced to the Mexican-American war and Mexican revolution, especially in the US-Mexico borderlands. *Corridos* most often praise the deeds of a heroic protagonist, especially of an outlaw such as Gregorio Cortez or Joaquín Murieta. *Narcocorridos* first emerged in the 1960s and 1970s and took as their subject matter famous drug smugglers. Mark Cameron Edberg, *El narcotraficante: Narcocorridos and the Construction of a Cultural Persona on the U.S.–Mexican Border* (Austin: University of Texas Press, 2004).

7. Authorship distinguishes the decapitation video from other gore, snuff, and mondo imagery that circulates online, such as recordings of a drone strike or combat, body-camera footage of police murders, or surveillance recordings of fatal accidents.

8. Adriana Cavarero, *Horrorism: Naming Contemporary Violence,* trans. William McCuaig (New York: Columbia University Press, 2008), 7.

9. This contemporary spectatorship marks the inverse of historical precedent. At the beginning of the twentieth century, Rielle Navitski argues, the display of cinematic violence (for example, the fictionalized reenactment of the real execution of a band of criminals) laid the foundation for Latin American spectatorship and contributed to the creation of the public sphere. Horrorism, in contrast, seeks to neutralize the public. Rielle Navitski, *Public Spectacles of Violence: Sensational Cinema and Journalism in Early Twentieth-Century Mexico and Brazil* (Durham: Duke University Press, 2017), 11–12.

10. Galli's term refers to the rise of new forms of violence that erase the borders between peace and war, friend and enemy, criminality and legality that have traditionally defined the battlefield. These trends emerged at the end of the twentieth century with the mutation of space and time in postmodernity. Globalization and neoliberalism drive this transformation, and the confluence of capital and violence is a central theme in accounts of Global War. Carlo Galli, *Political Spaces and Global War,* ed. Adam Sitze, trans. Elisabeth Fay (Minneapolis: University of Minnesota Press, 2010), 162.

Modern war was spatially defined within a field of battle and temporally limited as a state of exception inaugurated by a declaration of war and ending with a peace treaty. Globalization and postmodernity have redefined these concepts, resulting in the spatial and temporal homogenization of war. The state of exception has become permanent, and any place or time is a possible war zone. Similarly, the distinction between state and nonstate or legal and criminal actors enters into crisis: anyone is a possible terrorist or *narco,* including the police and military. The resulting nexus between politics and crime is especially powerful in the Mexican context. Sergio González Rodríguez, *El hombre sin cabeza* (Barcelona: Anagrama, 2009), 42.

11. Here I recall Maurice Blanchot, who, in the wake of the horrors of the twentieth century, wrote, "The disaster is related to forgetfulness—forgetfulness without memory, the motionless retreat of what has been treated." Maurice Blanchot, *The Writing of the Disaster,* trans. Ann Smock (Lincoln: University of Nebraska Press, 1995), 23.

12. Sergio González Rodríguez, *Campo de guerra* (Barcelona: Anagrama, 2014), 79–80.

13. In this overwhelming and unfinished work, Warburg traced a formalist history of affect (*pathosformel*) from antiquity to the Renaissance by juxtaposing nearly one thousand images across forty black panels. Warburg believed that montage held the potential to illustrate the survival of forms and images throughout the history of art. For Didi-Huberman's extensive engagement of Warburg's thought and practice, see Georges Didi-Huberman, *The Surviving Image: Phantoms of Time and Time of Phantoms. Aby Warburg's History of Art,* trans. Harvey Mendelsohn (University Park: Pennsylvania State University Press, 2017).

14. Georges Didi-Huberman, *Images in Spite of All: Four Photographs from Auschwitz,* trans. Shane B. Lillis (Chicago: University of Chicago Press, 2012), 3.

15. In the context of the Southern Cone, Didi-Huberman's arguments on montage and memory have offered a model for critics navigating the recent horrors of dictatorship. His influence has also extended to Colombia, where Juan Felipe Ureña has explored the potential of historical montage to represent the memory of the country's armed conflict. Juan Felipe Ureña Calderón, *El montaje en Aby Warburg y en Walter Benjamin: Un método alternativo para la representación de la violencia* (Bogotá: Editorial Universidad del Rosario, 2017). The same may be said of Ileana Diéguez, who borrows Didi-Huberman's concept of the surviving image—taken, in turn, from Warburg—to reflect on the genealogy of the severed head in the visual culture of Mexico's narco-conflict. Ileana Diéguez, *Cuerpos sin duelo: Iconografías y teatralidades del dolor* (Monterrey: Universidad Autónoma de Nuevo León, 2016).

16. *Inextinguishable Fire,* directed by Harun Farocki (Harun Farocki, Berlin-West for WDR, 1969), 1:15–2:06.

17. Niamh Thornton observes that Mexico's history of political violence has led to a tradition of curating screen violence. Filmmakers and curators have displaced violence to cultural spheres, implicating screen violence in questions of taste and tastemaking. While I agree with Thornton that violence offers a productive avenue for theorizing taste—for example, the distinction between gratuitous or lowbrow screen violence and more "refined" representations in arthouse cinema—this argument centers on how cultural practitioners aestheticize violence. Yet in the case of the narco-conflict, the perpetrators of violence

themselves aestheticize their cruelty explicitly. Scholars and cultural practitioners often respond to this spectacle of violence by privileging realism. While I concur, we cannot forget that realism is not itself anti-aesthetic. Furthermore, as this summary of Farocki demonstrates, not all modes of aestheticizing violence are necessarily unethical. While the risk of collateral damage always exists, a risk that it strives to always minimize, critical montage offers a method for dispelling the aesthetics of spectacle that empowers the perpetrators of violence. Niamh Thornton, *Tastemakers and Tastemaking: Mexico and Curated Screen Violence* (Albany: SUNY Press, 2020), 1.

18. In juxtaposing screenshots of decapitation videos with similarly violent images from film history, I take inspiration from Godard's montage in *Le livre d'image.* In his final essay film, Godard reflects on the audiovisual production of ISIS as the most recent example of cinema's commitment to representing violence throughout the history of the medium, juxtaposing ISIS's assassination of prisoners with the execution of partisans in Rossellini's war trilogy.

19. Agamben ties his account of the state of exception to the biopolitical function of the modern state. Echoing the conclusion of Achille Mbembe, Reguillo argues that the theories of biopolitics proposed by Foucault and Agamben are insufficient to account for the mutation of politics in contemporary Mexico. Giorgio Agamben, *The State of Exception,* trans. Kevin Attell (Chicago: University of Chicago Press, 2005), 33–34.

20. Rossana Reguillo, *Necromáquina: Cuando morir no es suficiente* (Barcelona: Ned, 2021), 34.

21. Reguillo, 34–35.

22. On the night of September 26, 2014, forty-three young men enrolled at the Ayotzinapa Rural Teacher's College, out of a group of approximately one hundred, disappeared en route to a protest in the Mexican state of Guerrero. The municipal police of the town of Iguala apprehended the students on a stretch of rural highway. Subsequent testimonies have documented that those students who were unable to flee were beaten, tortured, and assassinated. The case has become emblematic of the impunity with which state and nonstate actors exert violence in Mexico, as the families of the disappeared still seek answers more than a decade after the events. Rosaura Martínez Ruiz, "Ayotzinapa: Truth and the Economy of Mourning," *Critical Times: Interventions in Global Critical Theory* 2, no. 1 (Spring 2019): 107–9.

23. Reguillo, *Necromáquina,* 56.

24. Reguillo, 24.

25. Explaining the shift in terminology, Reguillo writes, "It's not that the *narcomáquina* had lost its heuristic value for fieldwork, but it seemed insufficient to me to give account of the growing cruelty and brutality directed at the body

and, what's more, the systematicity with which disappearances have increased transformed my understanding of this violence." Reguillo, 24.

26. Franco, *Cruel Modernity,* 14–15.

27. María Victoria Uribe, *Matar, rematar y contramatar: Las masacres de La Violencia en el Tolima, 1948–1964* (Bogotá: CINEP, 1996), 167–68.

28. Lev Kuleshov, "The Art of Cinema," in *Kuleshov on Film: Writings by Lev Kuleshov,* ed. and trans. Ronald Levaco (Berkeley: University of California Press, 1974), 44.

29. Kuleshov, 53.

30. The protocinematic logic of these shocking scenes recalls the concept of the "montage of attractions," which Eisenstein coined to theorize his early approach to montage in theater, prior to his career in cinema. The montage of attractions shocks the spectator through its assemblage of "pieces of representation." Sergei Eisenstein, "Montage of Attractions, An Essay," in *The Film Sense,* ed. and trans. Jay Leyda (New York: Meridian, 1957), 232. The final work relies on an expressive grammar that relates these fragments in a new composition. Like the authors of this expressive violence, Eisenstein employed this strategy to shock the spectator and heighten the audience's senses. Eisenstein, 230.

31. José Alejandro Restrepo, *Cuerpo gramatical: Cuerpo, arte y violencia* (Bogotá: Universidad de los Andes, 2006), 21.

32. Rita Segato, *La guerra contra las mujeres* (Madrid: Traficantes de Sueños, 2016), 22.

33. Jonathan Crary, *24/7: Late Capitalism and the Ends of Sleep* (London: Verso, 2014), 33–34.

34. Sayak Valencia, *Gore Capitalism,* trans. John Pluecker (Cambridge: Semiotexte, 2018), 20.

35. Crary, *24/7,* 33.

36. Initially, decapitation videos were uploaded to YouTube. When they grew in number and spectatorship (and as the site itself transformed from an outlet for amateurs to a corporate media platform), these were removed by the site and began circulating on forums with more lax content regulation. Eventually, *El Blog del Narco* (formerly *El Mundo Narco*), a website dedicated to tabloid-style news of drug-related violence in Mexico, became the principal archive for such videos. On *El Blog,* these are accompanied by open comment threads that invite spectator interaction. *El Blog* became a sensation, garnering an average of three million unique monthly viewers in 2010. Spencer Ackerman, "Mexico's Top Narco-Blogger Comes Forward," *Wired,* September 14, 2010, https://www.wired.com/2010/09/mexicos-top-narco-blogger-comes-forward/. Regardless of the platform hosting them, these videos also circulated widely on social media, expanding the digital reach of horrorism.

37. We cannot isolate the images produced under gore capitalism in Mexico without considering the global war on terror and the aesthetic regime born of it. The violence of terrorism surpasses its utilitarian value; its purpose is not merely to inflict harm on a group of bodies but to create an image of itself that will paralyze the public sphere. Those exerting terror by means of the electronic image rely on the liveness of televisual transmission and streaming, the logic of the video loop, and the spectator's ability to replay imagery on digital devices. W. J. T. Mitchell, *Cloning Terror: The War of Images, 9/11 to the Present* (Chicago: University of Chicago Press, 2011), 62.

38. Cavarero, *Horrorism,* 9.

39. Because postcinema refers to a constellation of aesthetic practices, investigating the remains of cinema in relation to a range of digital media from streaming platforms to video games and virtual reality, it risks becoming reductive. Shane Denson and Julia Leyda defend the utility of this term because it permits theorists to grasp the landscape of contemporary practices. Nonetheless, they insist, "it is incorrect to speak, in the singular, of *the* post-cinematic perspective." Shane Denson and Julia Leyda, eds., *Post-Cinema: Theorizing 21st-Century Film* (Falmer: REFRAME Books, 2016), 4.

40. Denson and Leyda, 2.

41. Jennifer Malkowski, *Dying in Full Detail: Mortality and Digital Documentary* (Durham: Duke University Press, 2017), 5.

42. Boris Groys, *Art Power* (Cambridge: MIT Press, 2013), 54.

43. These transformations to the representation of violence mirror the shrinking of cinematic productions as a result of neoliberal reforms. Gonzalo Aguilar describes this in the case of the Nuevo Cine Argentino, which responded to the shrinking of the media economy by significantly downsizing productions. Under this same structure it is not uncommon for the same person to take on the duties of writer, producer, and director. The reforms in Argentina pioneered the regional abandonment of state support of cinema—what was once a hallmark of national cinemas across Latin America, and especially true in the case of Mexico. Gonzalo Aguilar, *Other Worlds: New Argentine Film,* trans. Sarah Ann Wells (New York: Palgrave Macmillan, 2016), 9.

44. Seth Price, *Dispersion* (New York: 38th Street Publishers, 2008), 9.

45. Price, 9–10.

46. Hito Steyerl, *The Wretched of the Screen* (Berlin: Sternberg, 2012), 41.

47. Steyerl, 39.

48. The same is true of other examples of global conflict, such as the case of ISIS and what Hatem N. Akil terms "the snuff film production of its media machine." "What ISIS poses as a 'state,'" Akil continues, "is basically a B-rated

movie set." Hatem N. Akil, "Cinematic Terrorism: Deleuze, ISIS, and Delusion," *Journal for Cultural Research* 20, no. 4 (2016): 377.

49. Valencia, *Gore Capitalism,* 156.

50. Galli, *Political Spaces and Global War,* 146.

51. A criminal organization infamous for its brutality, Los Zetas had not yet formed its own drug-trafficking operation at the time the video was uploaded. Composed of veterans from Mexico's elite military forces, the organization initially provide security services to the Cartel del Golfo. González Rodríguez, *El hombre sin cabeza,* 26.

52. Sergio González Rodríguez, *The Femicide Machine,* trans. Michael Parker-Stainback (Los Angeles: Semiotext(e), 2012), 106–25.

53. Blanchot, *The Writing of the Disaster,* 6.

54. Walter Benjamin, "The Work of Art in the Age of Its Technological Reproducibility," in *The Work of Art in the Age of Its Reproducibility and Other Writings on Media,* ed. Michael W. Jennings et al., trans. Edmund Jephcott et al. (Cambridge: Belknap, 2008), 35.

55. Murch, *In the Blink of an Eye,* 60.

56. Georges Bataille, "Rotten Sun," in *Visions of Excess: Selected Writings, 1927–1939,* ed. Allan Stoekl, trans. Stoekl et al. (Minneapolis: University of Minnesota Press, 1985), 57–58.

57. Jean-Louis Comolli, *Daech, le cinéma et la mort* (Paris: Verdier, 2016), 11.

58. Lisa Downing observes that the violence of snuff is gendered; in the cultural myths that surround the snuff film, the victim is typically female. Lisa Downing, "Snuff and Nonsense: The Discursive Life of a Phantasmatic Archive," in *Porn Archives,* ed. Tim Dean et al. (Durham: Duke University Press, 2014), 279.

59. In the North American imaginary, snuff has historically been tied to the criminal politics of Latin America, beginning with the dictatorships of the 1960s and 1970s. The 1976 sexploitation film *Snuff,* filmed in Argentina by Michael and Roberta Findlay, bore in its publicity materials: "The film that could only be made in South America . . . where life is CHEAP!" In the twenty-first century, the specter of the snuff film reemerged in Mexico amid the surge in the disappearance and murders of women in Ciudad Juárez. The scale of impunity gave rise to conspiracy theories claiming that the femicide was evidence of an underground snuff ring on the border with the United States.

60. Paul B. Preciado, *Testo Junkie: Sex, Drugs, and Biopolitics in the Pharmacopornographic Era* (New York: Feminist Press at the City University of New York, 2013), 344. Drawing on Preciado's argument, Valencia nevertheless distinguishes *gore* from *snuff:* she argues that gore is, in a sense, a *work in progress,*

with snuff (the recording of death live on video) being the *telos* of gore capitalism, its most extreme form. Valencia, *Gore Capitalism,* 31–32.

61. Preciado, *Testo Junkie,* 346.

62. Valencia borrows this term from the medieval romance *Amadís de Gaula,* in which the *endriago* appears as a monster that is part human, hydra, and dragon. Valencia, *Gore Capitalism,* 53.

63. Valencia, 12.

64. Valencia, 32.

65. Laura Mulvey, *Death 24x a Second: Stillness and the Moving Image* (London: Reaktion, 2011), 15.

66. Mulvey, 23.

67. This excess of montage in modernist aesthetics poses a critical challenge to any overarching, transmedial theory of this practice. I do not attempt one here, though I do engage other (noncinematic) genealogies of montage when discussing the politics of countermontage in chapter 4. Mario Slugan, *Montage as Perceptual Experience: Berlin Alexanderplatz from Döblin to Fassbinder* (Rochester: Camden House, 2017), 6.

68. Slugan, 2.

69. I am drawing here on a phenomenological tradition of film theory first laid out by Vivian Sobchack and continued by Jennifer Barker, which theorizes the material film that is fed through the projector as a body.

70. Vicente Sánchez Biosca, *Teoría del montaje cinematográfico* (Valencia: Filmoteca de la Generalitat Valenciana, 1991), 13.

71. Adorno, *Aesthetic Theory,* 154; Bürger, *Theory of the Avant-Garde,* 80.

72. Bürger excludes cinematic montage from avant-garde practice because it is a technical requirement of the medium. It does not necessarily expose the non-organic composition of the film as a modern aesthetic object. Indeed, despite its reliance on fragmentation, montage quite often serves to preserve the illusion of a temporal and spatial continuity. Bürger, *Theory of the Avant-Garde,* 73.

73. For a comparative analysis of literary and cinematic montage, see Slugan, *Montage as Perceptual Experience.*

74. Mulvey, *Death 24x a Second,* 186.

75. In considering how Mulvey's theory of digital spectatorship might allow us to subvert the logic of the decapitation video, there exists the danger of falling into a possessive spectatorship that objectifies the victim. Throughout cinema's history, practices emerged to allow the spectator to possess the images that traditionally would float past her in the movie theater. With the arrival of digital technology, however, "the spectator is able to hold on to, to possess, the previously elusive image." Mulvey, *Death 24x a Second,* 161.

By controlling the image, the spectator is thus capable of objectifying the body on-screen and possessing it. This is one consequence of treating the decapitation video as spectacle. A possessive spectator might go back and revisit the goriest parts of the video, repeatedly moving the cursor back so that they can see the beheading over and over again. They seek to possess the severed head, which is the total eradication of the victim's subjectivity, their absolute objectification: the transformation of the face into the head. This is the mode of spectatorship imposed by the *necromáquina,* which must be subverted.

76. Steven Shaviro, *Post-Cinematic Affect* (Winchester: Zero, 2010), 2–3.

77. Ariella Azoulay, *The Civil Contract of Photography* (New York: Zone, 2014), 86.

78. Azoulay, 17.

79. As I have already suggested, the *necromáquina* has established a short circuit with Hollywood when it mimics the sexualized violence of blockbuster action movies. Hollywood, in turn, reciprocates by citing the imperfect images produced within Global War. Industrial cinema increasingly draws on low-resolution and imperfect images. Online videos, surveillance imagery, body-camera footage, webcam recordings, and archival imagery are frequently assimilated into high-definition and big-budget productions. Francesco Casetti attributes this appropriation of poor images by Hollywood to two postcinematic phenomena. First, this is a self-conscious gesture by cinema to highlight its uniqueness as a high-definition medium in a low-definition age of compressed media. Second, and more important for my argument, Casetti argues that the poor image has come to be associated with the visual expression of truth and authenticity. The high-definition image assimilates the imperfect image to acquire this truth effect. Thus, the convergence of perfect and imperfect images within audiovisual industries complicates a straightforward distinction between them. There is a feedback loop here between Hollywood and poor images, such as those produced by the *necromáquina.* Francesco Casetti, *The Lumière Galaxy: Seven Key Words for the Cinema to Come* (New York: Columbia University Press, 2015), 121.

80. Didi-Huberman, *Images in Spite of All,* 36–37.

81. This emphasis on the primitive or animalistic violence of the masculine through the use of a rural setting is reflected in Carlos Reygadas's *Post Tenebras Lux,* which (in the director's own words) responds to the violence of the *necromáquina.* I discuss the film at length in chapter 4.

82. Jens Andermann, "Exhausted Landscapes: Reframing the Rural in Recent Argentine and Brazilian Films," *Cinema Journal* 53, no. 2 (Winter 2014): 52.

83. "Global War, by contrast, manifests itself in the nonspace of globalization (where, to be clear, 'space' is understood in a specifically modern sense)." Galli, *Political Spaces and Global War,* 161.

84. Walter Benjamin, "Theses on the Philosophy of History," in *Illuminations,* ed. Hannah Arendt, trans. Harry Zohn (New York: Schocken, 1968), 257.

4. *Contramáquinas*

1. Reguillo, *Necromáquina,* 68.

2. Sánchez Prado, *Screening Neoliberalism,* 5–6.

3. Cavarero, *Horrorism,* 8.

4. Martine Beugnet, *Cinema and Sensation: French Film and the Art of Transgression* (Edinburgh: Edinburgh University Press, 2007), 28–30. This reaction against apparatus theory is not exclusive to critical accounts of new extremity. Appearing about a decade earlier, Steven Shaviro's *The Cinematic Body* accelerated the affective turn in film studies and shaped theoretical interest in new extremity, including Beugnet. Steven Shaviro, *The Cinematic Body* (Minneapolis: University of Minnesota Press, 1993).

5. Tanya Horeck and Tina Kendall, *New Extremism in Cinema: From France to Europe.* (Edinburgh: Edinburgh University Press, 2011), 8.

6. Eugenie Brinkema, *The Forms of the Affects* (Durham: Duke University Press, 2014), 40.

7. This debate between the primacy of ethics and politics has featured prominently in Latin American cultural studies in recent years. Bruno Bosteels, *Marx and Freud in Latin America: Politics, Psychoanalysis, and Religion in Times of Terror* (London: Verso, 2012); Erin Graff-Zivin, "The Ethical Turn," in *New Approaches to Latin American Studies: Culture and Power,* ed. Juan Poblete (New York: Routledge, 2018).

8. Patrick Dove, *Literature and "Interregnum": Globalization, War, and the Crisis of Sovereignty in Latin America* (Albany: State University of New York Press, 2016), 2.

9. Dove, 17.

10. Horeck and Kendall, *New Extremism in Cinema,* 7.

11. Horeck and Kendall, 1–2.

12. My reading of Reygadas's bourgeois, international, and predominantly white audience draws on Ignacio Sánchez Prado's research on the creation of the "art film" market following the neoliberal reorganization of media production in Mexico and the rest of Latin America in the 1990s. Sánchez Prado, *Screening Neoliberalism,* 156–57.

13. Laura Mulvey, "Visual Pleasure and Narrative Cinema," in *Visual and Other Pleasures* (Basingstoke: Palgrave, 1989), 14.

14. Kuleshov, "The Art of Cinema," 53.

15. Fernanda Solórzano, "Reygadas contra la interpretación," *Letras Libres,* November 30, 2012, https://letraslibres.com/cine-tv/reygadas-contra-la-interpretacion/.

16. Marina Galletit and Alastair Brotchie, preface to *The Sacred Conspiracy: The Internal Papers of the Secret Society of Acéphale and Lectures to the College of Sociology* (London: Atlas, 2017), 15.

17. Georges Bataille, "*Acéphale*," in *The Sacred Conspiracy: The Internal Papers of the Secret Society of Acéphale and Lectures to the College of Sociology* (London: Atlas, 2017), 130.

18. Manohla Dargis, "Ducking Rain and Competition at Cannes," *New York Times,* May 16, 2013, https://www.nytimes.com/2013/05/17/movies/at-cannes-film-festival-ducking-rain-and-competition.html.

19. Glaria Leticia Díaz, "Polémico y cuestionado, el informe de la CNDH sobre el normalista Julio César Mondragón," *Proceso,* July 16, 2016, https://www.proceso.com.mx/reportajes/2016/7/16/polemico-cuestionado-el-informe-de-la-cndh-sobre-el-normalista-julio-cesar-mondragon-167438.html.

20. Rossana Reguillo, "Rostros en escenas: Ayotzinapa y la imposibilidad del desentendimiento," *Magis* 443 (Winter 2014): 2, https://magis.iteso.mx/nota/rostros-en-escenas-ayotzinapa-y-la-imposibilidad-del-desentendimiento/. The photographs of the faceless Julio César Mondragón are another example—in addition to the many *narco* videos—of the archival function of the *necromáquina.* Like the death camp in Georges Didi-Huberman's analysis, the *necromáquina* compulsively produces documentary images of its work. If Auschwitz contained a darkroom, there is a digital camera and internet connection in the pocket of every *narco,* police officer, and soldier. This results in a sophisticated production and circulation of extremely violent digital imagery. Didi-Huberman, *Images in Spite of All,* 24.

21. Reguillo, "Rostros en escenas."

22. *La libertad del diablo* demystifies the criminals and does away with the cult of personality that envelops them in representations by the culture industry. Wearing identical masks, the criminals appear deflated. Instead of grand cartel bosses, we encounter anonymous, soft-spoken young men who nevertheless have proven themselves capable of committing atrocities. Despite their histories of violence, González renders them unattractive, meek, even vulnerable. Nonetheless, like other recent documentaries that feature the voices of the perpetrators of violence, such as Joshua Oppenheimer's *The Act of Killing* (2012), this documentary strategy risks humanizing executioners.

23. Nevertheless, this tactic ultimately does not manage to overcome a humanist impulse in the film. In its final scene, we see one of the witnesses remove her mask and reveal her face, though it is not clear whether this symbolic act occurs at the direction of the filmmaker or is a spontaneous decision on the part of the witness.

24. Georges Didi-Huberman, "The Site, Despite Everything," in *Claude Lanzmann's Shoah: Key Essays,* ed. and trans. Stuart Liebman (Oxford: Oxford University Press, 2007), 116.

25. Susan Sontag, *Regarding the Pain of Others* (New York: Farrar, Straus and Giroux, 2003), 30–31.

26. Giuliana Bruno, *Surface: Matters of Aesthetics, Materiality, and Media* (Chicago: University of Chicago Press, 2014), 19.

27. Bruno, 5.

28. Colectivo Los Ingrávidos, "Piezas sueltas para una máquina de guerra," *Desistfilm,* March 7, 2014, https://desistfilm.com/colectivo-los-ingravidos-piezas-sueltas-para-maquina-de-guerra/.

29. Reguillo, *Necromáquina,* 72. A prominent example of this was the assassination of Arturo Beltrán Leyva by the Mexican military in December 2009. Following the killing, photographs of the manipulated corpse began to circulate in the media. These images further eroded the boundaries between the security state and its adversary by mimicking the *necromáquina*'s symbolic violence. Nasheli Jiménez del Val, "Government Gore: The Images of Beltrán-Leyva's Body and the Mexican (Failed) State," *Journal of Latin American Cultural Studies* 20, no. 3 (2011): 293.

30. Miguel Errazu, "Barrar las imágenes, las palabras, los sonidos, las voces: Sobre *2 de octubre/Lejos de Tlatelolco,* de Los Ingrávidos," *TOMA UNO* 6 (2018): 121–40, https://revistas.unc.edu.ar/index.php/toma1/article/view/20901/20501.

31. Elisabeth R. Anker observes that the security strategies enacted by the United States during the war on terror were presented to the American public through a melodramatic narrative in which freedom triumphs over the evils of terrorism. In what Anker terms "melodramatic political discourse," the Bush administration employed melodramatic tropes—emphasizing the suffering of virtuous and innocent American victims at the hands of barbaric intruders—to justify the expansion of state power. Elisabeth R. Anker, *Orgies of Feeling: Melodrama and the Politics of Freedom* (Durham: Duke University Press, 2014), 2–3. Reguillo notes that this post-9/11 rhetoric of security constituted a transnational discourse that soon extended to Mexico and shaped the state's response to narco-violence. Reguillo, *Necromáquina,* 40.

32. Colectivo Los Ingrávidos, "Los Ingrávidos," *Proyecto Idis,* November 15, 2014, https://proyectoidis.org/colectivo-los-ingravidos/?fbclid=IwAR3aKOI79s0s06ExZzLeDyZyD0wjEqInhx2IIQjRJeig7x5WuD-Vb0zxfNI.

33. Federico Windhausen, "Deframing Evidence: A Transmission from Los Ingrávidos," in *Unwatchable,* ed. Nicholas Baer et al. (New Brunswick: Rutgers University Press, 2018), 99.

34. While shaped by the transnational security rhetoric that emerged from the war on terror, the political melodrama of the security state has a deeper history. Melodrama became the preferred genre of Mexican national cinema, and was crucial in its institutionalization of the revolution. For a critical study of the enactment of the Mexican national imaginary through melodrama, see Susan Dever, *Celluloid Nationalism and Other Melodramas: From Post-Revolutionary Mexico to* fin de siglo *Mexamérica* (Albany: SUNY Press, 2003).

35. Errazu, "Barrar las imágenes."

36. The ideological function of golden age cinema, as well as Fernández's central role in cinematic projects of cultural nationalism, has been discussed extensively in Mexican film studies. For an account of how *La perla* operates within this ideological framework, see Dolores Tierney, "Emilio Fernández 'in Hollywood': Mexico's Postwar Inter-American Cinema, *La perla/The Pearl* (1946) and *The Fugitive* (1948)," *Studies in Hispanic Cinemas* 7, no. 2 (2010): 81–100.

37. Colectivo Los Ingrávidos, "Shamanic Materialism: 77 Theses on the Audiovisual," in *Expanded Nature: Ecologies of Experimental Cinema,* ed. Elio Della Noce and Lucas Murari (Cham: Palgrave Macmillan, 2025), 229.

38. Colectivo Los Ingrávidos, 235.

39. From Gloria Anzaldúa to Alicia Gaspar de Alba, the tradition of Chicana feminism has similarly related the Coyolxauhqui myth to gendered violence in contemporary Mexico.

40. Segato, *La guerra contra las mujeres,* 35.

41. In this regard, *Coyolxauhqui* bears striking resemblance to *Corte del florero,* a photographic series by Juan Manuel Echavarría that reimagines the memory of the Colombian armed conflict by creating a montage of bones.

42. Colectivo Los Ingrávidos, "El lenguaje de los huesos en la Nuevo Tenochtitlán," in *La radicalidad de la imagen: Des-bordando latitudes latinoamericanas sobre algunos modos del cine experimental,* ed. Florencia Incarbone and Sebastian Wiedemann (Buenos Aires: Hambre, 2016), 147.

43. Georges Bataille, *The Accursed Share: An Essay on General Economy,* vol. 1, *Consumption* (New York: Zone, 1988), 55–56.

44. Colectivo Los Ingrávidos, "El lenguaje de los huesos," 147.

45. David Carrasco, "The Exaggerations of Human Sacrifice," in *The History of the Conquest of New Spain,* ed. Davíd Carrasco (Albuquerque: University of New Mexico Press, 2008), 442.

46. Underscoring the ritual character of its violence, the anthropologist Claudio Lomnitz compares the narco-conflict to the *guerras floridas* (flowery wars) waged by the Aztecs in the fifteenth and sixteenth centuries, the objective of which was to produce sacrificial victims. Claudio Lomnitz, *Sovereignty and Extortion: A New State Form in Mexico* (Durham: Duke University Press, 2024), 2.

47. Colectivo Los Ingrávidos, "El lenguaje de los huesos," 154.

5. Capital Visions

1. Mulvey, *Death 24x a Second,* 161.

2. Daniel Dayan, "The Tutor-Code of Classical Cinema," *Film Quarterly* 28, no. 1 (Fall 1974): 22; Stephen Heath, *Questions of Cinema* (London: Macmillan, 1981), 93.

3. Coincidentally, Argentine filmmaker Fernando Birri also adapted this narrative in his experimental feature *Org* (1978), which I discuss in chapter 2.

4. Anand Mahadevan, "Switching Heads and Cultures: Transformation of an Indian Myth by Thomas Mann and Girish Karnad," *Comparative Literature* 54, no. 1 (Winter 2002): 24.

5. Margaret Barton-Fumo, "An Interview with Alejandro Jodorowsky," *Film Comment,* January 9, 2012, https://www.filmcomment.com/blog/an-interview-with-alejandro-jodorowsky/.

6. Janes, *Losing Our Heads,* x.

7. Jacques-Alain Miller, "Suture (elements of the logic of the signifier)," *Screen* 18, no. 4 (Winter 1977): 34.

8. Jean-Pierre Oudart, "Cinema and Suture," *Screen* 18, no. 4 (Winter 1977): 40.

9. Kaja Silverman, *The Subject of Semiotics* (New York: Oxford University Press, 1983), 205.

10. Freud, *Writings on Art and Literature,* 264.

11. Kristeva, *The Severed Head,* 12–13.

12. Kristeva, 23.

13. Mulvey, *Death 24x a Second,* 162.

14. Mulvey, 161.

15. Maite Conde, *Foundational Films: Early Cinema and Modernity in Brazil* (Oakland: University of California Press, 2018), 106.

16. Conde, 93.

17. Tsivian, *Early Russian Cinema,* 196.

18. Oeler, *A Grammar of Murder,* 13.

19. Nicholas Balaisis, "Modernization and Ambivalence in Octavio Cortázar's *Por primera vez.*" *Cinema Journal* 54, no. 1 (Fall 2014): 10.

20. Critical accounts of the film have vacillated between embracing and critiquing Cortázar's representation of Cuban peasants. Julianne Burton praises the film for expanding the documentary gaze to traditionally marginalized communities, while Anne Marie Stock's revisionist argument critiques the filmmaker for his paternalistic treatment of rural Cubans. Julianne Burton, "Democratizing Documentary: Modes of Address in New Latin American Cinema," in *The Social Documentary in Latin America,* ed. Julianne Burton (Pittsburgh: University of Pittsburgh Press, 1990), 67. Anne Marie Stock, *On Location in Cuba: Street Filmmaking During Times of Transition* (Chapel Hill: University of North Carolina Press, 2009), 84. Balaisis synthesizes both sides of this polemic and inscribes *Por primera vez* in the tradition of experimental ethnography, arguing that the problematic elements of Cortázar's representation are ironic and intended to estrange the spectator.

21. Balaisis, "Modernization and Ambivalence," 9.

22. Balaisis, 16–17.

23. In Beller's words, "Early cinematic montage extended the logic of the assembly-line (the sequencing of discreet, programmatic machine-orchestrated human operations) to the sensorium and brought the industrial revolution to the eye." Jonathan Beller, *The Cinematic Mode of Production: Attention Economy and the Society of the Spectacle* (Hanover: University Press of New England, 2006), 9.

24. Participation in this politics of modernization was initially limited to urban centers. As Cortázar documents in *Por primera vez,* rural inhabitants were excluded from such a politics of modernization for decades.

25. For example, Rielle Navitski has documented how the first narrative films to gain widespread popularity in Mexico and Brazil restaged spectacular cases of real violence. As it contributed to national modernization projects, cinema gave rise to what Navitski terms sensational subjects. In other words, the subject positions created by the cinematic apparatus mediated the violence that characterized the uneven transition to modernity. Navitski, *Public Spectacles of Violence,* 12.

26. Mulvey, "Visual Pleasure and Narrative Cinema," 14.

27. Laura Mulvey, "Fears, Fantasies, and the Male Unconscious, *or* 'You Don't Know What is Happening, Do You, Mr. Jones,'" in *Visual and Other Pleasures* (Basingstoke: Palgrave, 1989), 6.

28. While Mulvey argues that visual pleasure is produced in narrative cinema through the image of the female body in pieces, feminist film theorists have

traced a deeper archaeology of the symbolic violence that the apparatus directs at the female form. Linda Williams identifies such processes in early cinema, arguing that the impulse to master the threat of difference posed by the female body—that is, to violently resolve the threat of lack posed by the castrated form—preceded cinematic narrative. For example, Williams understands the spectacle of female dismemberment and decapitation in the films of Georges Méliès as an early example of cinema's fetishization of the female form. As in the example of narrative suture examined by Mulvey, the female's severed head resolves castration anxiety by converting the female body into a fetish object through fragmentation. Linda Williams, "Film Body: An Implantation of Perversions," in *Narrative, Apparatus, Ideology: A Film Theory Reader,* ed. Philip Rosen (New York: Columbia University Press, 1986), 523.

29. Paulo Antonio Paranaguá, *Tradición y modernidad en el cine de América Latina* (Madrid: Fondo de Cultura Económica, 2003), 250.

30. Schroeder Rodríguez, *Latin American Cinema*, 265–66. Film historians are presently revising this historiography, which tends to isolate women's cinema as a development that follows the dissolution of the NLAC. For example, Isabel Seguí has addressed the erasure of female labor within radical film collectives such as Bolivia's Grupo Ukamau, arguing that the historiographic tendency to approach collectively produced films through an auteurist lens has suppressed women's contributions. Isabel Seguí, "Auteurism, Machismo-Leninismo, and Other Issues. Women's Labor in Andean Oppositional Film Production," *Feminist Media Histories* 4, no. 1 (2018): 11–13. Similarly, Lorena Cervera Ferrer has examined the feminist film collectives that arose alongside the Latin American feminist movements of the 1970s, such as Cine Mujer in Colombia and Grupo Feminista Miércoles in Venezuela. Lorena Cervera Ferrer, "Militancy, Feminism, and Cinema: The Case of Grupo Feminista Miércoles," *Journal of Italian Cinema & Media Studies* 10 (2022): 267–84. Lorena Cervera Ferrer, "Towards a Latin American Feminist Cinema: The Case of Cine Mujer in Colombia," *Alphaville: Journal of Film and Screen Media* 20 (2020): 150–65.

31. Matt Losada, *Before Bemberg: Women Filmmakers in Argentina* (New Brunswick: Rutgers University Press, 2020), 125.

32. Laura Mulvey, "The Spectacle Is Vulnerable: Miss World 1970," in Mulvey, *Visual and Other Pleasures* (Basingstoke: Palgrave, 1989), 3–5.

33. Isabel Seguí and Marina Cavalcanti Tedesco, "Feminist Ironic Montage to Dismantle Gender Essentialism," *Framework: The Journal of Cinema and Media* 63, nos. 1–2 (Spring/Fall 2022): 68.

34. Judith Butler, "Capital/Punishment," Annual Meeting of the American Comparative Literature Association, March 21, 2014, New York University.

35. Laura Mulvey, *Fetishism and Curiosity* (Bloomington: Indiana University Press and the British Film Institute, 1996), 40. See also Tom Gunning's discussion of Griffith's close-ups of Florence Lawrence, one of cinema's first female stars. Gunning, *D. W. Griffith and the Origins of American Narrative Film: The Early Years at Biograph* (Urbana: University of Illinois Press, 1994).

36. Mulvey, *Fetishism and Curiosity*, 43.

37. Mulvey, 48.

38. Martel has acknowledged the influence of Bemberg in her work, citing the similarities between *La ciénaga* (*The Swamp*, 2001) and Bemberg's *Miss Mary* (1986). Deborah Martin, "*Planeta Ciénaga:* Lucrecia Martel and Contemporary Argentine Women's Filmmaking," in *Latin American Women Filmmakers: Production, Politics, Poetics*, ed. Deborah Martin and Deborah Shaw (London: I.B. Tauris, 2017), 243.

39. Throughout her career, Martel returns to the theme of the fragmentation of the female body. For example, the correlation of framing and decapitation in *La mujer sin cabeza* can already be seen in *La ciénaga*. The title sequence of Martel's debut film features a collection of broken bodies around a swimming pool. A disembodied hand enters the shot to reach for a drink. Next, the other aging bodies begin to move slowly and in unison, dragging deck chairs behind them. The figures move mechanically, and the sound adds an unnerving tone to this parade of headless bodies. The scene culminates with Mecha, the matriarch, drunkenly falling onto a glass and literally cutting herself. With this symbolic fall, Martel playfully stages the visual cutting of the body in the frame.

40. For example, in *La niña santa* (*The Holy Girl*, 2004), the trilogy's second entry, Martel develops an oedipal narrative in which the young protagonist's desire "exceeds the patriarchal bounds of appropriate female behavior." Paul Schroeder Rodríguez, "Little Red Riding Hood Meets Freud in Lucrecia Martel's Salta Trilogy," *Camera Obscura* 29, no. 3 (Winter 2014): 101–2.

41. Valeria de los Ríos, "Look(ing) at the Animals: the Presence of the Animal in Contemporary Southern Cone Cinema and in Carlos Busqued's *Bajo este sol tremendo*," *Journal of Latin American Cultural Studies* 24, no. 1 (2015): 35.

42. Patricia White, *Women's Cinema, World Cinema: Projecting Contemporary Feminisms* (Durham: Duke University Press, 2015), 51.

43. Tania Modleski, *The Women Who Knew Too Much: Hitchcock and Feminist Theory* (New York: Routledge, 2005), 89.

44. Laura Mulvey, *Afterimages: Cinema, Women, and Changing Times* (London: Reaktion, 2019), 20.

45. Martel is not among those filmmakers who melancholically reject the digital image as the death of cinema. In an interview regarding *Zama*, she

remarks: "It would be very difficult, in fact nearly impossible, to shoot analog nowadays. . . . There is a certain nostalgia for analog film, and I think it reflects a mediocre way of thinking about the image. Things are changing, and we have to accept that this technology is more affordable and that it allows us to do what we want to do. And we need to master it." Gerd Gemünden and Silvia Spitta, "'I Was Never Afraid': An Interview with Lucrecia Martel," *Film Quarterly* 71, no. 4 (Summer 2018): 38. With the move to a new apparatus, a process once familiar to Martel undergoes metamorphosis and the filmmaker becomes estranged from her medium. The title of Martel's video *Muta* captures this, as it derives from the imperative form of the Spanish verb *mutar,* "to mutate." This is the command issued to Martel. With the changes to cinematic technology, Martel must mutate alongside the apparatus if she is to continue making films. Martel's comment implies that there is a pedagogy required by this transition, one that provokes a nervous meditation on the digital image.

46. Technology functions as an agent of uncertainty throughout Martel's Salta trilogy. In *La ciénaga,* a blurry television broadcast mediates the image of the Virgin Mary that has allegedly appeared on a water tank. Based on the imperfect quality of this electronic image, neither the characters nor the audience can be certain of this apparition. The distortion that is characteristic of television, the scan lines and grain that mask the image, generates doubt as to the veracity of this event. This trope reappears in *La niña santa,* when Martel repeatedly includes a theremin to heighten narrative tension through acousmatic sound; the ambiguity associated with the theremin generates an uneasy atmosphere. Finally, in *La mujer sin cabeza,* when viewing a home recording of a wedding, Tía Lala claims to see a family member who was deceased at the time of this event. As in *La ciénaga,* the scene emphasizes this medium's imperfections to sow doubt in the spectator. In these examples, Martel draws on electronic sounds and images to create an ambiguous and unsettling atmosphere.

47. In Gemünden's words, Martel "has repeatedly stressed the significance of YouTube. The platform has provided her not only with inspiration . . . but it has become a medium that for her exceeds the possibilities of cinema." Gerd Gemünden, *Lucrecia Martel* (Urbana: University of Illinois Press, 2019), 89.

48. Quoted in Gemünden, 89.

49. Emphasizing the agency of algorithmic autoplay over human creativity, Martel also signals an interest in posthuman aesthetics, a theme that appears in her experimental videos.

50. William J. Mitchell, *The Reconfigured Eye: Visual Truth in the Post-Photographic Era* (Cambridge: MIT Press, 2001), 5.

51. *Muta* emerged as part of a trend of fashion films in the 2010s, spurred on by the rapid expansion of YouTube and growing accessibility of digital devices.

The fashion film is an intermedial object: produced for digital platforms as advertisements, it draws on cinema for cultural capital. Filmmakers are typically given creative control over their shorts, though they must feature a collection from the commissioning brand. Other examples of auteurist engagement of the fashion film include David Lynch for Dior (2010), Harmony Korine for Proenza Shouler (2010), Roman Polanski for Prada (2012), Wes Anderson for both Prada (2013, 2015) and H&M (2016), and Spike Jonze for Kenzo (2016).

52. Marianna Souto and Mônica Campo, "*Muta*: Monstrosity and Mutation," in *ReFocus: The Films of Lucrecia Martel*, ed. Natalia Christofoletti Barrenha, Julia Kratje, and Paul R. Merchant (Edinburgh: Edinburgh University Press, 2022), 68.

53. Jussi Parikka, *Insect Media: An Archaeology of Animals and Technology* (Minneapolis: University of Minnesota Press, 2010).

54. In analog cinema, the projector creates the illusion of movement as it continuously rotates the reel and projects light through the film at a rate of twenty-four frames per second. In the digital image, movement is instead simulated through the constant transformation of a set number of pixels on-screen. Like the insect, the pixel is constantly morphing to simulate a new image. Together with hundreds or thousands of others—depending on the resolution of the image and screen—the pixel swarms: in this cloud we can distinguish an image.

55. This conceptualization of the insect helps explain their cultural association with the weird and creepy, an affect that Martel explores in *Muta*. In Eric Brown's words, "It is partly this innate distortion, derangement, and fragmentation—their world ever fractured from our own—that marks insects as humanity's Other, even as their swarming, hiving, and colonizing behaviors reproduce various self-identifications in human beings." Eric C. Brown, "Introduction: Reading the Insect," in *Insect Poetics*, ed. Eric C. Brown (Minneapolis: University of Minnesota Press, 2006), xi.

56. This representation of digital surveillance aligns with Martel's public statements on YouTube's autoplay feature, cited above, since this digital montage of videos is generated by an algorithm that draws on the user's data.

57. The video bears a striking similarity to the tradition of psychiatric photography, which finds its earliest expression in Charcot's photographs of hysteria. Medical discourse was quick to incorporate the moving image, and film historians have identified a physiognomic impulse in early cinema.

58. García Canclini, "Will There Be Latin American Cinema," 255.

59. Sara Ann Wells, "Jet Lag: Late Cinema in South America," *Revista de Estudios Hispánicos* 50, no. 2 (2016): 409–37.

60. While interest in expanded cinema has grown substantially following the eclipse of cinema's hegemony over the moving image, such practices did not originate in response to the digital turn. The popularity of television first challenged the theatrical exhibition of film decades earlier. Box-office sales fell drastically as a result, up to 75 percent between the mid-1940s and early 1960s. Expanded cinema emerged in the context of this crisis, the first in a series that would mark cinema's progressive decline over the second half of the century. Andrew V. Uroskie, *Between the Black Box and the White Cube: Expanded Cinema and Postwar Art* (Chicago: University of Chicago Press, 2014), 13. Though it first emerged in avant-garde circles in Europe and the United States, expanded cinema has rapidly gained popularity among artists and filmmakers from Latin America. Latin American film studies is beginning to catch up with the region's growing engagement of this form.

61. For example, *Oedipus Marshall* (2006) was commissioned by the Aspen Art Museum, *Caligari and the Sleepwalker* (2008) by the Haus de Kulturen der Welt in Berlin, and *Nosferatu* (*The Undead*, 2018) by the city of Rochester. The decision to select a particular hospital largely depends on its geographic proximity to the commissioning institution. In each work, Téllez follows the same method. After receiving a commission, the artist finds a nearby psychiatric facility that is open to collaboration. Téllez then selects a film or series of films relating to the main themes of the work. He organizes an extended workshop with the patients, screens the relevant film(s), and works with his collaborators on a script. Finally, Téllez films his collaborators' performance and consults them in the editing process. Although Téllez includes references to the surrounding area or city at times, these are not site-specific works. The artist selects Rozelle Hospital not for its institutional history but because of its proximity to the Sydney Bienniale and its openness to collaboration. Michel Faguet and Cristóbal Lehyt, "Madness Is the Language of the Excluded: An Interview with Javier Téllez," *C-Magazine* 92 (Winter 2006): 28.

62. Faguet and Lehyt, 29.

63. Georges Didi-Huberman, *Invention of Hysteria: Charcot and the Photographic Iconography of the Salpêtrière*, trans. Alisa Hartz (Cambridge: MIT Press, 2003).

64. Elaine Showalter, *The Female Malady: Women, Madness, and English Culture, 1830–1980* (New York: Pantheon, 1985), 3–4.

65. Didi-Huberman, *Invention of Hysteria*, 27.

66. Consequently, *Rozelle Hospital* approximates what Tobin Siebers terms a disability aesthetics, which challenges the tradition of disembodiment in aesthetics and "summon[s] images of disability" by enacting affective and corporeal modes of perception instead. By privileging bodily over cognitive perception, such works draw on disability as a mode of aesthetic experience. Disability thus

becomes an aesthetic value and critical framework. Tobin Siebers, *Disability Aesthetics* (Ann Arbor: University of Michigan), 2–3.

67. *Rozelle Hospital* continues a project on madness, exhibition, and the image that Téllez has developed early in his career. The artist has explained that his long-standing preoccupation with mental illness stems from the fact that both his parents worked as psychiatrists in Venezuela. Immersed in psychiatric spaces as a child, he began associating the silence, white walls, and enforced discipline of the clinic with another modern institution: the museum. Téllez's first installation, *La extracción de la piedra de la locura* (*The Extraction of the Stone of Madness,* 1996), meditated on the confluence of power and pathology in these spaces by introducing objects taken from the Hospital Psiquiátrico de Bárbula—hospital beds, archival documents, artwork created by patients, an electroshock therapy device—into the Museo de Bellas Artes in Caracas. While displaying the clinic's infrastructure of power, the work critiqued the museum as a disciplinary institution in its own right, one that constructs the discursive categories of art, artist, and viewer through its exhibitionary complex. This installation inaugurated a project dedicated to excavating the historical ties linking the image and madness that has spanned Téllez's artistic career. The destabilization of the positions of patient, doctor, and viewer through mimesis that organizes *Rozelle Hospital* is already present in *La extracción.* Faguet and Lehyt, "Madness Is the Language," 26–27.

68. David Bordwell, *Narration in the Fiction Film* (Madison: University of Wisconsin Press, 1985), 164.

69. Bordwell, 39.

70. David Bordwell, *The Films of Carl Theodor Dreyer* (Berkeley: University of California Press, 1981), 66.

71. Kristeva, *The Severed Head,* 127.

72. Laure Murat, *The Man Who Thought He Was Napoleon: Toward a Political History of Madness,* trans. Deke Dusinberre (Chicago: University of Chicago Press, 2014), 33–34.

73. Faguet and Lehyt, "Madness Is the Language," 29.

74. Didi-Huberman, *Invention of Hysteria,* 62.

75. Georges Bataille, *Inner Experience,* trans. Leslie Anne Boldt (Albany: State University of New York Press, 1988), 3.

76. Deleuze, *Cinema 1,* 120.

Conclusion

1. Reguillo, *Necromáquina,* 17–18.

2. Benjamin, "The Work of Art," 42.

3. Janes, *Losing Our Heads,* x. Janes observes that beheading is both "a communal act" and "the first sign that hominids are thinking in symbols" (x). Kristeva echoes this sentiment when she defines decapitation as the genesis of figuration and human creativity, of the expression of inner experience through images. Kristeva, *The Severed Head,* 4.

4. Oswaldo Zavala, *Drug Cartels Do Not Exist: Narcotrafficking in U.S. and Mexican Culture*, trans. William Savinar (Nashville: Vanderbilt University Press, 2022), 5.

5. Gunning, "The Cinema of Attraction[s]," 384.

6. Podalsky, *The Politics of Affect*, 21.

7. Traverso, *Revolution*, 87.

8. Bellour, *El cuerpo del cine*, 31–32.

9. Michel Foucault, "The Confession of the Flesh," in *Power/Knowledge: Selected Interviews and Other Writings, 1972–1977,* ed. Colin Gordon, trans. Colin Gordon et al. (New York: Vintage, 1980), 194.

10. Brinkema, *The Forms of the Affects,* 40.

11. Brinkema, 37.

INDEX

Thomas Matusiak is assistant professor of Latin American cultural studies in the Michele Bowman Underwood Department of Modern Languages and Literatures at the University of Miami.